To my Friend
My Friends Will
Rise and Fall ....
With you here ....
In turn I share it
with you —
Ardis 2012

BROKE
BUT NOT BROKEN

MICHAEL ROBERTS

To my Friends
At the "Pink House"
Enjoy!
Mike

DEDICATION

For my family and friends

Contents

Acknowledgments

I can hardly let this moment pass without expressing my sincerest thanks to those who believed in me, even in the darkest moments. This book is a reality because of your belief. Initially, I set out to write because I thought I had a story worth telling. But then I discovered a compelling need to write as a way to show my love and respect for each and every one of you. To prove to you that we can win, and that every day we do win. This book is my oath to the people who believed in me and in themselves. I am extremely filled with gratitude to all of you who inspired me to inspire you.

To my children, Hannah and David, for never failing to believe in me. To them I always give my best so that they know what the best looks like. I am filled with the utmost joy and pride to be both a father and friend to them. To my mother, who has never given up on me and has never stopped dreaming. To Shea and Lauren Farr who have filled my life with much joy and have given me a reason to win. To my ex-wife, Ann, who has never stopped believing in me, even when we divorced. An amazing person and a better friend there is none. To my sisters, who always look up to their big brother no matter how tough it gets. To my uncle Bob, who lived his life by loving and worshiping his family and placing them first ahead of all else, and to my aunt Barbara, who showed me that the secret to a good life is a happy family. No sacrifice is too big for Uncle Bob and Aunt Barbara when it comes to their children and grandchildren. To my aunt Joyce, who lives her life every single day as a winner, never missing a single chance to find the good in all she knows. Her shining example is legendary to all who know her. To Kristina, who wanted me to be the best I could be and made me want to be a better person. To so many of you, all the readers of the Daily (a daily blog) , who gave me support and examples by which to follow: Rodney Schoemann, Renae Dabney, Cindy Brown, Lisa Brown, Chris Sabin, Greg and Brandi, Robin and Mark VanDette, Najib, Jeff, Evanello and son Chris, Holly Baker, Larry Bjurlin, Dan Coury, Marie Barrett, Jon Moffitt, James Preacher, Robert "Bobby" McGregor, Phil Pisano, Clare Morse, Beverly Vineyard, Cheri' Valentine, Phyllis Stemmons, Beverly Hoffman, Kim Wilson, my roommates from Michigan State, Cathy Wilson, Tim Acre, Ken "Bonehead" Galecki, Dan-O and my childhood heroes from Flint, guys like Rocky Chamberlain, who always had my back and to this day remains my dearest friend, his wife Glenda, Scott Middleton, who is like a brother to me, David Middleton, Tim Lamb, Mike and Dana Rutherford, Mark Rothwell, Janie and Marc Gall, Dave and Krista Dungey, and so many of my buds from Flint. Perry and Cheryl Best, Dr. Rose Richards, Joyce Haver, Brian Hughes, Suzette Hrubes, Darla Brandon, Angelo Tullo, Peter Stronjik, Shay Williams, Jaycob (and Amy) Hanlin, Scott Hainey, Delene Kettleson, Jen Brown, Patrick Brown, Pat Brown, Erin Brown, Jeanine Steibel and all the Steibels, Andy Valdmanis, Nelleke Cooper, Richard, Kyle, and of course Kirstin, Mitch Ange, Joanne and Dennis, Scott Stearns, Dana Stearns, Roberta Greenberg, Alan Howard, Fred Kron, Mark Gulow, Luis Rodriguez, James Hansen, John Allinder and Kindra Allinder, Chris Wilson, Jon Tullo, Bobby Russo, Jim Piccolo, Tom Garcia, Dr. Frank Gulino, Mark Scharmann, Ron Hoon, George Staples and his beautiful wife Lynda, David Schwartz, Scott Schwartz, Becca and Bobby, Debbie Earle, Rachel Sanger, Lisa Lassiter, Sonya Lee, Fat Lever, Bruce Mayberry, Mike Briody, Valaria Ianco, Mark Dunaway, Lee Durst, Whitney Wolff and Chris D', Greg Price, Elysha Anderson, Angela Sabin, Cindy and Francine, Chef Doug and Camey, Craig Pauly, Daniel Coury Jr., Tom Grohs, Michelle Adkisson, and also my buds Nickolas, Mathew and Alexandra Anderson(A-Girl), my long-lost love Shea Farr, and so many, many more. I am grateful, for you have inspired me to give my best and to never give up. To all my friends in Flint, Michigan, who are not mentioned by name but needed to know that you can get out and you can be somebody. They lived through me and were all very proud of me. Finally, to those who turned on me, spoke poorly of and doubted me, the greatest of thanks to you all. It was you who so deeply motivated me to write this book.

Death is nothing, but to live defeated and
inglorious is to die daily.

—Napoleon Bonaparte

I would also like to pay homage to those who have departed this life. To them I owe the greatest of gratitude. You are my heroes. I salute you, and I will forever remain in your debt. Thank you! My father, Milton Arnold Roberts, taken from me too early by life. My grandpa Van, the greatest man I ever knew. I miss you, my hero. To Granny Van and Granny Roberts. Scott Simkins, Amy and Steve, Dick Wensel, John Belushi, Freddy Mercury, Bob Hope, Michael Jackson, all the lost souls, my friends from Flint, Michigan, who died from alcoholism, drugs, and violence.

I also give honorable mention to Little Blake. I am puzzled as to why he had to be taken so soon. Lately, I am trying to make sense of all the people that God has taken. I am simply not sure I am following his plan.

A SPECIAL DEDICATION

In deep regrets, I add to this list my dear cousin of fifty years, Susan Marie VanDette Brown. It seems lately there have been many deaths that have touched my life, but none harder than this one. Sue passed away, a victim of a ravaging cancer that could not be held at bay. She was a loving wife, a best friend, a mother, a daughter, a sister, a niece, an employer.

I would not have completed this book without her support. Sue had been reading my Daily's (blogs) from almost day one, which I began writing in 2008. She saved them all in a notebook and reread them. Sue would reply to the Daily's, and it would read like this: "Mike, you make a difference."

When I first began the Daily's, I was highly criticized by a reader. This individual believed writing the Daily's was an unproductive use of my time and a bad decision for a CEO. Listening to the early thoughts of this person, I hit a moment of great uncertainty. Two people convinced me to go forward—my son David and my cousin Sue. David's opinion was very important because I will never give up on anything my children believe in. Sue's request had equal meaning because she was simply one of the people in this world I respected most. Sue was so concerned that she sent me an e-mail and called me. She said, "Mike, you must go on." Every single time I think it may be time to stop writing, I am reminded of Sue's comments. And I thank her for encouraging me to go on when the road seemed dark.

I wish I could say that due to Sue's suffering in the last weeks of her life, I rejoice in her death and celebrate her leaving. But, for me, it has never worked that way. I am a man of much faith. I do not think, I know. I attend mass more than most Catholics, although Father Patrick reminds me often that going to mass does not make me a good Catholic, just a Catholic that goes to mass. I go because it is my medium for God and me. I am a man of much faith. I am not rejoicing in Sue's death today. Instead, I am crying that one of my greatest heroes has left and she is gone far too early. I cannot change this, and oh boy do I wish I could. I have to accept she is gone, but I do not want to. I think it was said best by Nicole Kidman in the movie *Rabbit Hole*. In the film, Nicole has lost her six-year-old son, and she is with her husband in a group grief counseling session. One of the other mothers who has also lost her son remarks to the group, "I miss my son, but God needed another angel!" Nicole, very upset, says, "Why? Why did he take our son? God did not need our son, he can make new angels. He did not need to take our son!" Yes! God can make angels.

Often, when people die suddenly, they become extra-special, and we identify all their good points. We will say something nice like "They were very special and never had a bad thing to say." Well, in Sue's case, this is 1,000% true. I am not trying to say nice things about Sue because she has died. I am simply saying nice things about her because they are true, and it is my honor to do so. There are a certain number of people in this world you can count on. She was always one sure person you could depend on. Every single person has good qualities, and I always look for those qualities in a person. But, in Sue, I never had to look; they were always right there.

She was an exceptional person, a true hero with a heart of gold. She would be the first person there to help you change a flat or look for a lost dog. You would not have to ask; she was smart enough to be there. She always felt it very important to listen to and try to understand a person's point of view. Sue never put a person down but always tried to put them up. Truly, I never heard her say a bad thing about a single person. This was her cornerstone. This is how Sue thought. It was her life, and it was the way she lived. Sue knew the value of life and never questioned its cost. Sue worked hard every day of her life and always found the path to moving forward and never the path to quitting. Even as she was dying, Sue was the most positive of any of us. She was in tremendous pain during the whole process. I believe her pain regimen started at 30-something of morphine, and it advanced to 1,500-something in days. She did not cry or quit; she plowed forward *and she smiled for her family*. I guess the good news is at least the pain is gone.

I never truly heard her say a bad thing about a single person. Sue's only complaint in this world was the political system. She wanted it changed so that it worked the way we all hoped and dreamed it would work—for the people and by the people. Sue was a best friend to her children. She never faulted them for a single minute and was always there to love them and support them. She gave them guidance and not the back of her hand. She gave them love and not hate. She gave them her whole life. Her children, Patrick and Erin, are devastated up to this day, and there is nothing that anyone can say or do to help with their hurt. A better mother there was none. And a better wife there was none. She and Pat were married almost twenty-eight years. In that time, I can assure you that Pat never once slept on the couch. I can also guarantee they never were apart. In this sometimes-challenging world for marriages, theirs was a true gem, a dream marriage that you do not always see. They did not have or display any of the behaviors that decimate so many marriages today. They never screamed at each other. They never fought with each other. They always put the other first. I remember last year when they picked up David and me from the airport. As we rode to their house, Pat and Sue were holding hands. Pat actually loved his wife, and there was never any other consideration. Sue was his best friend, and Pat was Sue's best friend. Pat is devastated, his world ripped apart. Today, he is asking a lot of questions, for which he will not get any answers. He has lost his best friend, his partner, and his soul mate. But Pat will stay strong for his children, Patrick and Erin.

I think there is a heaven, and I know there is an earth—and it is a darn good one. A better warrior in this world there was none. Today it is one warrior less. I am certain that Sue has gone to Valhalla, the great warrior heaven. And there she continues in her winning ways. A champion she has always been, and a warrior she remains. Today, God and the Vikings have a great cause for celebration. As for me? Well, I am very sad. I will miss Sue, and that is a mighty big cross to bear. Her loss will be felt for all the years to come. She was one person who really wanted this book. I had pledged to finish my book for Sue. She wanted an autographed version. When I discovered she was sick, I went to work and finished it for her. The first signed copy was to be delivered to her in the week she died. This book is now dedicated to Sue's life and the way she lived it.

Sue, you made a difference every day of your life. We all love you forever.

PREFACE

—Maya Angelou

I decided to write this book as a result of total financial and life meltdown. I went from a net worth of $46 million and a happy marriage, darting about the planet in our private jet, piloted by me, to a man left with $150, a nasty divorce, and a 9mm to comfort me. I replaced success with a bottle of Jack and a "Why me?" attitude. As I left the boardrooms for the bedroom, I found out that there was more to life than dying; there was living, and in this I found my greatest victory.

This book takes you from the best of times to the worst of times and then back. You will feel the power of wealth and the despair of failure. It is harsh, real, and you will grow. You will want to win and be the best you can be, not because you fear losing everything, as I did, but because you have a hunger for success, a thirst to win and be the best you can be. This book will help you understand what it means to get it, lose it, and then have to go get it again. Call it a guide to success, defeat, and victory. As this book takes you on a ride, strap in and prepare yourself for a ride that you might not want to go on.

For my family and friends, I am sorry if this book reveals aspects of our lives that you would rather not have revealed. I figure if I am going to tell the story, then I better tell it right. Sometimes telling it right has its downside. This is real and I lived it. I am very proud of who I am, I make no apologies, and I offer no quarter. This story needs to be told.

This book was written because I believed that it needed to be. It was not written for money. It was written for the realization that this book could help someone to make a difference in this world by understanding the importance of life and being a warrior in their life.

As I wrote this book, it became a mission to win. I spent many nights and days alone with my writing as well as running our young company. The balance was necessary as I needed to earn a living as well as earn a life. It helped me regain my momentum and my drive to win. It saved me as much as I saved myself.

The book was always for you and never for me, but as it unfolded, we both became winners. I fought back from the worst time of my life, and when I wanted to quit, I found a strength that I did not even realize existed. I came back to the world, and I made a difference. I came back to life, and I fought with a tenacity that would not accept the defeat that so rattled my world. I felt like a soldier with fifty bullet wounds who somehow was able to pick up his rifle and go back to the front.

The book started out for you, but along the way, it helped me. I originally wrote this because I felt I needed to tell you of the world I had built for myself, the greatest of the American dream, but that I must warn you of both sides. I felt I had to do this for you more than any other single reason. But as the story was told, I soon realized we were in this together and we were both winning. Thank you for reading this book, and thank you for allowing me to write it for you. It is a pure honor, and I will forever be in your debt.

CHAPTER 1
ROCK BOTTOM AND GOING DEEPER

Despair is the price one pays for setting oneself an impossible aim. It is, one is told,
the unforgivable sin, but it is a sin the corrupt or evil man never practices.
He always has hope. He never reaches the freezing-point of knowing absolute failure.
Only the man of goodwill carries always in his heart this capacity for damnation.

—Graham Greene (1986)

When I put the barrel of the Colt 9mm in my mouth, I remember thinking, *This is so easy, and I can make all the pain stop. I can make all the crap go away.* Loaded and cocked, the weapon felt heavy in my hands. I ran my finger over the trigger; my life was one-eighth of an inch away from being over. I wasn't sure I gave a damn. Who was to say being alive beat being dead? I'd lost everything. My multimillion-dollar business had gone bust. My wife had taken off. Debt was eating up

4

everything that I'd worked day and night to create. There would be nothing left—nothing. My world had somehow mutated from an entrepreneur's kingdom of big-dollar deals, famous friends, civic awards, and a skybox at Suns' games into this giant toilet called bankruptcy that was flushing me down, down, down. So what was so great about staying alive?

On that night on October 2008, I couldn't come up with a single decent answer to that question. I'd been binging on cocaine for three days straight, roaming around my thirteen-thousand-square-foot home with the Colt tucked into the waist of my pants. A friend had given me the coke. It had been many years since I had been on that shit. The will to fight had long left me. Blitzed out on blow, I pictured investors knocking on the front door, out of their mind, angry over lost money. Maybe they'd be packing, too. and I'd need to protect myself or protect my children. Maybe I'd just plug the person and pull them inside the house. No one would ever find out. Or we might fire our guns at the same time and do each other a favor. Was it less chicken shit to go that way? My mind raced with dark possibilities.

I wasn't a cokehead and never had been. But by nighttime of that dreary fall, I didn't care. The Phoenix housing market, considered by many to be the epicenter of the national real estate collapse, had imploded. I was in it for $131 million of my own and my investors' money. Cash was running down the drain. All the toys would be taken away—the two Cadillac Escalades, the Hummer, the Jaguar, and the Mercedes. Worst of all was my ten-seat CJ-2 corporate jet; this one I piloted myself and really loved. I knew what it felt like when a short guy had his trucks dually taken away. The toys were the lifeblood of the phony rich, and I was one. I was so far gone from reality that the stench soaked my body like a corpse at the morgue.

I loved life, but I wanted to die. I was on a collision course; the autopilot had been engaged, and it was set on self-destruct. I was losing all the toys that I had, foolishly allowing them to consume me.

They had become more important than life itself. I was also totally alone and unresponsive. This all summed up to a very grim life in the future. Death seemed like the best OFF switch.

For me, the point of all the work, all the deals, and all the glitzy people was the main event of my life. And now I thought I had no one and nothing. I snorted lines of coke in between shots of Cuervo and followed both of those with a glass of Jack on ice, anything to numb out the total disaster zone that my life had become. I hoped it would prepare me for impact.

By 2:00 a.m., I was destroyed—literally wasted in every sense of the word. But which 2:00 a.m. of which day, I did not know; I just knew it was 2:00 a.m. Did it matter? Not to me!

Alone in the master suite, lying naked on a king-size bed that was worth more than I was, it seemed like the bedroom walls were collapsing on me. The only light in the dim room came from the sick blue glow of the flat-screen TV that had gone blank. "Californication" by the Red Hot Chili Peppers was looping over and over again in the background. It felt like there was no air to breathe, like my chest was paralyzed with the weight of self-hatred combined with self-pity. *How much more of this could I take?* I wondered. At what point would I just say enough's enough, time to turn out the lights?

That was when the phone rang. I was so lost in my own black web of thoughts that it made me jump like an alarm going off. I'm lucky I didn't pull the trigger then and there just from being startled. Instead, the gun barrel jabbed up and scraped the roof of my mouth so hard that it left a cut; I could taste the blood.

On the line was a male, and in a matter-of-fact voice, he said to me in an all-too-professional tone, "You're a dead man, Roberts. You hear me? A fucking dead man."

It would have been hilarious if it hadn't been so completely sick. My suicide interrupted by a death threat? Strangely, it felt like I'd made it happen, like I'd rubbed some genie bottle and had been granted my wish. That's how upside-down and twisted my life had become—that the wish my genie would grant me at that moment would be a death wish.

Still, thoughts raced wildly through my mind. *Who wanted to kill me?* It could have been any number of investors or creditors. *Would they really follow through on their threats? How the hell should I know? Should I call the police? Would they care anyway? Hell, do I even care? I think not.*

As I slumped down on the floor next to the bed, my head dropped in my hands. You don't get to the level of success that I had reached without pissing off a few people along the way. But what the hell are you supposed to do when somebody says they're going to kill you? And did I even give a damn?

A Ball Buster of a Day

I was not a quitter. Not even close. You don't get out of the hardcore poverty of Flint, Michigan, to make $2.5 million annually by giving up easily, or giving up at all. But that day, and after a bunch of days like it, I just about punched my last ticket. The calls from creditors thirsty for blood, being deposed before the Arizona Corporations Commission (which was convinced I was a criminal), the ongoing emotional and mental attacks from Colleen, my soon-to-be ex-wife, had all been enough to take me down. Almost.

At ten that morning, I had dragged myself to the office of Attorney Michael Lane, the bankruptcy trustee's hired gun. I was expected to give a deposition known as a 2004 exam. The trustee Lane, a stenographer, my lawyer, lawyers from about five different creditors, my CFO, and I were all crammed into a small dimly lit room. It felt a lot more like an interrogation than a deposition; then again, that is exactly what it was. Their goal is to find where you are hiding the loot. Bad news for them, even worse for me, is that there was no loot to be found.

This band of thug lawyers questioned me nonstop for three and a half hours. They asked me the same questions over and over again to see if I'd slip up. They were looking for inconsistencies in my story. They believed I was hiding information about my assets. But I didn't have a "story." All I had was a hard dose of reality—my reality. When you are reiterating your reality, it doesn't matter how many times you are asked the same question; you always come up with the same answer. The line of questioning only made these idiots look like even bigger jackasses than they actually were.

"Michael Roberts—is that your name?"

"Yes."

"Where do you live?"

"Scottsdale, Arizona."

"Did you file bankruptcy?"

Seriously? Why the hell else would we be here? "Yes."

"Why did you file bankruptcy?"

"My debts far exceed my ability to pay them." *Isn't that why anyone files bankruptcy?*

"Have you reviewed the schedule of assets compiled by the trustee?"

"Yes."

"Is the report of your assets accurate?"

"Yes."

"Do you own any assets not listed in the report?"

"No."

"Have you sold any assets listed in the report?"

"No."

"Did you sell any assets prior to the report being compiled?"

"No."

"Where would we look for assets not reported?"

"I don't have any assets not reported."

By far, the most dumbass conversation I had ever had in my entire life ended with them interrogating me about flights I'd taken in my jet. I was ultimately ordered to turn over my flight logs. The trustee said he received "anonymous tips" that I had flown to the Cayman Islands several times, presumably to deposit money in an offshore account. I've never been to the Caymans in my life. Either there were no such "anonymous tips" and they just wanted an excuse to dig further up my ass or some bastard cooked up the stories to make my life even more hellish than it already was. I think people watch too many TV shows and think every lug nut out there hides money in the Cayman Islands. Hell! I am not even sure you can do that. The reality is that I was desperately trying to save the company, and I put every dollar I had into that effort.

They were especially interested in a flight to Nassau, Bahamas, on December 2007—the one international flight I did make. My wife, Colleen, had already testified that she had packed all my bags herself, and none of them were stuffed with bills, as their questioning had implied. *Since when is taking your family on vacation for Christmas a crime?*

But that Bahamas vacation was a distant memory now. When you've got flies swarming all over you, it's not that hard to feel like shit. Being treated like a monster was getting to me. I had built my fortune by treating people the right way, caring about them not just myself. Now, having my honor questioned over and over again burned me up inside. They were talking to me like I was some street punk from Flint when my whole life had been about getting away from all that.

When I had the cash, I was invincible, so there was no need to hide it. But I now understand why people do that. Doing the right thing didn't protect me from newspaper articles making me out to be a greedy, self-serving tyrant. Doing the right thing didn't protect me from investors and creditors wanting my head on a platter. Instead of taking huge payouts as my company grew, which I could have done many times, I put money back in. When things started to go downhill, I even took out a second mortgage on my home to generate some operating capital for the company. But this proved to be an even bigger mistake. When you are going down, you might as well just go down instead of digging a bigger hole.

All News Is Bad News

Out in the parking lot after the deposition, I felt my guts knot up on me. Would my Escalade still be there? I had only missed one payment; still, when everything's being taken away from you, you can't help but wonder what's going to go next. The Escalade was there, but I soon found out I had bigger things to worry about.

My attorney called about the status of my house. The trustee was laying down the law. I would have to be out in two weeks. He actually seemed like a good-enough guy, except that he liked his work too much. I don't think I could have done his job. His decision on my home only confirmed my opinion of him.

What the hell was the hurry? The housing market had gone soft as mud. No way were they going to sell a $6.5 million home in the next few months. People in the area were actually *paying* thousands of dollars to stage vacant homes to make them look lived in. Why not let me stay in and do the job for free until the house is sold? The trouble was that the trustee's ear had been poisoned by people telling him they'd been ripped off by me. He had no interest in making my life easier. Later, as he got to know me, he lightened up on me quite a bit. Once I got over my distrust of him, I really liked him. He had been through his own wars in his life, and we found a common bond.

"You want me to tell my kids they have to pack up their stuff and get out right before the holidays?!" I raged at my attorney. "You need to go back to him and work something out."

Ultimately, the trustee petitioned the court to let me stay longer, and I was given until January 19 to vacate. Happy New Year!

As if the bankruptcy meeting and the trustee's bad news weren't enough, Colleen called me. I loved Colleen, and I know she loved me. But when our high-flying lifestyle went up in smoke, she couldn't deal with it. I can't say I blame her.

Now she was calling me telling me *not* to go through with the divorce. At that point on the worst day of my life, nothing should have surprised me. But this just blew my mind. Why hold off on the divorce? We weren't together anymore. We lived in separate houses. We hardly even talked. I sure as hell could have used some support at that time, but we stopped talking. All she could do was give me grief over what *I had done to her.* So why should she suddenly give a rat's ass about the divorce getting filed?

The thought crossed my mind that she was holding on to the knowledge that Mike Roberts always comes back. She knew about the drive and passion I had, which is what made me be me in the first place. Maybe she was worried about missing out on what I might create in the future. My nerves were shot, and I was being fired at from all sides. Colleen had her battles, and they all led back to me. As it turned out, she wanted to not file because of her own financial needs. And she certainly had no problem getting all over my ass.

From Dream House to House of Nightmares

Just four years earlier, as my real estate developments were taking off, I decided it was time to shop for my dream home. When I saw this almost-seven-acre-walled equestrian estate in North Scottsdale, I knew it was *the one.* Five huge bedrooms and bathrooms; thirteen thousand square feet of living space; the massive kitchen with Viking appliances, granite countertops, and cherry wood floors; the grand fireplace in the family room; and a master suite larger than most apartments—it was everything I was looking for. My daughter was thrilled that she could have her horses there. My son was psyched about the pool, tennis courts, and the size of his new room.

The $4.8-million price tag was a bargain, but Mike Roberts always gets a better deal. The original owners were Tom and Joan Van Welden. Tom was the CEO of Allied Waste. Tom, a great guy,

11

started his first waste management business operation in 1975 in Danville, Illinois. He had two trucks, and he built the business into a billion-dollar company. He and Joan had moved out of the house several months before to relocate to their new mansion, and I knew he just wanted to get rid of it.

Wealthy people will brag about saving ten bucks by buying chewing gum in bulk and balk at paying retail for a piece of furniture, but when they really want to get something done, they'll make financial decisions normal people would consider nuts. I offered Tom $2.5 million. We finally settled on $3.125 million, and we moved in on October 4, 2004.

A big factor in the decision to buy the house was a friend's insistence that I would never be able to afford the $25,000-a-month payment. Thirteen different banks agreed with that friend, but the fourteenth gave me financing. Looking back, I must admit that a lot of what I've accomplished in life has been because somebody told me I couldn't do it.

Back to the Master Suite

But that night, my dream home felt like a chamber of horrors. It was a palace where life was good, the family was together, and the bank account was loaded. But now the emptiness of the house only fed the hollowness. I felt alone inside, and all those rooms seemed haunted with the ghosts of what I'd lost.

My life had become a daily war to keep my sanity. Every time the phone rang, my guts twisted with fear. There was no good news coming, only bad. In the court of public opinion, I'd already been convicted of being a scoundrel. So why not just end it? What was the point of going on? Who would even care? I knew I could come back from this. I'd lost everything before. But was this struggle worth it? Was it worth taking the chance of coming back only to feel this hell again someday? The alcohol and drugs were in control of my emotions, and they were giving me first-class passage to the final countdown. I wallowed in self-pity, and all hope for living was a dim light at best.

I just said over and over again, "Fuck this life." How the hell did this all happen? I never imagined it could be so unbelievably damaging to my mind. A smart guy on this day I was not. Suicide was a shortcut, and I wanted a shortcut out. At that instant, I thought of my grandfather who had told me several times in life, "Shortcuts never work; you want to get anywhere, you need to work for it." This day I needed to work harder than I ever had in my life. However, today I was not up to task.

In the end, it wasn't the hit man on the phone who saved me from suicide, let's be clear about that. It was the thought of my daughter, Hannah, fifteen, and my son, David, fourteen. I felt my love for them like a laser cutting through the darkness, through the coke-induced haze, through all the bad news coming my way, through all the people who had turned their backs on me. There was Hannah and David. I could feel them with me as if they were in the room. With all the mental strength I had left, I forced myself to focus on them. I knew they loved me, and they needed me. I visualized Hannah's beautiful smile and the spark David gets in his eyes when he's excited. I felt the warmth of hugging them; and I knew that no matter how sick, scared, angry, or helpless I felt, I just couldn't leave them without a father. I couldn't do that to Hannah and David. They were my life.

I made a promise to myself to be the very best father in the world, and no matter how bad and shitty things had gotten, it was not fair to the only good thing in my life that I should ruin that too. This is not what they had signed on for, so for today or any other day, there is no OFF switch.

I always felt that taking one's own life was the coward's way out. On that night, all that I was and all that I am told me that I am not a coward. I put the gun down. It was time to fight again, so I picked myself up, and the fight started. I was beat, and I was beat hard.

I was broke, but I was not broken.

Chapter 2
Now What?

Don't go around saying the world owes you a living.
The world owes you nothing. It was here first.

—Mark Twain

I looked around and asked myself: Now what? Now what was I going to do? Since I decided not to end it all, now what? It was time to man up. Well, the Jack and coke was not going to get me anywhere. It was time for those things to leave my life.

Writing about this shit isn't the smartest thing I'm ever going to do, but I will be honest. I will hurt some of those who love me. And I will make those whom I do business with question me. But you know what? All I can do is tell the real story—say I am sorry and rely on my character to guide me through this. It has been said it is better to seek forgiveness than ask permission; in this case, that is the best approach.

Drugs are destroying people. I have not done drugs since that fall evening, nor will I ever. I had hit a point so low that good judgment left me. I felt like Sigmund Freud when he wrote the *Cocaine Papers*. Freud experimented with cocaine and wrote about it. He felt the powers and the addiction. Cocaine changes you. I have watched drugs destroy so many people I have known in my life, not to mention many famous people. Drugs killed the greats like John Belushi, Elvis Presley, Michael Jackson, Jimi Hendrix, Janis Joplin, Jim Morrison, even Judy Garland—what the hell went wrong with Dorothy? The loss of Toto must have been too overwhelming.

The one that really hit home was Freddie Prinze. Freddie shot himself dead—while on drugs. It was initially ruled a suicide. Freddie had hit rock bottom, and there was an out. Not a very good one. The official cause of death was later changed to accidental. I still believe it was no accident that drugs and a loaded gun fell into his hands. We will never know. I, however, will know about me. And at this point, that is what seems important. I liked Freddie a whole bunch.

Many make it back from the death clutch of drugs. But then again, many more do not. I guess the story, as it goes, is that drugs are bad, and the world would be a better place without them. However, that is another battle. Just as the following group of people won their battles by defeating drug and alcohol addictions: Betty Ford, Kirstie Alley, Robert Downey Jr., Mel Gibson, Michael Douglas, Paula Poundstone, Matthew Perry, Ray Charles, Richard Dreyfuss, Bela Lugosi, Mickey Rourke, Ted Kennedy, Dick Van Dyke. I needed to rally! I needed to move on from this certain death and find success once again. I had to crawl out of this shit hole and quit feeling sorry for myself. I needed to pull myself up and get after it. I figured other people had their own "Come to Jesus" meeting, so it was simply my turn. I was tired of feeling sorry for myself. It was a new dawn. My own battle took me to the forefront of a different comeback. But to get to this new dawn, I have to tell you how I got to this point.

I have a great story to tell, and you need to hear it. It is a story of a man who pulled the Colt 9mm from his mouth to fight back. He pulled it out of his mouth to save his life and his children from a fate worse than death. I have been in business my whole life, and I have had many success stories. I also realize that if I am to tell a story, it needs to be interesting, it needs to be true, it needs to help guide each and every one to a higher worth. I am going to give you something to believe in. I promise that although I cheated death, I will give you a great story about life.

I am not writing this book for the money. Truth is most writers never make any money, so I am writing because I have to. I need to save someone's life, and it may just be yours. I have to help someone get up off the floor and believe. I need to help someone rise—to a better place. I need to give just one person the hope and the dream that there is a better day. Screw the money. I will probably lose more by writing this book than I will ever make, but I need to save just one life. Someone will read this and believe. They may believe, just enough, to not give up—but go make a difference.

I had a dark moment. The moment where you say, *Why go on anymore?* For me the answer was Hannah and David, my two children. I was beat, but I was not beaten. I was down, but I was not out. I was broke, but I was not broken. I got as close as you can get. Now that I am back and now that I am asking, *Now what?* I have an answer, and as you read, hopefully you will find the answer. Then again, most of you are not at that point. Most of you want to hear of a success story, not a survival story. I met the devil, and *his* day was not mine.

I often wonder if there is a magical moment, a moment where you look to the heavens and say, "This is it." I have to make a change. I truly believe that we are all exactly where we have gotten ourselves. We are victims, but we are our own victims. We are winners, but we are winners because we made it so. The phrase that is so often said,

17

"I have to deal with the hand I was dealt," has no place in life. We are where we are because of the choices we made to get here. We are the dealers, and we deal ourselves the cards.

Victims! Aren't we all?

The simple reality is that we all have a good life; it is the understanding that it is good which is so important. We often busy ourselves with dim views or with the cup-half-empty way of thinking. Life is exactly what we make it. I had faced my biggest demons, and the world was caving in on me; I had to make a choice—to rise up. It was time to find the new world that I was about to create. It was time to quit feeling sorry for myself.

I knew what it would take. I had been fighting adversity my whole life. I had always won, so why should this time be different? Truth is, it should not be different! I had the tools! I had me! I had the ability to believe and to make a difference. I had the ability to rise above.

My mind raced with so many thoughts. Was this the end? Would it get worse before it got better? Was this penance for being such a bad person growing up in Flint, Michigan? I was street-smart; I was a little too street-smart. I then thought that God wanted me to go through this so that I could experience forgiveness, so that I could experience this misery, so that when I returned to the top, I would be a better person. Maybe it was God's plan that I understand the value of the world around me and that I become an instrument to serve this world.

I am not a very religious man. I am Catholic and I go to church a little more than the average Catholic. I do not push the Word of the Lord. My relationship with God is between God and me. I consider it private. However, I was not sure God and I were talking at this point. I definitely knew we were not on the same page. We both have a deal—to always see that Mike does his best. I continued to wonder why on earth I had to fall so hard.

I had no idea that my fall had just begun. I was about to learn many more lessons while I traveled back to my road of success. It was the initial writing of this very book that helped me find my feet again. It was the need to come back and fight this terrible monster we call "adversity." I was tired of getting my ass kicked. It was time to fight back.

I was beat and beat hard. I was asked for the first time in my life to doubt. I was asked to doubt! This is the most horrible mistake one can ever make. And I was about to make it. I was about to surrender to defeat. I could not see any reason to continue. But I knew I that I needed to fight. I needed to protect the very two children I brought into this world. I knew that no matter what anyone thought of me, what was most important was what I thought of myself.

You never know how strong you are until being strong is the only choice you have.
—Author Unknown

As for me, I was fresh out of choices. Being strong was all that was left.

I was six when my father died. My mother was asked to deal with a life much tougher than I faced. She was a mom without her husband and four little children in tow. I was the oldest at six and Julie, the youngest, at five months, Tracy and Janet in the middle. It was my grandpa Van who aided my mother in raising the four of us, or at least me. It was really me he took to. He was a man who himself had never made it out of the third grade. He was one of thirteen children. His parents, both from Germany, needed another hand in the fields; and his going to school never made much sense. So after three years of school, off to the crops Grandpa went. Just like Jethro Bodine, from the TV show *Beverly Hillbillies*, and Jethro's third-grade education.

I spent many days with Grandpa Van. He in turn taught me to be a man, and he taught me how to think. This is where I learned the most important lesson of my life. Grandpa Van would always pull me aside and say, "Mike! You must always remember that you cannot feel inferior without giving your permission." This has served me well all my life. He was one hundred percent right on the money.

You must give your permission to feel inferior. This is why my first thought was that it was important what I thought of me and not what others thought of me. It was the only way I could start on my road back. It was my decision to rise above and to move on. The decision was made for me when I was six; I just didn't realize it then. It was time to man up and take that first step back to success while fighting the evil villain of adversity. I needed to fight back and kick adversity right in the ass.

I was now in the fight of my life. I had decided not to take the coward's way out and kill myself. It was time to look in the mirror and realize that it was me who needed my help. It was me who needed to win this fight if I were going to protect my children, Hannah and David. It was me who needed to man up to protect my mother, my sisters, and all the people who needed me. It was me who had to find the road back. It was me who had to step up to the podium.

I soon realized that I could not blame the housing meltdown. I could not blame my ex-wife, Colleen. I could not blame the government. I could not blame bad timing. I could not blame the world economy. I soon realized I could not blame anyone or anything. I did not need to look for blame. It was not time to blame. It was time to fix. It was time to look for the answers. It was time to step forward. This is the story of a guy who wanted to end it all and decided instead that he must go forward. He must win and never ever give up. It is not a pretty story, and there are still many challenges to fight along the way.

It is now time for the story, how this guy found the tools and the belief in himself to rise above and to follow the road that he would need to take to find his path back to success. This time the path will be harder. This time the lessons learned will take their place. This time I will not do it for the money. I do it because it is what I must do. I must rise above defeat and I must emerge victorious. Along the way, I will help families, and I will make a difference. I will find success once more because that is what I do. I will not fail. I know no other path. I know no other dream. I have to do this thing because it is what I believe in.

It is me who must pony up now and do all that I can. It is me who must step up to the line and take another shot. To give up—to kill one's self—is just not an acceptable alternative. I must do whatever it is I was sent here to do, with the heart of a champion, not the mind of a loser.

There is a reason for all this adversity. I have often heard, "What does not kill us makes us stronger." I am now convinced that this is true. I believe writing this book and returning to the pillar of success is my destiny and that I am being tested. So I say, "Bring it on!" I am ready for the challenge, and I will emerge a champion. I will emerge a champion because I believe. I believe in me. My fears almost won out, and I almost accepted defeat. I was beaten and I was broke, but I was never broken.

I have to tell the story. It will not be easy. There are many more fights ahead, but I will never lose sight of the victory that I seek. I promise that if you stay with me, you will find out what it takes to win. You will discover what it takes to be a champion.

You will discover many things along the way. You will glimpse into the boardrooms and you will hold a hand in their final hour. You will cheer and you will cry, but through it all, you will become the better for it. It will not be easy. I have spent some forty years in business. I have been behind closed doors, and I have cut ribbons. I filed bankruptcy for $131 million, and I have put a check in my personal bank account for $9.2 million.

I have dined with celebrities, and I have sat with pro athletes of the highest caliber. I have seen many, many things in both life and in business.

It is time that these stories are told. It is time we all get a glimpse into the heart of a lion. It is time we all experience what it feels like to have a net worth of $46 million one minute and to be left with only $150 the next.

I have ridden in parades and sat in jails. I have met famous people, and I have dined with a janitor. My biggest challenge, however, has inspired this book. My biggest challenge was, for the first time in my life, that I doubted *me*. I almost fell victim to defeat. I was broke, but I was never broken.

As for *now what?* now it is time to go and do this thing! I am broke, but I am not broken.

Chapter 3
Cruising on the *Titanic*:
The Real Estate Boom Gone Bust

> *Get the facts, or the facts will get you. And when you get them,*
> *get them right, or they will get you wrong.*
>
> —Dr. Thomas Fuller (Gnomologia, 1732)

The First Iceberg

Being CEO of Charlevoix Homes in Phoenix, the epicenter of the entire country's real estate collapse, was a lot like being the captain of the *Titanic*. Heading into it, I didn't think anything could sink us. We'd had a three- or four-year run in which everything we touched had turned to gold. It had been one big deal frenzy. People were pushing deals at us ten times a day, faster than we could analyze them. We were closing them constantly, just trying to keep up. We were making daily bank deposits of $200,000, $300,000, even a half million. We were like a machine.

Sure, we thought home sales would slow down sometime. In fact, we knew they would; they had to. The market was so overheated it glowed red like a desert sunset. Or a warning beacon out at sea: iceberg! What iceberg? Depending on your point of view.

We knew home sales would level off; we just didn't know when. And until they did, we were hell-bent on riding that wave as long as it lasted. We were cranking out homes and selling them so fast we didn't have time to think about anything but building and selling, building and selling. It was a blast. When the slowdown did hit, we thought we were solid enough to get through it. We weren't. We were buzzing on our success, high on our own speed and power, like this unstoppable luxury liner cutting through the ocean.

What we couldn't see is that we were speeding right into an iceberg. It did not matter anyway because, just like the *Titanic*, we were unsinkable.

I can tell you the exact point of impact—it was May 2006. If you knew what to listen for, you would have heard a sickening crunch just below the waterline. But we were rockin' and rollin' too hard to hear it. The engine drowned out the crash, and it was not until we looked over the starboard side that we began to ask questions that were mostly ignored. Only one month before, in April, we had delivered and closed escrow on forty-eight homes. Not a bad month at all. We were smashing our own high goals. Just three years before, we were delivering homes at a rate of three a month and thought we were doing pretty well then. Now we were blowing that away by 4,600 percent. It was a real rush. We were on our way to being a big-time player and not just in Arizona. Morale was way up. We were like a factory running twenty-four-hour shifts to get new homeowners moved in.

But in May, our closings suddenly went down to twelve homes. That's 75 percent in the wrong direction—in one month! People who had been lining up to buy were now backing out of deals quicker than water through a screen door. They were walking away from thousands of dollars in deposits. On paper, we had three hundred contracts. In March and April, we started another one hundred homes due to buyer demand. Within thirty days, 268 of those contracts had cancelled, but the homes were started or nearly completed.

This knocked us back on our heels, no doubt about it, but we thought it was just a matter of regaining our balance as we motored through some rough waters. We were invincible! We would be okay! What iceberg?! The band played on and the ship's purser served champagne. No worries! But June was worse than May. In June, we sold one home. One! We had 160 houses in inventory across our 14 communities, another 150 under construction, and another 1,000 lots waiting to be built on, and we moved only one whole house that month.

It was a lame eight weeks, but we still didn't have a clue what we were in for. We were having a bad little run—that was obvious. To the war room, we assembled the brain trust, as we collectively called ourselves. We discussed useless minute adjustments, like reassessing new home starts. *Really? No shit!* I thought. We decided to slow down on looking at new deals. Another brilliant plan! We speculated the market would take six to twelve months to correct itself. *(Today, they say it's more like ten years.)* We were tweaking our business strategy when we should have been abandoning ship. Instead of running for the lifeboats, we poured more champagne. We were on the *Titanic*, and we were just changing seats, still oblivious to the fact we had just hit an iceberg. We were unsinkable, yet we were taking on water—and lots of it.

We kept looking ahead for better news. No such luck in July—again we only managed to sell one home. July sucked, but it would actually get worse from there. We started selling about one home every *three* months. We became so desperate; we actually put money in to close transactions. We were trying to stop the bleeding. We went from making anywhere between $20,000 and $100,000 per home in April to paying the same just to get the loans off our books. We were coming to the table with more money than the buyers— until we ran out.

It was time to face the music. We had a serious long-term problem on our hands, and this was where I missed it. I was stuck on saving the company. It was the only way I knew how to think. My mind was fixed on keeping us afloat. In my head, it was the only option. I started borrowing from wherever I could. I took out a second mortgage on my home. When I should have been manning the lifeboats, I was still bailing water.

It was like someone had thrown a switch; home sales were turned off. The whole Valley of the Sun had gone under a thick black shadow. Bring out your dead! There was no light coming through. No home sales meant no cash was coming in, but plenty was going out. We were paying out to the banks for homes we were building and the home sites we were holding.

I still didn't believe we were going down and neither did the employees. The brain trust was guiding us right into the path of another iceberg. Like the *Titanic*, I kept telling myself we were unsinkable. No matter what we faced, I thought we could make it through. I always saw us on the other side of the slowdown—cashing in again. What I didn't get is that it wasn't a slowdown. It was a meltdown—a total meltdown.

We bailed water for a while, sweating to renegotiate terms with our lenders and reel in small bridge loans. Our investors were getting edgy. We did conference calls every week to try to calm them down. We looked at different ways to get stable. We hired guys like the financial firm KPMG and paid them thousands of dollars to put together a private placement memorandum, which was supposed to get us some money to keep us afloat. We didn't realize we were already sunk. When the doctor came in and informed us that we had stage 4 cancer, we still believed we could go to Germany or Mexico and be saved.

As we became more desperate, we put out an SOS signal: Save Our Ship really meant send money now, or Save Our Shit. But instead of first-aid, we attracted a shark. He must have smelled blood in the water.

In stepped a business associate. He acted as if he was coming to our rescue. But the truth was he had brought a bunch of his investors on board who had millions of dollars trusted with him, and now he was afraid they'd come after him—if we went down.

Before the bust, we were like best buddies. I used to have him out to our Phoenix Suns box, which was the sweetest in the whole arena. It beat the owner's box hands down. We could put seventy-two people in there and make them all feel like VIPs, including a private bartender serving us. People want to invest in success, so strutting our stuff was always an important part of doing business.

But now that I was down, he started treating me like shit. I couldn't get a call back from him if I was on the floor bleeding to death. And all his people treated me the same way. I soon figured it out—I had leprosy.

For a while, his money propped us up. But the truth was that nothing was going to save us. On the *Titanic*, the band was still playing. And we were reassuring the passengers that we were okay. In the office, we kept reassuring ourselves that somehow everything would be just fine. We renamed the company Copper Leaf Communities, as if that would help jump-start sales. We kept making payroll. We still had our luxury boxes at the Coyotes and Suns games, but we were starting to shed them—again we were way too late.

The Second Iceberg

The first iceberg that nailed us was the collapsing housing market. But the second iceberg that finished the job was the banks. The banks took us down. The banks had made loan commitments to us in the millions. For a while, we figured out ways of paying the interest, treading water and staying alive. These commitments were based on 75 percent of the appraised value of our real estate. Without even telling us they were doing it, one of our major lenders did a new appraisal based on the current property values that obviously had tanked. It didn't take a genius or a bank appraiser to know that the values were no longer there and would never be there. In just one of our communities, the value went from $21 million to $14 million. We soon received a formal certified letter letting us know that we had exceeded our loan limits. In other words, we had just been cut off.

I had personal relationships with these people going back years, but suddenly it was all new names and faces. My buddies of fifteen and twenty years were gone. The banks had brought in the vultures. My banker pals wouldn't even return an e-mail—they were too scared of losing their jobs, which most of them ended up losing anyway. Heads had to roll, and it was a mega bowling alley out there.

It reminded me of a saying my grandfather would often use: "Be leery of banks, they will loan you an umbrella until it starts raining and then they will want their umbrella back." Boy, was it ever raining!

This was bad business any way you look at it. There was no way we would ever be able to pay back what we owed without having cash to keep going. They were killing us and themselves. But that's how badly the banks were starting to spin. They didn't know which way was up, so they sent us straight to the bottom, and many of them would join us.

That was the death knell for the company. We had subcontractors waiting to be paid. One contractor got stiffed for $800,000.

Everyone in the office had much confidence in me; they thought I would figure it out, like it was something that could be figured out.

The Lord, it is said, gives us challenges according to our ability. It is thought that the Lord knows we can handle what he gives us to deal with. I started to wish the Lord did not have so much confidence in my ability.

Probably the toughest thing for a hard-driving entrepreneur, like me, to swallow was that I didn't have a chance—I was helpless. The *Titanic* was going down; we were done. At its peak in mid-2006, Charlevoix Homes employed about sixty great people. Most of them were like family to me. I looked forward to seeing them every day. I lived for it. Then, *kaboom!* In one sixty-day period, I had to lay off thirty-two of them.

It felt like one long funeral. I valued those people. We had put together a truly awesome team. When the market was rockin', we kicked ass.

I took a lot of pride in our people, and I knew damn well what they had done for us and the company. None of this was their fault. I hated letting them down. I hated that I couldn't pull us through it together.

Investors Gone Wild

Investors do not like losing their money. That's obvious. But during the housing bubble, it seemed like people forgot that losing money was even an option. Everyone was riding high, clearing outrageous returns and getting way too used to it. But when the bubble popped, so did the investments. And people got seriously pissed off.

We had about 150 investors in the company. Seeing they were going to lose their money, some of them got mean. They tried to make me out as a Ponzi scheme operator. A *Ponzi scheme* is a scam in which someone pays big-time returns to early investors with money from other investors. Word gets around that an investment is really paying out and people rush to dump in their money, which they never see again. This was no Ponzi—just a real estate meltdown.

We were no scam. We were a company in major growth mode. We used investor money to create explosive growth. We jumped into deal after deal. But when the sales dried up, we had no money to work with. I tried desperately to generate cash for the company. I even took out a second mortgage on my home from Chase Bank just to help keep our doors open. The second was for a cool half million. This infusion gave us another ninety days of *breath*. But, of course, it was like putting a Band-Aid on a mortal wound.

People asked me, why didn't I see this coming? The answer is I did see it coming. But, by then, it was too late. Before the bubble burst, everyone in the home-building business would ask themselves, *When is it going to end? When is it ever going to end?* We were all racing to get in on the boom while it lasted. Just like the investors. But our investments were much bigger—we were all-in.

The market was on fire, and everyone was picking their number to cash in. Now serving 146, please! Home prices were blowing up—10, 20, 30, 50, 100, 200 percent. There were bidding wars for every scrap of buildable land out there. No one wanted to think about it ending. No one wanted to kill the buzz. It wasn't just us builders; the banks led the craziness. Everyone wanted to believe that this could somehow just keep going.

We builders were blown away that all home buyers had to do to get a loan was pass the mirror test. You put a mirror under the prospective borrower's nose. If any fog shows up, meaning they are still breathing, they're approved. The same people who five years ago couldn't get credit to buy a TV were now having $250,000 mortgages dropped in their laps.

That was the juice that kept people buying homes and sending prices up, up, up. Common sense said it couldn't just keep going and going, but we didn't want to look real hard at that. No one in the business did. One story going around was that the credit was coming from overseas, like that meant there was some kind of unlimited supply. Lenders and mortgage brokers were bragging about the low quality of the borrowers that they were approving. They were running out of mirrors; pretty soon the borrowers did not even have to pass the mirror test. We were all getting rich and there seemed to be no end, but it was beating down on us like a meteor.

To show you how quickly the boom was here and gone, think of this: just as home sales were completely drying up, the municipalities of the greater Phoenix metro area raised the impact fees they charged for building houses. What were they thinking? It was totally nuts. We couldn't sell a house, and they were bumping up the fees we had to pay for the privilege of building in their fair city. *Typical government BS, the slowest to react and usually by the time those idiots figure it out, the* Titanic *is at the bottom of the ocean. Didn't they watch the news and read the papers like everyone else? Or were they too lost in their own little bureaucratic world? It took them three years to get their new fee structure approved and in place.* By then, the boom had already passed us by.

I was into building this mega company. That was my vision—to be one of the biggest in Arizona. By the time the end was in sight, I was all-in. I'd bet my entire pot of gold and lost. I couldn't get out—the only way out was to sell homes, and no one was buying.

By mid-2007, we were totally wiped out. By 2008, I was in bankruptcy. And there wasn't one damn thing I could do about it. There was nothing left but the abuse, the depositions, the newspaper stories, and the pissed-off investors. The hurricane cometh, and it cometh hard with a fierce vengeance. It was one thing to be broke; it was another to be under constant attack. I was a bad guy, and this was a brand-new role for me. I was well-liked and well-respected, but not today or any day at this point.

Over the years, I'd made my investors a ton of money. In one deal, I'd bought fifty-one-acre lots in Litchfield Park for $3.4 million. We put $900,000 in to develop it and then sold it for $9 million to another home builder. This was known as Cottonwood Estates. This was in the boom days of 2005. In eleven months, my investors had doubled their return on their money. We paid out $5 million in profits to the investors. They loved me on that day. I got kisses—even from the guys. But that wasn't the only jackpot we paid out to our investors. We were more than a one-hit wonder. We had a damn good track record of paying out and paying well. Fremont Cove, 900 Devonshire, Maryland Lakes, Casa Lomas, Happy Trails, The Ravines—all these communities made great returns for our investors. They had plenty of love for us then.

However, now that the company and the entire industry had gone bust, they wanted my head. They threatened to have me arrested. They called me a crook and attacked me in the media. The *Arizona Republic* drank it up. That rag of a paper didn't even bother to fact-check the spelling of my wife's name. Why not print whatever they wanted? It sold newspapers, at least for a while. Besides, what were we going to do? Sue a newspaper? Our plate was full. Freedom of the press and all that garbage—another losing battle.

Of course, in the end, investors lost money. But that's what always happens to investors who come in late or stay in too long. *Investing 101: Early money earns the returns.* When you're following the pack, eventually you get left behind. And it ain't a pretty sight. The great Phoenix real estate gold rush was over, and most of us weren't left standing. The only ones making money now were the undertakers, the people paid to carry away the corpses.

I lost everything right along with our investors. Talk about having skin in the game, I had my flesh and blood in it too. I'd put my whole life into the company. When my children were born, we had more money in the bank than we could count. Now there would be nothing for them. My income would drop from $200,000 a month to $25,000 a year.

But the court of public opinion seemed to have passed its verdict. *Truth is, when the shit hits the fan, you either step up or you don't. You are the guy—good or bad, you are the guy. Period!*

Having lots of money is a beautiful thing. I know that firsthand. Don't ever let anybody tell you otherwise. They're full of it if they do. Money can make it hard to know who your friends really are. When I lost my money, I found out quick. Ed Gaylord, who owns Gaylord Hotels, along with the Grand Ole Opry in Nashville, Tennessee, was supposed to be my buddy. We ate lunch together, had drinks, went out to dinner, the whole bit. We had similar business interests, family interests. But when the bad press hit, he disappeared under his rock. He wouldn't return my calls or answer a single e-mail. It was the coldest thing in the world. Our wives were friends, they were good friends. But then again, my wife was long gone. He didn't respond to a single e-mail. Furthermore, there were several others who did the same thing.

There were people who stood by me. Gary Geitz, a custom builder in town, who was a guest at my wedding. Gary and his wife, Camille, are longtime friends. He's the salt of the earth—the real deal. And she's one of the best people I've ever known. She truly has a caring heart. When he saw the smear job in the newspaper, he called me right up and invited me out to lunch. He said, "I just gotta make sure my friend is okay and see what I can do to help."

Others who stood by me include my accountant, Gary Fleming, of Henry & Horne, and Keith Hendricks, my lawyer at Fennemore Craig. Guys like these are pure gold. You can't ask for better friends or colleagues. I was now a poison, a freak, a bad guy. Don't get too close or you may catch leprosy. Still, guys like the two Gary's and Keith knew I would be back. And they knew I was a good guy. They were close to the war zone and knew the real story. Guys like these I will always welcome into my foxhole.

The Bitch of Bankruptcy

Twenty-five homebuilders in Arizona went bankrupt, from Trend and Engle to Pulte and Fulton. I wasn't alone. I was in good company on the way up and on the way down. But it was a brutal thing to go through. Creditors swarm over everything you've got, grabbing up any assets they can get their hands on. I expected to be roughed up this way. Still, I didn't think my kids would get the same treatment. I would have thought that women and children would have had some sort of diplomatic immunity. Boy, was I wrong!

Meridian Bank sucked out $105,000 in cash from the children's accounts. These were Hannah's and David's accounts. AmTrust Bank grabbed another $300,000 worth of Certificates of Deposits, which were also Hannah's and David's. Like any good father, I had set up their education accounts. You know the dream, right? Put money away for our children so they will get through school and all that! Yeah right! The vultures were circling, and when they swooped down, they ate the young. Bankruptcy is a tough pill to swallow, but you'd think your children would get some kind of protection.

When the bankruptcy trustee walked through my home, he told me what to expect. Everything would be auctioned off. Every single book, table, lamp, and curtain would go. He said that anything left over would be put in a pile on the floor and sold for some ridiculous price like two dollars. Just to make sure I had nothing left. It almost seemed spiteful, like they wanted to punish me. Not just pay off creditors, but make me pay a price in my heart. My LLC(s) couldn't protect me. My past achievements couldn't protect me. I was going to be zeroed out, returned to nothing, just like where I had started. Or like a bad night in Vegas and all the chips were gone. Where did that big pile go?

The Dawn of a Comeback

This kind of loss can make you think seriously about killing yourself. I did!

When you're suicidal, you can't see the whole picture. All that shows up in your head is darkness and death. It's all you can hear, see, taste, and feel. Death is like a cold dish that does not warm up in the microwave. But when you go through this kind of ordeal, it almost feels warm, as if to comfort you.

But once you put the gun or the pill bottle down long enough, the clouds can clear. That's what happened to me. I started to see a future. It was like a light had been buried under shovelful after shovelful, and still another shovelful of bad news. But then the light started to shine through again. I realized it wasn't over for me. Not by a long shot. No matter what hell I'd been through and how much I had lost, it wasn't over.

I love the glitz; I'll be the first to admit it. But that stuff doesn't make me; I make the stuff. I had to let go of the attachment to it all. What good did it do me to hold on to what I had lost? It could only kill me. I grew up poor in Flint. I knew what it was like to come from nothing. I'd been on the comeback trail all my life.

The hell with all the junk! I was happy to breathe the air and be sunny-side up. I now knew more than ever that I was in the fight of my life. I decided to fight for my life—I no longer had a choice. I was all-in, and the game was life. I was beat hard and I was broke, but I had the power to believe. I had never been beat like this, but I knew no matter the odds, there was a way out. That way out was me.

Chapter 4
Bad from the Bone in the Vehicle City

People are always blaming their circumstances for what they are. I don't believe in circumstances. The people who get on in this world are the people who get up and look for the circumstances they want, and if they can't find them, make them.

—George Bernard Shaw (1904)

I was born and raised in southwest Flint, Michigan, a tough part of a town that was pretty much tough all around. I lived within walking distance from "the Hole," the Chevy manufacturing plant where my grandfather worked, my dad worked, and I would work. Right by the Hole ran the Flint River. You couldn't fish the river or swim in it, but you could drown in it. It was more for accidental drowning than anything else.

Also in the neighborhood were GM Truck and Bus, Flint Metal Center, and Powertrain South. By the time I got to high school in the mid-70s, Flint had seen better days. The auto industry that had fed us was in shambles. They started building crap cars, and the oil crisis of 1973 didn't help either. "White flight" was in full swing. Disinvestment, deindustrialization, and depopulation were sucking the life out of the place. Manufacturing plants were closing and the jobs weren't coming back.

Your best bet for starting a career in Flint was in crime. The largest city in the United States with a one-syllable name, Flint, earned the title of "Murder Capital, USA"—the preferred place Detroiters went to get shot. *Money* magazine rated Flint the worst place to live. What an honor.

Flint wasn't always like that. Around the time I was born in 1959, Flint was a "happening" city. GM employed 83,000 people. If you didn't work for Chevy, you worked for AC sparkplug, Buick, Fisher Body, or some other local plant. Jobs were easy to find, and they paid good money. Flint was your basic blue-collar town filled with good, down-to-earth people who could put food on the table for themselves and their families.

We had our civic institutions, too. Whiting Auditorium, Sloan Museum, Bower Theater, and the Flint Institute of Music—all set on an amazing thirty-acre site near downtown—were just a few of the perks playing host to the thriving auto industry of the '50s and early '60s. With a population of about two hundred thousand, Flint was a great place to raise a family. It wasn't quite the big city Detroit was, but you could still find plenty to do in Flint; and most of all, you had a good job.

My Flint roots run deep. My parents both grew up in Flint. My mother's father, my grandpa Van, worked in management at the Chevy plant. He was there for the sit-down strikes of 1936–1937 that got the United Automobile Workers union off the ground. They forced GM to cut a deal, and the labor unions were in business.

Grandpa Van didn't go for unions. To him, they were trying to break the backs of the company that was putting food on our table. He had strong opinions about that and about everything else in life. I couldn't have become a man without him.

My mom, Delores Jean, went to St. Matthews High School. My dad, Milton Roberts, went to Flint Tech, where advanced students took their classes. They got married right after graduation. That's how people did it back then; they got it right. If Dad had not died at an early age, he and Mom would still be married; they were that kind of couple, and it was that kind of world. Not like today. Not like Scottsdale where marital life expectancy is eight years.

Mom was from a Catholic family; my dad's family was Mormon. Neither family liked the idea of them crossing that line to be together, but they didn't let that stop them. It got really hot when my dad's mother insisted on inviting the whole church. My mother's father, who was paying for the big day, said, "No way." He gave her leeway for twenty guests max. It was a real standoff.

My parents solved the problem by eloping to Indiana. It wasn't the last time my mom took a risk and did her own thing. I got a healthy dose of freethinking from her.

I was the oldest of four kids, and we were doing all right. Dad had graduated from the General Motors Institute, where they trained automobile tradesmen, and he was hired on as a tool and die maker. Mom stayed home raising the kids. We were an all-American family living the middle-class dream. Then the roof caved in.

A Hole in the World

My dad was twenty-eight years old and in good shape. He used to pick me up and put me over his shoulder like a sack of potatoes. But as a child, he'd been sick, growing up with rheumatic fever. When he was sixteen, he went for a job at the Chevy plant. They gave him a checkup, and it turned out he had a heart murmur caused by a leaking aorta valve. He had surgery, and that was the end of it—for then.

On July 2, 1965, he collapsed on the assembly line of Chevy Plant 2A, "the Hole." The sutures the surgeon had put in his heart years earlier broke, and he bled to death internally. No way my mother could have seen this coming; none of us could. She was with him when he died.

Mom and I never spoke a word about it until recently, nearly forty-five years after Dad's death.

It was the holiday weekend, and Mom was home packing us four kids up, preparing for the Fourth of July up north. Mom and Dad had just put a deposit on a new home the day before. They were signing the papers when they got back from the holiday weekend. Mom got the call. She did not think it was that serious, so she went to the hospital. When she arrived, she was in shock. It was only then that she realized Dad was in big trouble. It was all happening so fast. She did not have time to call anybody. Her worst nightmare coming true and she was all alone. She told me that Dad knew he was not going to make it. The family doctor finally arrived, but it was too late. Dad was gone. Mom was with him alone as he passed.

To this day, she will not go to a hospital or visit a doctor's office. It's been forty-five years and she's stuck by her decision. Not a single exam or checkup in all that time. The whole family knows that Mom does not go to hospitals. If you are there, she will join you in spirit. I can't say I blame her. To her credit, she is not, nor has she ever been, on a single medication; she won't even take an aspirin if she has a touch of the flu. She just toughs it out.

With her high school sweetheart gone, she was left with four kids to bring up on her own. At six, I was the oldest and the only son. Janet had just turned five two weeks before. Tracy was three, and Julie was just six months. It must have looked like a pretty horrible situation, but my mom kept her head.

While she was in mourning, my grandparents came and took us with them. We didn't know what was going on. My grandparents' place was on forty acres in Gladwin, Michigan, about one hundred miles north of Flint. I remember driving the long dirt road to their house. They always kept the place perfect. At that time of year, the gardens next to the house were loaded with vegetables: corn, tomatoes, potatoes, onions, you name it—everything was in bloom.

They had this huge oak tree in the front yard that was exploding with new leaves and under a great big picnic table where we enjoyed the summer breeze. It's strange that on the day my dad died, the world was so full with new life, and we had no idea he was gone. I didn't know it yet, but I was about to start on my first comeback.

I ended up staying there for more than a month and loving every minute of it. I helped my grandpa Van clean up around the property. When I wasn't working, I would hang out by the creek that ran through the forty acres of land, cool and slow moving. I sat on the rocks and daydreamed about big things to come. Grandpa Van and I also watched baseball together on TV. He loved his Detroit Tigers and taught me about all their great players like Willie Horton, Norm Cash, Mickey Lolich, and of course, Al Kaline, "Mr. Tiger."

I really got to know my grandfather that summer for the first time. He was a great man. He never had much schooling. His father pulled him out after third grade to work in the fields. But the guy was a genius. I learned more from Grandpa Van than I ever would from any class I took or any book I ever read. He just flat out understood how things really worked in life. I didn't know it at the time, but he was getting me ready for what I was going to have to face. Without Grandpa Van, I would never have made it. It's as simple as that. I would have become a street punk, an inmate, or a drug addict—that's how it works in Flint.

He taught me so many incredible lessons, but most of all, he showed me that you have to respect people. He believed that there is value in everyone, that everyone has something to offer. I picked this up from him. You don't dismiss people. You listen to what they have to say. He said that people want to be heard. If you listen with real interest, they can feel it, and they will respect you and be loyal to you. It's so simple, but how many business people really do it?

Because of Grandpa Van's advice, I found talent in people they didn't even know they had. I saw that they could be brilliant, and I let them have at it.

We loved that summer at Grandpa Van's place and never had a clue as to why we were really there. Even after we returned home to Flint, no one told us our father was dead. I remember seeing my mother sitting at the kitchen table with the saddest of hearts. I watched her not knowing why she was so sad. And she didn't give any reason as to why. When one of us asked about Dad, we were told Grandpa Van would explain everything.

For us kids, it was really a weird and scary time. We lived in a strange limbo of sadness. Something bad happened or maybe something bad was going to happen—we just didn't know what it was. I don't know why they took so long to tell us. I think they were still in shock and couldn't figure out what to do next, even though it was pretty obvious.

Finally, the day came when my grandfather let me in on what was going on with my father. He took me to his house in Flint to do it. Even though it was forty-five years ago, I remember it like it was this morning. At around 10:00 a.m., on a mild Michigan fall day in September, we stood in the shade between my grandfather's house and the garage. Grandpa Van, who seemed huge to me, looked at me through his plastic-framed glasses. He didn't say anything for the longest time. I kicked around some little rocks and messed with the buttons on my tan plaid shirt. He put his hands on my shoulders, bent down, and looked me in the eye. He said, "Mike, your dad is gone and you are the man of the house now, you're gonna need to take care of yourself now, and you're gonna have to take care of them three girls and your mom too. You understand?"

I nodded my head yes, but I was six years old, what did I know? My heart suddenly got as heavy as a boulder. It was like a huge hole had been ripped in my world. My dad, my hero and my favorite person in the whole world, was never coming back. On top of that, I was supposed to get that I had to start fending for myself and look out for my family too? It scared the shit out of me! I kept thinking, *Dad is gone now, and all of a sudden, it is all up to me. I am six years old; this can't be happening.* But it was. I don't know how much I really understood, but for sure I knew that my life was not going to be the same. It was comeback time.

My family wasn't comfortable talking about deep feelings. *Love* wasn't a word they used. My mother never told me she loved me until I was thirty-two. I knew she did, but it's different than someone actually saying it to you. This way of communicating creates distance between you and other people; it also teaches you to be independent. Even though I really felt connected to them, I also felt alone. When I first saw parents love their children openly, it confused me. I thought the kids were pussies. Eventually, I found out that I was sadly mistaken with this line of thinking.

Later in my life, it's probably one reason why I worked my butt off to build businesses. It gave me a way to be with people and do something great together. When I was a seven-year-old kid, I used to pray to God to give me children so that I could love them with all my heart. I make good on that prayer every day.

Dee's Way

For my mom, known as Dee by her friends, it was a hundred times tougher. In 1965, it was still very much a man's world. Women were almost second-class citizens. There wasn't a lot a woman could do to earn good money. Like most women of her generation, all she had was a high school degree.

Dee could have looked at my dad's loss as the end of the world. She could have given up and adopted us out or maybe even try to start her life over again with another man. But that wasn't her way. Mom never quit. She never stopped believing it would be okay. What's even more amazing is that she didn't complain. And if anyone ever had an excuse to bitch about the cards life had dealt her, Mom did. My biggest lesson in life was coming at me like a speeding train, and it was all courtesy of my mother who was just trying to survive. She taught me to fight and fight for the future, not the past. Mom let me know we would win and that we needed to stay on track.

I simply cannot stress this enough. It was through this terrible loss that I saw that the world could be won—no matter the odds and no matter the adversity. You have to fight and you have to believe; to do these things was the only way Mom lived. It was Dee's way. She missed her husband, but she had to buck up and raise four children. That is what was real, and it was every single day.

It still blows my mind to think that I never once heard her say how much better everything would be if my father was still around. She didn't waste an ounce of her energy on what could have been. She never looked back, and that was a lesson for me. The past is the past, and you can't do a single damned thing about it. If I could, I would have brought my father back in a flash. But he wasn't coming back, and we had to move forward. *That's a pretty crucial understanding for anyone looking to get into business, or more to the point, to stay in business. You deal with what is, and you move forward. There is no room for backward thinking in business.*

Dee went to work as a typesetter for the *Catholic Press*. She didn't make much. Even with the Social Security benefit from Dad's death, times were tough, to say the least. To bring in a little more money, she took a second job teaching typing to adults in night school.. She worked herself to the bone so we could have a decent life. She taught me what determination looked like each and every day. You can either sit around and cry about what you don't have or you can move forward with what you do have and make the very best of it. Dee was a genius at this.

Dee was a true warrior, a fighter in every sense of the word. Not because she wanted to be, but because she had to be.

Winter was the hardest time of the year. Michigan winters are bitterly cold, and our little frame house wasn't exactly airtight. When the temperatures hit ten below zero and your heating oil tank is on empty, you really feel it. I remember waking up under three blankets, teeth chattering, and being so cold, it hurt. I'd go downstairs wrapped in a blanket, wake up my sisters and mother, and we'd all go into the kitchen to crowd around the open oven. We would open the oven door, crank that baby on broil, and *yahoo!* we had heat—it was the only hot thing in the house.

You might think we cried and whined about it the whole time, but it wasn't like that for us. We huddled together, joked around, and made the best of it. If anything, it brought us closer as a family. This adversity built strength in our family and we knew we were in the fight together—the fight to survive. We did what we had to do, and there was no complaining. We are still that way today, a lesson we learned from Mom over forty-five years ago.

We had one bathroom in the house, and we'd take turns making runs for it. We'd shower as fast as we could so we could get back to the warm kitchen. It seems like a crazy way to live, but it was all I knew. I thought everyone lived that way.

The best day in the world was payday. Mom came home with groceries, which was great, but we were really psyched to see the heating oil deliveryman show up. I learned firsthand what COD (cash on delivery) meant because that was the only way the oil company worked—at least with us. My mom would hand the deliveryman a check. He would then pull out the long hose from the truck and run it down the length of the driveway to the tank in our basement—and *voila*, we'd have heat! No check, no heat. That's the power of money right there. Don't tell a poor kid from Flint that money doesn't matter. Man, the warm smell of the furnace first kicking on after days of being off was better than the smell of my grandma's fresh bread baking.

Even though her life didn't turn out the way she expected, Dee took on the challenge. What choice did she have? It would have been the easiest thing in the world for her to become a "What if" or "Why me?" person. What if things had been different? What if our father hadn't died? Or, "Why did this happen to me?" But she never fell into that trap. She kept moving forward. That was her way.

Everything I ever achieved and will achieve comes from doing it Dee's way. Persistence pays off. I had the best teacher in the world to teach me that lesson. Sometimes when I hear people bitch about how tough their lives are, I want to laugh because their troubles are nothing compared to what Dee went through. When I ask her about it now, Dee says, *"Everyone is always worried about keeping up with the Joneses. The Joneses? Hell, we were just worried about keeping up."*

How true it was, she was in survival mode, and she was just trying to keep up. She had only one thing to prove and that was she was going to take care of her children no matter what she encountered.

Ten Going on Twenty-One

With Mom working two jobs, by the time I was ten, I was pretty much on my own. I learned to take care of myself because I had to. I made myself meals, got myself to school. Pretty soon I was making money, too. My first paying gig was as an altar boy—I got a $2 tip for doing my cousin Joann's wedding ceremony when she wed her new husband, Dennis.

The money in my pocket got me fired up about making more. I started cutting lawns. I'd just show up at people's doors with the lawn mower. *That's the key to sales—you don't wait for them to call you; you go out*

45

and find the business. Half of this country is broke because people are sitting around waiting for the phone to ring.

As an entrepreneur, at the age of ten, I paid big dividends when they needed to be paid.

That summer I got an awful toothache. It hurt like hell, but I ignored it as long as I could. I remember drinking soda out of the side of my mouth, the side where the cavities weren't bothering me. I would drink in such a way so that the soda going down would not hit the blaring cavity and give me that sharp hurting sensation.

Before long, I constantly drank from that side of my mouth, even if the cavities were not acting up. People would ask if I realized I drank from the side of my mouth—I mean *a lot* of people would ask.

At one point I had a tooth that was hurting so bad I wanted to cry. It was a monster of a toothache. I finally went to the family dentist, Dr. Wiesendal, the next morning. Imagine a ten-year-old walking into the dentist's office without a parent. Today, they would send you right out the door. I did not want to bother Mom. I knew how hard she worked, and after all, it was my problem. It was my tooth, and it was time for me to man up. Like Grandpa Van said, I was the man of the house, so it was time to step up to the plate.

Doc whistled as he checked my tooth, told me it looked pretty bad and that it had to be dealt with. The good doctor gave me three options. Option one, root canal, would run me $90. Option two, a filling, would cost me $45. Option three, he could just yank it out for $30. I told him to give me until 4:00 p.m. I would be back then. He agreed.

I spent the rest of the day hustling up lawn-mowing jobs at $4–$8 a pop. By 4:00 p.m., I had the thirty bucks I needed to get the tooth pulled. I walked into Dr. Wiesendal's office and told him I'd take option number three. In his chair, he noticed my Pro-Keds stained green from cut grass. He asked me about the stains, and I told him

I'd been out mowing people's lawns. He did a double-take. He was putting it all together. He stopped for a minute to think about it.

"You were out cutting lawns to raise the money to have your tooth pulled?"

"Yes, sir!" I exclaimed.

He was stunned that a ten-year-old would take that kind of initiative.

"My tooth is killing me," I told him, "I had to do something."

Dr. Wiesendal was stunned; he was also touched. It was like he was proud of me and wanted me to know it. He pulled my tooth and said, "Today, I have a new rate, half-price." I paid him the $15 bucks, and I was on my way. I realized that hard work pays off in more ways than one. If I had asked Dr. Wiesendal to pull the tooth for free, he would have said no way. I was willing to do whatever it took. He saw that, and it made him want to help me. People respect hard work— you step up for them, they'll step up for you.

Working with Grandpa Van

My best times were with my grandpa Van. I'd spend the whole summer at his place. It was no country estate—he just barely got by on his retirement, between Social Security and his personal savings. It was the best forty acres in the whole world to me. I felt special when I was there. He taught me to hunt for deer, rabbit, squirrel, and duck, and to fish. But mostly I worked. He needed my help, and I was happy to give it. I loved him. He was my only real friend. He treated me like no one else in the world. If I had to work to be around Grandpa Van, that was a good deal to me.

That's how I learned to connect work with a larger purpose. So many people aren't willing to do the work it takes to really get somewhere in life. They get bored too easily. They give up. They think it's all about doing stuff you like. News flash: *Nobody enjoys everything about running a business or doing a job. It's your purpose that keeps you going. My purpose was simple—getting to be with Grandpa Van. It was more than a purpose; it was a passion. Passion is the key to success, and that is exactly what winners are made of—hard work and passion. If you do not have passion for what you are doing in life, then you are doing the wrong thing.*

When it comes to work, I remember many things about Grandpa Van. He was afraid of fire and had these fifty-gallon drums all over the property. I had to make sure they were full of water, just in case a fire broke out and the fire department couldn't get there in time. That was a job. So was the wood-chopping. Seems like I was chopping wood all the time, or picking worms off the tomato plants, mowing the lawn, working in the gardens, scraping the lane, mending fences, burying garbage, or something. He even had me clean the chimneys. We would put bricks in a burlap bag and drop it down. That was his system. You pull that bag up and down the chimney and it knocks all the soot loose. I was his chimney sweep.

Grandpa Van once told me something really amazing. He said, *"Once you start thinking you're better than somebody, you're not. I don't want to know anybody who's better than someone else."*

That stayed with me all my life, and I can tell you that as a businessperson, my biggest strength by far is connecting with people. I meet people where they're at, whatever level that is. I always treat people well because I want to be treated with respect myself.

Another big lesson Grandpa Van taught me was to face my fears. In the eighth grade, I had the biggest, meanest kid in class wanting to whip my ass. Gordie was all muscle. He was such a badass that he even beat up high school kids. His girlfriend, Polly, took a liking to me. We didn't fool around or anything, but Gordie found out and he thought the worst. It was all Polly's doing, but I was going to pay the price. That was on a Friday. I was in for a royal butt-whopping.

Word got around that Gordie was coming for me, so I took off early. I went to Grandpa Van's that weekend. The whole time, all I could think about was Gordie knocking my head in and beating the living snot out of me. I decided to tell Grandpa Van so he could talk to the school principal.

I told him about it while we were out working. He really loved me and wanted the best for me. I knew that, so I expected him to tell me he would take care of it. Instead he said, "You need to face this guy. If I step in to stop this, it would be worse than getting beat up."

I kept thinking, *I can't believe he's not going to help me.* What could be worse than a beating at the hands of Gordie? But he said I had to face my fears for myself and I accepted his judgment.

I went to school the following week feeling sick to my stomach, looking for Gordie around every corner. But he never got in my face. Turns out, Polly let him know that nothing went on between us, so he didn't come after me. Grandpa Van said it would work out okay, and it did.

What if Polly hadn't talked about me to Gordie? I probably would have gotten my ass kicked. But at least I would have faced up to it and gotten it over with.

As a friend said to me much later after my bankruptcy, *"There's no disgrace in falling down, the disgrace is not getting back up again."*

I remind myself of that every single day.

Chapter 5
Too Much Time for Trouble

In the absence of clearly defined goals, we become strangely loyal to performing daily trivia until ultimately we become enslaved by it.

—Helen Keller

For Christmas, when I was eleven, my mom got me an air-pump BB gun from Kmart. Don't ask me why, but I used it to shoot out the back window of a cop car. I was at my bedroom window when the squad car pulled up to the stop sign at our corner. So I took a shot. The BB should have bounced off, but it was so cold, a typical Michigan winter, that the glass just exploded. The cops probably thought they'd been fired on by an M16. They searched the whole street house to house for hours. I hid up in the attic. Fortunately, my mom didn't even know I was home and the cops never found me. All

I could think was what a lucky shot that was. What the hell was I doing taking a shot at a cop's car? Today, the FBI would have brought in J. Edgar Hoover, and I would have been in prison longer than Nelson Mandela was. It was a miracle shot, and to this day, I don't know why I made such a shot. That's just what we did in Flint. You were raised to hate the police—everyone you knew had had some kind of run-in with the law. It was us versus them. Maybe most of them were trying to do the right thing, but they came across like they were so much better than us—like we were nothing but street scum. I guess looking back, we were on the edge. Then again, kids do stupid stuff.

Maybe we weren't really mad at them at all. Maybe we were pissed off about the factory layoffs or our dads dying or becoming drunks or a thousand other things. Flint was a city of misplaced passion and random violence that could hit at any time. The reasons for it were like this giant knot you could never really untangle. Today, as then, Flint was and is the murder capital of the United States. You have to compare it to Afghanistan and Iraq to have manageable numbers. If you look it up today with respect to the FBI crime statistics, Flint shamefully leads the way. I kid you not! Google it.

It doesn't matter that I love Flint and I am incredibly proud to have been raised there. I would not have my children go through it, but it made me tough. It made me smart, real street-smart.

You know the film producer Michael Moore? I love that guy! He did *Fahrenheit 911* and *Bowling for Columbine*. We are about the same age, but I was truly from Flint—the belly of the snake. I think he was from Burton, a lot more upscale. His first big hit was *Roger and Me*, which I loved. Roger Smith was a greedy scumbag, and Michael showed it to the world.

Michael upset a lot of people in Flint with the way he portrayed the town. My uncle was pissed off. Oh man! I love Flint. Flint has a lot to offer. I wish Michael would have shown that Flint is where you get the *real* Coney Island hot dogs, not Detroit. In Detroit, they put

51

chili sauce on 'em and call 'em Coney's. Flint has the *real* Coney sauce. And for the number 1 Coney Island in Flint, see Dave at Atlas Coney Island on Corunna Road.

Unfortunately, Flint is not all about Coney Islands. It's a very dangerous town. Flint takes lives as often as Scottsdale delivers new breast implants. Stay off Saginaw Street after sundown; it is a war zone. This is the advice the sheriff gave me.

Maybe we were just numb and were trying to feel something—anything—and violence was the only way we knew how. Personally, I don't remember actually being angry. I just did all the things angry people do. I was a dumb kid in a dangerous town, and I'm lucky I made it through.

I have a file that I keep in my drawer called "The Lost Souls File." In this file are twenty-three names. They are all friends of mine from Flint and Flint Southwestern, the high school I attended, who are now dead. They are dead due to drugs and alcohol. It is the hardest file to pull out of my desk, but it is there.

It wasn't all child's play. If only it had been. By the time we hit our late teens, death or jail seemed the best bet for filling in the line in our yearbooks about what our future would be. One night, I was making the rounds, picking up my buddies, just before a football game between our high school team, Flint Southwestern versus Bay City Central, from a neighboring town. Our last stop was Scott Maslak's place.

Scotty was a character right out of *Pulp Fiction*—the one named Lance, played by Eric Stoltz—right down to his long reddish hair, his wiry frame, and the bathrobe he walked around in. Scotty was a live wire, full of energy. He was type A all the way. He always had a plan, he always had something to say, and he was funny as hell. When he walked into a room, it was like someone switched on the lights.

I had called Scott a couple of hours earlier and told him we'd be there, so he should have been out front. But when we pulled up, he wasn't. I honked, and he still didn't show. So we went to go get him. The front door was slightly ajar and we just walked in. That's Flint hospitality for you. But as soon as I got inside, I got a weird feeling. All the lights were out, and when we called for Scott, no one answered.

Scott had converted the basement into his own little party pad and hung out down there most of the time. It's also where he grew his pot under hydroponic lights. We could see the glow of the lights from the top stairs. There was also the slow thumping sound of a record that had played through to the end but hadn't been taken off the turntable. We thought he might have fallen asleep or passed out. But at the bottom of the stairs, I saw Scotty lying on the floor with the end of a shotgun barrel in his mouth and blood everywhere. His head had been blown apart. There was no point in checking for a pulse. We were in shock. Our best friend was soaked in his own blood.

The Flint police figured it was a suicide. We all knew better. We knew Scotty. He would have never have offed himself. But the cops weren't too interested in any details we could offer. To them, he was just another street punk who ended up where he had always been heading, just maybe a little sooner than expected. They had no CSI, no forensics. Just two patrolmen with an opinion, and that's it. Scott was one of the first in the file of twenty-three "Lost Souls."

We couldn't know for sure, but most likely Scotty was killed over some kind of drug deal. He grew much more dope than he could ever smoke himself. He'd been dealing and had probably pissed off somebody he shouldn't have. Scott had a sharp tongue and a slightly weird sense of humor, and your typical dope dealer doesn't have patience for all that. I also knew he had ripped off some guys from the north side for some hash. I always figure that they got their payback.

He should have been more careful. But *careful* wasn't exactly our thing. By the time I got out of high school, I'd been to the funerals of six close friends. That's a lot of death in your face before even hitting the age of twenty. A lot of the ones who didn't get themselves killed ended up in jail doing serious time for everything from drug dealing, robbery, or deadly harm–type charges. Drugs were always in the picture. Every story in my Flint neighborhood involves drugs—someone, somewhere, somehow. It is like a virus that is wiping out the city.

Doing Business on the Dark Side

Even as a kid, I was always looking for an opportunity. And I didn't just limit myself to legal ones. Pretty soon I figured out a way to make more money than by mowing lawns. I began to sell pot. I never smoked it much, but the cash came in handy. I hated the pot buzz, but I was never afraid to profit from it.

All my friends were stealing record albums, so I got in on the action. I must have boosted fifty copies of Pink Floyd's *Dark Side of the Moon* and sold them to people. They should have had a billboard chart for that—what album was getting stolen the most. In Flint, Pink Floyd would have ranked pretty high. I wore one of those parkas that had a fur hood and I could get about fifteen albums out under it in one shot.

I wonder how I even got away with it. I think being a little white kid helped. The store security was so uptight about the black kids that came in that I got away with the petty theft on a regular basis.

When I wasn't shoplifting, I was pulling tape decks and CB radios out of cars. I never thought about how much I was hurting people by ripping off their gear. It just never occurred to me. All I thought about was the cash I was going to pocket for it. Later, when I had my own video rental store and someone tried to shoplift from us, I thought back to that time. It was just normal then to live a criminal way of life. All my friends did it. I did it. That's how we rolled.

I once outfitted an entire junior high school football team with sports shoes. Zimmerman Junior High—the Clippers. They played on Astroturf at the Atwood Stadium, so Pro-Keds worked the best. They wore white and gold, and I got them shoes to match. I just didn't pay for them. When any of his players needed shoes, Coach Brody sent them to me. "Go see Roberts," he'd tell them. He didn't even give it a second thought, and he was the coach!

I'd walk into the shoe store with a paper in my pocket that had all the size information written on it and sneak peeks while I worked my way down the aisle. The tricky part was that football season started in August, so wearing that parka was a stretch. I must have made a hilarious sight wearing a heavy parka during that time of year, looking pregnant because of the shoes stuffed underneath it. But nobody stopped me.

Only when I got out of those surroundings and away from those people did I get a conscience about it all. It was like I had a complete conversion—from a criminal way of life to an honest life. I wanted something more for myself than being a screw-up from Flint. I felt I was better than that, and I was right. After I "crossed over," I never went back. This was to be my second big drive in life. The comeback—the chance to be something instead of nothing. To make a difference and to do the right thing. Albert Einstein once said, "Try not to become a man of success, rather try to become a man of value." It was a hard sell, but I bought in.

Rent a Con

Sometimes I wonder how I even got away with half the crap I pulled. By age nineteen, I'd gone to jail a couple of times for one or two days, usually for screwing up behind the wheel, and I'd gotten my license suspended. Of course, that didn't stop me from driving. I was never very good at following the rules of the road. Even now people say they feel safer with me as their pilot than as their driver!

It all came to a head one Friday night, in 1977, after I got off from work. I was working at GM Plant 2A, "the Hole," the same place where my dad had collapsed twelve years before and died three hours later at McLaren Hospital. I was a gas welder/repairer, a card-carrying member of UAW 659. My job was to fix radiator supports that busted coming down the line. We called them horse collars. I drank Jack Daniels at work; everyone did. One time when I wasn't paying attention, a horse collar came off the line and clipped my arm and cut it wide open. They sent me to the GM on-site hospital, patched me up, and got me right back to the line where I continued welding.

That Friday night after work, I got pulled over for speeding. My license had been suspended, so I got busted. The judge gave me three days in jail. I was making good money for back then—$12 an hour. I didn't want to miss the work, and of course, I didn't want to spend more time in lockup. I paid a guy named Rick Chamberlain to pose as me for the three-day stint. It was perfect, I thought. Rick looked enough like me that my ID would pass when he showed up at the jail. Anyway, who would think of someone sneaking *in* to jail? Once in, all he had to do was sit on his ass for three days and he'd make a hundred bucks.

The plan worked like a charm until day 3, when they told ol' Rick he also had to pay the $116 fine to get out. Rick tried to reach me every which way he could, but no luck. Remember, no cell phones back then. See, he either had to catch me at home or on the job, or he was out of luck. Actually, I was the one out of luck.

Rick had had enough of being behind bars. So Rick finally called his brother, Randy, to pay the fine and spring him. Of course, he couldn't exactly explain our little scam to his brother from the jail, so Randy wasn't clued in. When he arrived to pay Rick's way out, he asked for Rick, not Michael Roberts. So much for trading places!

They ended up letting Rick go. They couldn't figure out what to charge him with. Technically, he hadn't broken any laws! What do you charge a guy with for going to jail under the wrong name? Think about that one! I'm sure they have a charge for it now that probably carries the death penalty. They weren't so easy on me. Apparently, the judge didn't see the humor in my stunt and slapped me with another thirty days in jail. This was the first time I made the front page of the paper, but it would not be my last. And the Sunday paper no less. The headline read, RENT A CAR, RENT A COP, RENT A CON!

It brings me much sadness to write the following. In my "Lost Souls" file, Rick Chamberlain just recently became number twenty-three. I cried. He was the best of the best. A mismanaged prescription, it is said. He was alive when I started writing this book.

So there I was, sitting on my ass and hating every second of it, when on day 10 of the thirty days, the turnkey comes to my cell and tells me I'm free to go. I thought it was some bureaucratic screw-up, so I just bit my tongue and got the hell out of there before they figured it out. I called my mom right away for a lift and was back on the line at "the Hole" the next day. What screw-up did the jailers do? Why was I set free? I was not in an arguing mood; I let them win.

Only after my grandfather had passed away did I find out the true story. My granny Van finally told me that Grandpa couldn't sleep at night once he heard I was in jail. Finally, he went into town to have a word with the judge. He wore his favorite hat and a clean shirt. This was big. He wore the dress hat he saved for only important meetings. I know he must have fought with himself over that one. He was a man who never liked asking for favors. I know, because I'm the same way. But sometimes you have to—it just better be for the right reason. Grandpa Van was a quiet man but carried himself with dignity and could dominate a room when he wanted to.

See, Grandpa Van knew the real Mike. He, along with Mom, raised me, and he knew I was one of the hardest-working guys he had ever run herd on. I could take all he dished out, and I would come back begging for more. I would say to Grandpa Van, "Is that all we got today? I figured we were going to do some real work! Guess I was wrong." And as I was rambling, the sun was going down. He loved that. He would laugh, but the next day he would try to pile it on. I loved being with him and never minded the work. I loved my time alone with him, and I got a lot of it. He was my hero. A better man there was none.

Granny Van told me that he said to the judge, "You've got my grandson, Michael Roberts, locked up in your jail. He's the one they put in the paper a couple Sundays ago. You don't know my grandson and what a good young man he is. Michael is always the first one I can count on, and he's got a good head on his shoulders. He comes up to my property and works whenever I need him, and he puts in a hard day's work without ever a complaint. In fact, he comes up a lot of the time without even being asked.

"He wipes his feet, he hangs his coat up, and he always thanks his grandmother for the food. My grandson is a good young man, Judge. And he needs to be out of your jail! Now! I respect your position, but I'm not asking. I'm here to set things right. He's learned his lesson, and you need to let him go."

The judge agreed and shook my grandfather's hand. Grandpa Van put on his hat, got in his Chevy pickup, and drove home. I was released that day and Grandpa Van never said a word to me or anyone else about it.

It's no surprise to me that he could persuade a judge. He had that kind of personal power, and some of it definitely rubbed off on me. It's just one of the many ways he touched my life. When I stop and think about everything Grandpa Van did for me, it blows my mind. Sometimes I wish I could have sat down with him and thanked him for it all, item by item. Of course, that could never have happened. We didn't talk that way in my family. Also, it would have taken the whole day—since he blessed me in so many ways—and Grandpa

Van would have never stood for that. So I guess it's really my way of remembering the man who was my best guide and my best friend.

Getting a Clue

Even though I got out early, ten days in the Genesee County Jail was enough time for me to get a clue. Sitting there staring at the crummy walls of my cell, I couldn't fool myself. My buddies and I talked cocky talk. You would have thought we were on top of the world or at least headed there. But we were going down—every last one of us, including me, unless I got the hell out of "the 313," the area code for Flint. If I didn't make a move, prison, drugs, and death were the only things coming my way.

I only knew of two ways out—college or the armed forces, the recruiters whom we called "the Body Snatchers." So I was sitting on a bench in a jail when my next comeback started to take form. I decided to do what no one in my family did before—I was going to go to college.

What made me different from all the guys who didn't make it out? It was something inside me that said there was more for me. Maybe it started when I was six years old and my grandfather told me I was to become the man of the house. Maybe I just started thinking bigger. In Flint, it's so easy for the demons to get to you. You see people struggling all around you and it becomes normal to think that crap is all there is.

I always felt like I had a destiny, like there was something bigger waiting for me that I had to go find. I had a desire and the ambition to better my life. It came from the inside. The two biggest influences in my life, my mother and grandfather, had it too. But they had families to care for and obligations to answer to. I was the one in a position to make a move. I could accomplish what they never had the chance to really try. Something in me said, *God put you here for a reason, so you sure as hell better find out what that is.*

59

When I was a little kid, I thought Flint was the perfect place. But then it went bad on me. So I had to move on. Too many people are afraid to trust that gut instinct. But it's all I had. I knew I needed to get out, simple as that. Do what you gotta do. Sometimes it's not easy to get up and leave a place you're used to, but it's a hell of a lot better than staying there and rotting. It is a damn sight better than becoming one of the twenty-three "Lost Souls."

That's what a comeback really is—it's when you just don't stop. You *can't* stop. You won't let yourself rot. No matter what you've been through, you know something more is waiting for you. Maybe you can't see it, but you feel it in your gut. You may have lost some money or someone you loved, you might think you've lost everything, but when you lie in bed at night, underneath all the static buzzing around your head, in the quiet of your heart, you can still feel it there, that sense of purpose pumping away.

Even if everything else in your life is so mixed up and it's like a blur, that feeling tells you the one thing you really need to know: you are unstoppable. You need to know you can win and win you will if you believe in just one person—and that person is you.

I knew I could escape. I knew I would make a better life, and I did. I was broke, but I *was* determined. The most important thing in the world was my own personal power—I believed in *me.*

Chapter 6
Run for the Future

This is the lesson: never give in, never give in, never, never, never, never—in nothing, great or small, large or petty—never give in except to convictions of honor and good sense. Never yield to force; never yield to the apparently overwhelming might of the enemy.

—Sir Winston Churchill (1941)

For some kids, the future is all teed up for them. High school leads to college, college leads to a career, and then the house with the white picket fence is just waiting for them to move into. For me, I was staring straight at a dead end. To even have a future, I had to make a run for it. If I just kept taking the lowlife road I was on in Flint, I would get sucked down into the muck forever.

College was my shot at getting out. But it was a hell of a long shot. Within the crowd I ran with, our idea of higher education was getting stoned in the back parking lot at school. We'd smoke grass before school and in-between classes. Sometimes we just cut class totally. The principal had to go out there to try and herd us back in. His name was Olasuski, Principal Olasuski; we called him "O" for short. His son was one of the biggest dope heads in school and was a friend of mine. When O showed up, we would scramble. It was like an immigration raid at a factory full of illegals. That's what we felt like— outlaws, outcasts, like we really didn't count for much.

When we saw O coming, some went back to class while others just headed to another parking lot. Some just took off, and we never heard from them again. In other words, education was more like an elective—one you never really picked. So when I started saying that I was going to college, people basically didn't believe me. They looked at me like I was a total dreamer, or they thought I was lying—that is, I was lying to myself because even though they knew I would never amount to anything, they were laughing inside knowing that I had no clue. When they finally accepted that I was serious, everyone was pretty sure I'd fall flat on my face. Behind my back they'd talk about me like I was on dope, like I was living in some pipe dream.

At home it was even worse. One Friday night at the kitchen table, I said to my mom, "I've decided I want to go to Michigan State." Before she could even get one word out, her boyfriend, Jimmy, said, "There's no way a shit-ass, little shop rat like you is gonna get accepted into MSU." Jimmy never missed a chance to put me down, but I didn't take it too personally; he was that way with everyone.

My mom had been seeing James "Jimmy" MacArthur since I was fourteen. The guy sold concrete, and sometimes I wish he would have bought himself a pair of concrete shoes and gone for a nice long walk in the Flint River. The first night my mom brought him home, in struts this 5'5" bulldog of a man, with a crew cut and so full of himself him that he could hardly see anyone else, especially considering he spent that whole evening talking about himself—

Jimmy. He was his favorite subject, if not his only subject. "I can kick anyone's ass. Nobody gets one over on Jimmy MacArthur."

Anybody who's been on the street at all knows that there's *always* someone out there meaner and tougher than you are. You just don't want to meet them. He made so many of these knucklehead statements that we started to call them "Jimmyisms." As my little nine-year-old sister put it, "Jimmy sure likes to talk about himself." He was truly a legend in his own mind.

Even my sister was not fooled by severe "little man" syndrome. The big mystery was what did Mom see in this guy? She was with that jackass for about ten years, and he never got any better. He smoked three packs of Marlboros a day, drank a six-pack or two of Pabst Blue Ribbon every night, and was as short on goodwill as he was short in stature.

At the time, I really didn't know why she was with him. Looking back, I realize she was always attracted to strong personalities. All her friends tended to have these huge, overbearing personalities. They were control freaks. So Jimmy just fit the profile. It didn't help that she was a widow with four kids to raise on her own. How many men, especially in those days, wanted in on that? "Pat, may I have an *S* please?" I'm sure she realized that her options were pretty limited and she took the best one she thought she had. Unfortunately, that was Jimmy.

The fact is that being poor, you learn to tolerate a lot of shit. A crummy car, a crummy neighborhood, crummy clothes, and crummy people. Jimmy was just another thing to tolerate. That's one of the reasons why I hate poverty so much. It wears you down. It makes you settle for less *every* single day. Pretty soon, you're so worn out by the daily grind that you just accept that you can't have what you really want. The clouds close in; that's just the way it is. You know the bum ain't no prince, but who remembers what a prince even looks like?

By the grace of God, along with my mom, I had Grandpa Van as my mentor. He was my hero, my best friend, and the one guy who loved me with all his heart. Much of who I am I owe to his guidance. He told me, "Never let anyone else decide what you're worth." He said that if I ever felt bad about myself because of something someone said, it was because I let them get me down. That was huge. That meant I was in charge. I had to take responsibility for how I felt.

This was incredible advice. We all face people who want to put us down. Guys like Jimmy are pros at it. That short little piece of shit went from 5'5" to 6'3" when he put someone down, and he spared no one. He was always out to hurt people if he could. I was always so surprised he did not drive a big-ass truck. He never got tired of calling me some nasty name or dumping on anything I said or did. It was the only way he knew how to build himself up. What a sad excuse for a human being. Me and my buddies used to crack up how he always started his putdowns with the word *little*—"little shitheads," "little, no-good bastards," "little this, little that." You didn't have to be Freud to figure out what his problem was. We were all like seven inches to a foot taller than him and maybe fifty to a hundred pounds heavier.

Why would he get all worked up about me going to college? That was a good thing, wasn't it? Not to Jimmy. He took anything positive happening to someone else as a personal affront or a threat to his insecurities. He heard "I'm going to MSU" as "I'm going to MSU so I can be smarter and better than you!" Like nothing could happen in the world without it revolving around *him*. He would squint his eyes and wrinkle his nose like something smelled really nasty. He hated me for wanting something better for myself and for going for it.

God rest his soul and fuck him. What Jimmy didn't get about me, what I didn't even get about myself, was that when someone tells me I can't do something, it lights a fire under me, and I get things done. I love the challenge. Proving someone wrong about me is as much fun as doing the thing itself. It's one thing to win when you are supposed to win, but it's so much sweeter when they don't think you can do it.

Jimmy didn't stop me. He just added fuel to my fire. He inspired me, which was exactly what he did not want to do. He thought he would defeat me, but he was wrong. He only made me want to fight for it more. You see, just because this guy did not believe in me had nothing to do with me believing in myself. Plus, why would I want to stay home to listen to him dump his failure on me on a regular basis?

The good news was that Mom was a true believer, and she learned to ignore Jimmy's defeatist, put-down comments. Mom knew I could do anything I set my mind into, and she was, without a doubt, my biggest cheerleader. When most moms put their little children to bed at night, they read them nursery rhymes. Not my mom. She told me about the world, and she told me that I could be anything I wanted to be. Mom always looked forward and always saw the light. This is why Jimmy was such a curiosity to me because he was nothing. However, one thing that Jimmy had was *confidence*, all about his own feats. Even if he were an asshole, he believed in himself, and he would tackle anything. I think this is what Mom liked about the little worm. It was, in fact, the one thing I did admire about him.

Making the Grade

As much of a loser as Jimmy was, and he could have been in the *Guinness Book of World Records*, he was right about one thing—my grades wouldn't get me into MSU. So I enrolled in Central Michigan University (CMU). I knew nobody thought I had a chance of making it. That didn't get me down. It got me fired up! All my life I've used criticism as motivation. I love proving the disbelievers wrong. Tell me I can't do something, please. Just say, "Mike, that's impossible for you!" and you've just sparked the fire in me to take another step forward in my life. Thank you very much.

That's how it was with getting into college. Poor white kids like me didn't go to college. It just didn't happen. I was the guy parents didn't want their children to hang around. They were afraid I'd corrupt them, mess them up for life. I lived on the edge of trouble all the time. I always wanted to be where the action was, and in Flint, the action was usually bad news.

The beauty of being that kid, the bad kid that parents did not want their kids hanging around with, was that if a friend ever pissed me off, all I had to do was go ring his doorbell and tell his mom we were supposed to meet up, and boom, they were grounded for life.

That's what went down with Donnie Leach, who happened to be the brother of Rick Leach, All-American quarterback for the University of Michigan and *Sports Illustrated* cover boy. Donnie was my best friend, but Donnie never wanted his folks to know he was hanging around with me. One time we were supposed to meet up but he blew me and the guys off. My assignment was to go knock on his door. So finally, I just knocked on his front door and said to his mom, "Hello, Mrs. Leach! Is Donnie home? We were supposed to meet up." Big trouble for him. The irony of that whole deal was that in the end, I was the guy who inspired Donnie to get out of Flint. After I moved to Phoenix, he came down too. I was happy he did; we are still good friends.

The neighborhood bad boy is not supposed to get into college. That just didn't happen. But I made it happen. I pulled up my grades and test scores together, and I made it in. I shocked the world, at least the world of Flint.

There's a famous story that Muhammad Ali tells in the book *The Right Words at the Right Time* by Marlo Thomas. I have read it many, many times. Growing up poor and black in Louisville, Kentucky, Ali had a vision of greatness. He would puff out his chest and tell everyone he was going to be the best in the world. He just believed, deep in his heart, he believed, and he let people know about it.

I am the greatest; I said that even before I knew I was.

—Muhammad Ali

Ali believed, and this is exactly why he was the best boxer in the history of the sport. Because he believed, he fought with his heart. He was a winner, he was a warrior, and he was the greatest champion of all times. Why? Because he believed it to be true, he went and made it true.

One day, one of Ali's teachers came up to him in the school hallway and told him straight to his face, *"You ain't never gonna be nuthin'."* She just couldn't stand it that he had big ideas for himself. This motivated him more than any other one thing in his life.

When he was seventeen, Ali won the Golden Gloves competition. Then the next year, 1960, he won the Olympic gold medal in Rome. Guess what? Suddenly he *was* the best in the world.

What was the first thing Ali did when he got home? He went straight over to that teacher's classroom and showed her his gold medal. He dangled it in her face so she could see exactly how wrong she had been. Then he walked out and never went back. Ali said it was the most important thing he had ever done.

It could have been that one spark that set him on fire, a pure rage and a champion he became. You never know what one thing may push us to greatness. One little step, one more extra effort, one more ounce of belief may be the one that makes you the winner. This is why Ali never gave up, and this is why you should never give up. Winners start where quitters stop.

For me, the acceptance from CMU was like winning a gold medal. Everyone figured I was just kidding myself. "College, Mike? Okay it's your story, tell it how you like." I pulled it off, and I wore my pride all over town. It was a huge win for me, a major comeback from the dead-end road I'd been heading down. When I told people I was going to CMU, they couldn't believe it. They'd written their own story about me. They thought the street punk Mike Roberts was all there was.

This was my first real big lesson. It didn't matter what others thought I was capable of; it was only important that I knew I was capable of accomplishing. I knew who I was. I made a decision then

67

and there that I wasn't going to screw this up. No matter what, I was going to get it done. Over and over again I told myself, *I'm not flunkin' out, I'm gonna make it. I'm not flunkin' out, I'm gonna make it. You will do this and you will not fail.*

I needed to do very well at CMU if I were to realize my ultimate dream, going to MSU (Michigan State University). It's a funny thing about the American dream—everybody loves that idea, but mostly for themselves, not for you. They don't want you to have the American dream because they think that means there's less of it left for them. If you think everyone wants you to succeed, you're in dreamland. It's one of the hardest lessons I was to learn.

> *That when people tell you you can't, that's not a sign to quit. That's the time to turn up the intensity, put your heart into what you're doing and prove the sons of bitches wrong.*
>
> —General George Patton

The Social Experiment

I remember sitting in my dorm room in Mount Pleasant, Michigan, near the mighty Chippewa River, and realizing I was in a whole new world. How the hell did I get here? I decided that no matter what, I was going to treat people with respect, even the stuck-up rich kids. In an effort to fit in, I went with the dormies to The Wayside, the popular campus bar, and made about thirty new friends. It was a blast. But I paid for it the next morning. That's when I learned the chair-in-the-shower trick. I was so hung over I couldn't stand up in the shower, so I brought a chair in with me. I sat there and relished the moment as the water beat down on me like a hammer on a nail.

Classes were tough, especially since I'd never had to study before. Where I went to school, it wasn't required; hell, at Flint Southwestern, studying was frowned upon. It was a transfer station and to where did not really matter, just be the hell on your way.

I hit the books hard and managed a 3.3 grade point average. It took about five hours a night in the library, but I got it done. My life was really simple: classes, library, bar. That was it. I had never been so determined in my life. All I could think of was the guys back in Flint saying I wouldn't make it, or little Jimmy telling my mom, "He will be home any day, you better not let him stay here, make sure you get him the hell out." What I learned later, and to wit, what became important, was that my battle changed from proving the guys in Flint wrong to winning the battle for them as well as for me. I needed to give them something to believe in, and I was that ticket. If they could see me make it, they would believe they could make it. I became a torch—a torch of hope.

I made friends easily; I had always been the popular guy. But it was different rubbing elbows with rich kids. They were from places like Farmington Hills, Bloomington Hills, Gross Pointe—all the places I used to drive by and say, "Someday." I felt like I was getting closer to where I wanted to be. For the first time, I had a sense of a future. My mentality went from trying to stay out of prison in Flint to thinking about success. That's what a different class of people will do for you. I had advanced to a new level—the top of the class. Now, the secret would be to stay there. The rich had let me in; someone left the barn door open, and I took my chance. My A game just got better. We are what we eat, and I was eating pretty well now.

Houston, Tranquility Base here. The Eagle *has landed.*
—Neil Armstrong

It's not like I thought I was one of them. I wasn't stupid. I was the government's social experiment—the kid from Flint. Give him a $10,000 Pell Grant and see what happens. That's one of the few advantages of being poor; the government gives you stuff. They give it to you for being poor; that's how it works. The rich let you know they are rich, and because you are poor, you notice it more than anyone. But I never felt they were better than me; they may have, but I didn't.

The most important thing is that I kept my focus, even when it got really hard. I didn't let the coeds or the drinking get me off track either. I had a plan, and I wasn't letting go of it. I wanted into Michigan State University. Yeah, the same place Jimmy MacArthur said would never take me.

I got good grades, and after two years, I applied to Michigan State University again.

I had other reasons besides just rubbing Jimmy's nose in it. MSU had a higher status rating than Central Michigan. CMU was a fabulous experience and a tremendous school, but MSU had always been my goal. I took the important step that would lead me to the ultimate prize. Going to MSU would mean instant credibility for me when it was time to make my move. Same reason I chose Ernst & Young as my accountant and Fennemore Craig as my law firm years later. The rich taught me all about credibility; people will give you money because of who you hang with.

Sweet Success

Michigan State would open doors for me, but first I had to get in the door. I sent my application and waited, and waited. Finally, one April morning, my mom called. She'd gotten a letter from MSU. I told her not to open it; I wanted to read it myself. As soon as classes were over Friday afternoon, I tore out of that place. I hopped in my 1974 Chevy Monte Carlo, cranked the radio, and hit the road at about 3:00 p.m. The whole hour-and-a-half drive to Flint, Pink Floyd, Grandfunk Railroad, and Led Zeppelin were doing their thing. Green fields whipped by me while I wondered what that letter was going to say. *Dear Lord, I need this win.*

Part of me was in suspense, but part of me knew better. If I didn't get in this time around, I'd just hit the books harder and apply again.

I was unstoppable. I'd figured out the difference between a winner and a loser—the winner is the one who keeps going. It's not always pretty, but it doesn't have to be. I wasn't about to give up, no matter what. I knew it, so I had nothing to worry about.

Mom was standing in the kitchen holding the envelope when I walked in. We both knew what this meant to me. I had no hesitation. I just took the envelope and opened it. The first three words told me everything I needed to know. "We are pleased . . ." But you better believe I read every single word of that letter. I read it and reread it and reread it. I took it everywhere with me. I was in! I was in! It felt so incredible to *finally* get the big win in my life. I still get chills thinking about it to this very day. Not just because I got accepted by MSU, but because I proved to myself that I could make it happen. No matter who called me a dumbass, or how bad I sometimes felt about myself, with my hard work and my belief, I could make it happen. Anything is possible!

When I showed the letter to my mom, she about flipped. I've never seen her so excited. She's always been my biggest fan, so it was especially sweet to be able to give her the good news. When people root for you, you want to show them it was worth their while. You want them to know they rooted for the right underdog. Mom had stood by me through some pretty low moments. She just always had this look in her eye that said, *You're better than this crap, Mike, you're a lot better than this.* She never quit on me. Not even close. Now, finally, she had something to show for her faith in me. I loved giving that to her. What a rush! It was better than any high I'd gotten from any drink or drug. I liked the world—in fact, I loved it. I was part of the success system. I could make a dream happen, and it was not going to be taken away by drugs or by Flint.

The next few days I showed that letter all around Flint. It wasn't just Jimmy MacArthur who had blown me off. My high school counselor, someone you would think should have been encouraging me to reach higher, tried instead to get me to lower my sights and go to Community College. She told me, point blank, MSU was not in the cards for a guy like me. Instead, I should focus on my job at Chevrolet. It was the best job I could get, and she did not want me to blow it. She hadn't wanted me to disappoint myself—well, I didn't want to disappoint her either, but I was going to MSU!

To be honest, it was easy to understand why people were so blown away by what I'd achieved. Success for someone like me wasn't supposed to read that way. For shop rats, you did your thirty years in the Hole for GM and then retired to a hunting cabin up north. And that was the best-case scenario. Short of that, we were all destined to end up on drugs, in prison, or dead. We were a bunch of inner-city fuckups. The idea of going to college and getting somewhere in life was like a dream—shit like this didn't happen to guys like us.

I remember the look in my buddies' eyes when I told them I'd gotten in to MSU—it was like my success was their success, like I had to make it for them too, not just for myself. I took that feeling with me when I left for East Lansing, that feeling that they were counting on me, that I had to be the guy that got out of Flint alive. I wore that badge with pride. I have never been ashamed of where I came from. Flint wasn't easy on anyone, but I learned loyalty there, and how to rise above tough times, and that no one is better than anyone else. I wasn't going to MSU to try to erase Flint from my mind. Flint would always be a part of me. But there was also more for me, and Michigan State was my way to get there.

I'm not sure what I expected from Jimmy. For some messed-up reason, part of me always wanted to impress him. He had been so 100 percent sure I would blow it; so of course, I wanted to show him how wrong he was. I guess I should have known he would never give me that satisfaction. His response was "typical Jimmy." I was all lit up, so when I handed the letter to him, he already knew what it would say. He didn't even look at it. He just tossed it on the table and said, "Just 'cause you got in doesn't mean you'll ever make it through. Besides, how you gonna pay for it?" It's one thing to be a complete asshole; it's even worse to be a predictable one. But that was Jimmy.

There have been other "Jimmies" along the way. In the long run, they all did me a favor. They taught me that there will always be people who put you down. *No matter how great your idea is or how much you've accomplished, there will always be someone who says you're nothing, that you can't do it, that you're nuts to even try. And at the first sign of something going wrong, they'll whisper "quit" right in your ear, if you let them. DON'T LET THEM! RISE ABOVE THEM AND RISE ABOVE YOURSELF.*

Because of Jimmy and people like him, I've learned to shut out those voices. I've learned to keep right on going and even to hit the accelerator. You have to realize that these guys aren't just speaking from the heart. They're not out to protect you or me. They've got their own agendas for opening their big mouths; you can be sure of that. They've brought the fear to themselves; they've quit on their own success. The last thing they want to see is me or anyone else "make it." That would only prove to them how badly they failed. They want you to quit or fail to show that they were right to pass on their own dreams.

Of course, these are the same people who, when you do succeed, tell you that you just got lucky. People will tell you that you happened to be in the right place at the right time. You had some special advantage they never had. Really? You mean like growing up in Flint without a dad? Was that my lucky break? Over the years, I've figured out something about luck—the harder I work, the luckier I get.

> *I find that the harder I work the more luck I seem to have.*
> —Thomas Jefferson

There's no mystery about success. You gotta get your butt out there and stay out there. Determination, persistence, and a passion for what you do—that's what makes it happen.

73

My first real big break happened, and it happened because nobody but Mom and I believed it would happen. I got out when I was supposed to stay. I was beaten down, but I was not beat. I rose above and I found the victory, the victory that we all want in our lives. We've just got to go and get it.

CHAPTER 7
NO U-TURNS

The reason most people never reach their goals is that they don't define them, or ever seriously consider them as believable or achievable. Winners can tell you where they are going, what they plan to do along the way, and who will be sharing the adventure with them.

—Dr. Martin Luther King, Jr.

Being accepted into Michigan State University was an awesome achievement. I amazed my friends and shocked the critics. But once you feel that first rush of achievement, you want it again and again. You can't live off of yesterday's glory.

I equate it to an interview I watched with Chuck Negron, lead singer of Three Dog Night, and ex-heroin junkie. In the interview, Chuck described his first heroin experience. He went to a place he had never been to before, and he literally threw up. He felt as if he

75

were going to die, the vomit spewed out as he fought to breathe, but the high was so intense that from that day forward, he spent every day in pursuit of that high one more time. He became a junkie and lost millions. Eventually, he was homeless and living on the scraps of the streets. He entered rehab some thirty-eight times, always turning back to that one high he could never ever again find. Although he never found it, he kept the feverish search for it. Ultimately, he married, and he became a counselor. He is now and is credited with saving lives. He found his new high, and he is the better for it.

I have never done heroin, so I am not sure what Chuck went through. But I am a success junkie, and I, too, am always searching with great fever for the next success. This is where you come in. You can find success and you can make success, but it is up to you. I figure why not become a junkie for a good cause—success.

Getting into MSU was my first true shot of heroin; I was a pure junkie at this point. A pure junkie for success and I have never given up my search since the first big one. Not for a single day. I had another big rush that I will describe in a later chapter that will make this point even more relevant. The rush was all I needed for me. I loved that others were impressed, but at the end of the day, it was all about me. It was about reaching a *dream. And the high was unbelievable.* It was official! I was a success junkie, and I had the thirst. I knew victory, and I wanted to know it again, and again, and again. For me the addiction could not be treated in rehab; it needed to be fed with more successes.

I was proud to be at MSU! Damn proud!

One ice-cold February day, I was walking across the intramural fields at MSU, which we affectionately called "the frozen Tundra," and I thought, *I will get out of the freezing weather.* It was more than that too. I was hungry to turn the page and to start my future.

It was here that I needed cash—cold, hard cash—to put myself through school. So I did what every good entrepreneur does. I found a way to make money. You couldn't keep an entrepreneur like me down. I started working as a referee, of all things.

I went with a friend to see her friend's little brother play a high school freshman football game. At halftime, I asked the ref how he got the job. For a guy who broke rules on a daily basis growing up, this was my first time to be on the other side—an enforcer of rules. Go figure! I was interested to be on the other side. He gave me the number for the Parks and Recreation Department, and I got my certification. Next thing I knew, I was officiating high school football games. Then I got into Community College basketball and adult-league fast-pitch softball. I possessed no special training or skills to be a referee. I read a book, took a test, and got my zebra stripes. I pretty much had no clue. The one thing I did know how to do was to stand my ground. Flint had taught me all about that. I knew, as I always have, that I can do it, so let's get it done.

Blowing a call in a game is a bad day, real bad day. What's even worse is getting pushed around by the players in such a way that no one's in charge. That's when all hell breaks loose. I learned to make a call and stick to it, even if it was the wrong call. Even if it was ridiculous and the players bitched like I'd just had sex with their mothers. Let 'em bitch. I was the ref; I had the whistle. *It's a great lesson in leadership. You're gonna make mistakes, that's a given, sometimes you just have to go with it. Stand by your decision and fix it the next time. Don't be chicken about making mistakes; mistakes won't take you down. It's making the same mistake over and over that will bury you. Try to make all new mistakes.*

Being a referee also provided a very practical business management lesson. If one of the other refs made a bad call, you stood behind him or her. I loved the "hers" by the way, something about a lady in a referee's outfit. Later in the business world, I discovered that I could never go against anyone who worked for me or with me. I had to stand by them, right or wrong. I put them there, and they needed my support. We would discuss the mistake in private and fix it in public; I stood behind them.

As a referee, I didn't back down. This got me hired back, and pretty soon, I had ten guys working for me, on my crew and in separate crews. Now I was climbing; I was the crew chief of my crews. I was the youngest crew chief in the system. Age does not matter; it is *confidence* that will win the day. A good entrepreneur cannot be a good entrepreneur without being a good leader and without being confident. To me it seemed simple. I took the bull by the horns and made it happen. I knew what needed to be done right, and I was the right one to do it.

When one of my guys made a bad call and I saw it, I had to run over there and support them. They needed to know that I had their backs. That was a critical management lesson. The worst thing I could do was to overrule that referee's decision on the field. It would have killed his confidence, made him quit wanting to make any calls at all because he didn't want to make the wrong one. So the first step was to back him up.

It's a lesson I follow to this day. When a manager makes a bad decision, I support them first, and then we talk it over in private. If they need to change direction with a team member, the change comes from them, not from me. That way, the chain of command stays intact. They keep their authority, and the game goes on. A lot of leaders are so hell-bent on letting everyone know how smart they are they just overrule a team member. Yes! They look smart, but they destroy their teammate or subordinate's confidence or their self-esteem. A real leader and a true genius never manages above or around someone, but through them privately!

Refereeing was a great little gig. It kept me in bar money and helped prepare me for the bigger things that lay ahead. But after four years, I was bored with college. I was ready to get on to those bigger things. When you get right down to it, I'm a doer. I like to get out and build stuff. I like to work hard and see the results. College was more like practice for real life. I was tired of practicing. I wanted to be in the game. There's only so much prep stuff I can take before I want to roll up my sleeves and get into it. I was ready to make my mark. I'd hung out with rich kids long enough. Now, I wanted to see what I could do in the real world.

Hitting the Road

I had a friend who lived in Phoenix who said I could crash on his couch. So, with $900 in my pocket and a girlfriend named Bunny, I hit the road. Bunny and I got as far as Effingham, Illinois, before our muffler decided it wasn't going with us any farther. With a smack on the pavement and a shower of sparks, we were stopped in our tracks. It cost me $480 to get it fixed; we'd just blown half our cash.

We never ever seriously thought about turning around and heading back to Michigan. My desire was stronger than my doubts. I wanted out, and I wasn't going back. Michigan was done for me. When it's over, it's over. We would make it happen somehow. We'd get our asses to Phoenix. Bunny agreed, and we were on our way again. We turned a three- or four-day trip into a day and a half. We couldn't afford hotels anyway, so we powered straight through; one of us driving while the other slept. By the time we got to Phoenix, we were wiped out. But we were there! I remember thinking, *So we finally made it——now what? Where are the band and the balloons?*

I had transferred to Arizona State University because I still wanted to finish college and get my degree. But by the time classes started, I was flat broke. I knew I had to do something to make money, something in sales. All I had was my mouth. I answered an ad for a sales rep for Mountain Bell's marketing division, selling the Bell Boy Pager. Remember pagers? At the time, that was cutting-edge stuff, the latest and greatest communication technology, and Bell was the best. They were the phone company. Not a phone company—THE phone company. I applied for the job and got it. Within twelve months, I was the regional manager, speeding up the corporate chain with so much speed that the older fellas hated me. I never paid them much mind, never. I was there to excel—and excel I did. I was an entrepreneur, and I took advantage of my opportunities. I gave my best, delivered the best that I could, and was rewarded for it.

How did I pull it off? The same way I've accomplished everything in my life—I saw an opportunity, and I took it. I just worked hard, and I had this mentality that there was always a way to make a sale. When it came to sales, I was very persuasive—honest, but persuasive. Typical things like objections didn't bother me one bit. I'd gotten them all my life. I started to see objections as a sure sign of interest.

I worked for a fella named Tim Denton. Tim had a beautiful saying that has never left my arsenal. "If someone objects during your sales pitch, oh baby, you got 'em; that shows a sign of interest and with interest, you can sell 'em. If they sit there for an hour and don't have one single objection or one single question, you're lost; they have no interest."

I have never forgotten that lesson, and Tim was 100 percent spot on. If they object, they are interested. Welcome those objections like a kitten welcomes a bowl of milk.

This serves up another reminder that went back to what Grandpa Van had taught me. He said, *"When people communicate, someone is buying, and someone is selling. The important thing is to never let anyone sell you on why you can't do something. You can either buy someone's bad attitude or sell them your positive one. It's totally up to you. If you're the seller, you need to sell what works about your product, or people will sell you on what doesn't. They can sell that negativity all they want, but if you don't buy into it you can't be stopped."*

It's pretty damn simple when you get right down to it.

I can tell you that I moved a ton of pagers—about 150 a month compared to 30, which was where most of the sales team members were at. Just like that, I was bringing down $100,000 a year in salary and commissions. It was a hell of a lot more money than I had ever made before in my life. But I wasn't surprised. If anything, I thought I should have been making more. It never surprised me how much money I made, only how little.

Hard work and belief put that money in my pocket. Underachievers don't get that; they look for the answers to the mystery of success, instead of just getting out there and making it happen. I don't have a problem with underachievers; they just make me look that much better. They always have.

While making that kind of cash, it was tough to stay interested in school. I did one term at ASU, and it was a disaster. I earned two Cs and two Ds, my worst grades in my college life. It wasn't like I'd suddenly turned stupid. It was just that work was taking off and I was putting so much of myself into it that there wasn't much time left over for classes and books. I was at a fork in the road. Actually, I was a little past the fork and didn't get it until I saw those lame grades.

My passion had always been to move ahead in my life. College had been my way of moving forward, of getting ready for a career, but now I actually did have a career. I was driving a brand-new Oldsmobile and had a corporate American Express card in my pocket. I was flying high and loving life. With a six-figure income, I was *outearning* by two to one or more other college buddies who had already graduated. It wasn't just about the money; it was a measure of success. I wasn't slacking off, I was revving up.

It didn't make sense for me to sit in a classroom when I was learning more on the job every single day. This was my first big excuse for not reaching a goal. I was copping out here. Instead of staying with it, I realigned my priorities and my story so as to accommodate my failure. That failure was not graduating. However, later in life, I went back, graduated, and earned my degree from ASU—after I took a break of eighteen years. Bottom line was that my heart just wasn't in it anymore. It would have been more "normal" if I had graduated first and then started making bank, but since when had anything in life been normal? I was twenty-four credits short of graduating when I took my hiatus from college. I had no idea that break would last eighteen years.

Meanwhile, my sales passion went to work for me big-time. The suits noticed how much product I was moving for them. I started cruising up the corporate ladder and was soon named regional manager. I was on the fast track and feeling damn good about it.

What would they say about me back in Flint now? Suddenly I was in charge of sales for Denver, Portland, Seattle, Oakland, Los Angeles, and Phoenix. That was like winning a gold medal. At the time, I was on such a fast track that I did not have time to be bothered by anything else, except for my own pursuits of considering myself a legend.

The stakes were high as the other managers were at least ten years older than me. I was starting to take a starring role in my own life. I started seeing who I really was. I wasn't some "nothing kid" from the street. I had value. I was an asset. This was a major boost for my confidence. Confidence is a beautiful thing. You start to let the brakes off and your life builds momentum.

I am a huge believer in momentum. It's the most powerful force in the universe. Momentum can make worlds or destroy them. It's so powerful most people are afraid of it. They don't want to lose control. They're afraid to step out of their small, little world. I couldn't get out soon enough. The folks staying in their boxes and trapping themselves with their own limitations and fear of change have always played to the advantage of any good entrepreneur. *Thanks to that box, entrepreneurs can excel. That is what sets them apart. It is what will make you a winner. I am talking directly to you, the reader, right now. This is for you. You want to win, then win big. Leave the box. Take charge and win. Be a champion, because you are. The way I figure it, if you are reading this, you are already a winner. I figure well that way.*

I once read a study that claimed 95 percent of people would rather go to Las Vegas and come back with the same money they went with rather than run the risk of losing; it meant they might lose what they came with. This fear kept them from going for it. Consequently, they will never win big; the fear of losing has its grip right on their balls. For me, I'm into betting it all every day. I have confidence in myself. I'm willing to put it all on the line. That's when you start to feel the power of momentum in your life. You feel the power because you're not holding back anymore.

You have to wake up every day believing in yourself. If you let someone tell you that you can't do something, then you are telling yourself that you're a loser. I'd rather put my whole heart on the line, my enthusiasm to achieve, than accept and fail. Small bets are boring. I can't worry about losing it all! I'd rather go down swinging for the fence than take a called third strike with the bat on my shoulders. How pathetic is that? If I played major league baseball, I'd be the leader in strikeouts and home runs. That's just the way I play.

When I filed for bankruptcy, I did it for a big number—$131 million—the largest in Arizona history at that time. Do I wish my company and investors still had all that money? You bet your ass I do! Filing bankruptcy offers no pride, but you have to deal with it and move on. Step forward; do your best. You need to pick up the pieces and just do your best. At the time, I thought I had hit the worst spot in my life, and I kept the 9mm by my side in case I needed to take the chicken's way out. When it all looks like it is over is when champions are born, the champion gets up and finds a dream, but the loser pulls the trigger. I was at that point where I had two choices: fight to live another day or die. Life may be bad, but it is never *that* bad. I know. I've been there.

Take a chance. Do something with your life. It's like this: let's say, you ask a beautiful woman to go out on a date with you. Worst thing that happens is she says no. You have to put that *no* in perspective. The world isn't going to end. Just ask the next one out. Think about it, all you need is one beautiful woman to say yes to you. If one hundred turned you down and one said yes, you're going out with a beautiful woman. That's the essence of success right there. You can't be so afraid of the nos that you stop before you even get to the yeses.

As a manager, I learned to pass that confidence on to the sales teams I worked with. I'd always been a salesman, but now I started to sell people on themselves. I loved it. I loved making a difference in people's lives. Doing something for me was great, but seeing someone else take off, that was awesome! That's when I started to understand what it meant to be a leader and how powerful the bond with other people could be.

The biggest mistake people make is that they spend too much time talking about themselves, telling their stories, which are, for the most part, just not that damn interesting.

My former father-in-law, Gerry Williams, who to this day is my very good friend and a man I deeply admire, taught me a brilliant lesson many years ago. It was not his purpose to teach me a lesson; I just watched and learned. Everyone loves Gerry; he is a very bright, cordial man. His biggest secret to success is that he truly cares about people. He wants to hear their stories, and he asks lots of questions about them, very good questions. And he listens, allowing the speaker the podium. Once again, he truly cares. People love to talk about themselves, as they are their own favorite subject. Gerry understands this, so he decided long ago to learn about others. I have never failed to profit from this lesson. I, too, want to learn about others and love to listen to their stories. Mostly because it makes them happy and it gives me a chance to bond with them. It is truly beautiful, and if you can develop this true skill and love it, you will triple your friends list; and you may just develop some really great friends.

Card Game

As an owner of several businesses, and a manager of even more, I have had the privilege of managing some ten thousand people in my business life. There are many lessons learned to be sure. It's a different kind of deal, teaching other people, instead of just teaching yourself. You have to figure out what is going to get to them. What makes them tick? What is going to make them click in and see the light? I will assure you, the one lesson I have learned is that people want a pat on the back a hell of a lot more than anything else you can offer. Sure, they want the Hawaiian vacation bonus or the performance bonuses, but they want recognition. I know! I do! A good manager will worship in public and criticize in private.

One day I took Lynn, a struggling sales representative from our Phoenix office, out on sales calls. I saw right away what her problem was—she sold everything but her product. When she talked to potential clients, she sold her car, her dog, her stamp collection, just about anything she had left, but not her product for which she hoped to earn a commission and a pay check. In short, she was afraid to sell her product, and Lynn had the wrong approach. After all, her product was pagers, and she was working for Mountain Bell—a great product and a great company at the time, and pagers were hot at that time, red-hot, on fire.

For Lynn, the worst part about doing it wrong was that it was killing her confidence. Even when she started doing it right, she still had that big fat question mark in her mind. That question mark that says, *Can I do this? Probably not.*

We made a number of calls together and sold a few pagers. But cold calling can be tough, and it was pretty slow. By the end of the day, I knew she'd picked up on what she needed to do, but she still didn't have the belief she was going to need to really make it. Without that belief, Lynn was just another success wannabe.

It's not enough to know how to do it, you simply have got to do it, and you've got to be able to picture it. See it in your head. Paint the picture. That's real belief—when you can see your goal as if it was already achieved and in front of your eyes. This takes something special, because if you have any guts at all, you set goals ahead of where you are already. That means it's not an obvious thing right under your nose. You can't see it just by opening your eyes. It doesn't exist yet. It's out there in the future, somewhere. So you have to make an effort, you have to exercise your imagination. You have to see what isn't there, and keep seeing it, until it *is* there. That's real confidence, and I knew it was going to take something more to get Lynn tapped in.

I suggested to Lynn, "Let's make one more call."

I picked a business with a "No Solicitation" sign in the window on purpose. In sales, the thought is that these signs are displayed because the people who put them up are people who are afraid to say no; they hide behind these signs like teenagers under a bed. For me, choosing that business was a risk because the odds were against us. However, I felt the tougher the odds, the harder the challenge would be; therefore, if it went well, as I knew it would, the victory, that taste of success, would be that much sweeter.

I wanted Lynn to get the feeling of being more than capable. I wanted her to feel unstoppable. We marched right in. I handed my card to the receptionist and asked her to give it to the decision maker. Like a good little gatekeeper, she said he was busy. How predictable is that? I said no problem, we would wait. That caught her off guard. She got this confused kind of look on her face, like I wasn't following the rules, and then she finally took the card back to the "big cheese" himself.

His office was right behind the reception desk. There was a big glass window blocked by blinds; they were cracked open just enough for us to see in without them knowing.

We could see the receptionist hand the fella the card and then he blew our minds; he ripped it up and threw it in the trash. Lynn was horrified. She knew in her mind it was all over. This is where Lynn lost and her game was over. Lynn was racing for the door. What Lynn did not realize was that at that moment we still had work to do.

Lynn was ready to go home, sit on her couch and watch *Wheel of Fortune* reruns, eat bonbons, and dream about what she was never going to have in real life. I wasn't going to let that happen. I knew we weren't done yet. In fact, the fun was just beginning.

When the receptionist came back out, she said her boss would get back with me. That was putting the typical polite corporate spin on it. I asked if she thought he would ever give us a call, and she said, "Probably not." I really didn't appreciate the guy's attitude. Everyone is trying to make a living, not just him. At that moment I got this weird inspiration. I said, "Well, the company makes us buy our business cards, and if he is not going to call, could I get my card back because they're expensive?"

Lynn totally freaked, which was fine with me. It's okay to make someone uncomfortable. Sometimes we need to go there to learn something new. Lynn was like, "Oh my god, Mike, you saw him tear up the card!" The receptionist got that confused look again. She didn't know what to do, so she went back to her boss. I had no idea what was going to happen myself. *What fun,* I thought, and I also wasn't into getting blown off that easily.

The receptionist returned and she's got a nickel for me for the price of the card. It was basically her boss's way of saying, "Fuck off." Being from Flint, I'd heard a lot worse, so I wasn't as fazed as maybe he thought I would be. Obviously, I could care less about her boss's nickel; it was his time I was after. So I pulled out another card. "They're two for a nickel," I informed her. The boss was listening, and we heard him laugh; the boss couldn't help but crack up. I'd taken his punch right on the chin and made a joke out of it. He might not have any idea what I'm selling, but he knew for damn sure that spending half an hour with me was going to be a hell of a lot more interesting than whatever else he's got on his desk.

He invited Lynn and me into his office and ended up buying four pagers. Now that was the right way to end a day! Would those four pagers set some new sales record in the office? Not even close. But it's all about the power of *believing.* If you can do it once, you can do it again, and again, and again. Lynn saw what it meant to hang in there, believe, and not quit, and I came away with a great story. This story became folklore in our office. People repeated and repeated it. But it was really just "balls out" sales in action.

It was about never giving up. It was about *believing*, and it was about seeing yourself with success in your pocket, seeing yourself in the future. This was one of the stories I thought of after I put the 9mm down.

I thought about how the impossible could become possible; all I had to do was *believe*. All I had to do was get up and fight. It is oftentimes not the victory but the fight that makes winners of us all. I was beat and I was beat hard, but I was not broken. I knew I could come back and I could rise, and that is exactly what I did.

Chapter 8
The Show Must Go On

If you want to build a ship, don't drum up the men to gather wood, divide the work and give orders. Instead, teach them to yearn for the vast and endless sea.

—Antoine de Saint-Exupéry

One of the most important business lessons I ever learned was to let my passions lead me to success. You have to have a passion to be successful. So many people are blinded by the dollar signs. They want to think, *I need a paycheck. I need to make a house payment. I want to buy a new car. Hmmm? Now let's see how do I do that? I know, I will get a job.* It is a job they get.

I found out what a job was at a very early age. Its letters tell the whole story. JOB! *J-O-B* stands for *Just Over Broke*, and that is where you usually are when you have a job. Don't just find a job, find a passion. Don't just look at business as a way to make money—it's the worst mistake you can make.

Look into your heart. Connect with something that turns you on. That will make working a blast, and then the money would just be icing on the cake. You can slave for money if you want to, but when you plug in your passion and the cash starts flowing, you'll realize it's the best money you have ever made. It won't be just because of the numbers; it will be because of how easily it comes to you.

When I was a little boy working with Grandpa Van, I loved it. It wasn't like pulling weeds, and cleaning chimneys were awesome, it was because it meant that I could be with him. He was my best friend in the world; so of course, I wanted to do a good job. I found a passion, a reason to love what I was doing. Ever since then, I've always looked for meaning in the work. Not just the money—something bigger than that, something that would fuel my fire. I knew that is what would keep me going, make me work harder than the next guy, and come out on top.

When you have passion in your work, you are, in effect, patting yourself on the back. I would rather be broke doing something I believed in than make money while hating what I do. I have never sold out; this is important because you must *never* sell out. Go home a winner every day; build something that really turns you on

I'm into movies. I like everything about them. I like watching them. I like thinking about them. I like owning them so I can re-watch a favorite over and over. *Apocalypse Now*, I've probably seen it fifty times. *Gladiator*, just as many times. *Silence of the Lambs*, the first one with Jodie Foster, is still incredible to me. I could go on and on. *Seven*—I love chick flicks too. *The Proposal*, what a great movie. By far my favorite number one movie of all time is *Casablanca*. Movies make the world go round, at least in my world.

Movies can also make a difference. Take a look at *Bowling for Columbine*, the documentary by fellow Flint native Michael Moore (actually, he lived upscale in Burton; I lived in the heart of the city). That movie and Michael Moore convinced Kmart to quit selling ammo. People see Moore as a fat guy in a slob's attire, but his films have had more influence than most politicians. While those guys are blowing hot air, Michael Moore changed how we think about things. I think Michael Moore is one of the most talented directors to have ever delivered a film.

The first film that really blew my mind was *Rocky*, released in the summer of 1976, when I was seventeen. I'll never forget sitting in the Dort Highway Theater with my buddy Scotty Middleton, watching that film and feeling my own hopes and dreams come alive in my chest. The film, starring Sylvester Stallone, was about a huge underdog that nobody was willing to give a chance. That wasn't just Sylvester Stallone's character on the screen. That was me! The music gave me chills. The down-and-out Philly neighborhood could have been Flint. It made my heart thump and my mind race.

If Rocky could do it, if Rocky could train with crap gear in a dump of a gym and come out a winner, then I could too. I could be the underdog who made it big. It didn't matter to me that it was just a movie. I got the feeling in my gut of being a winner, of making it to the top. That feeling was real. I never forgot it.

I walked out of that theater a different person—I was high with possibilities. I thought of all the shop rats in Flint going nowhere, hanging out in their rented apartments lit by a bare bulb strung from the ceiling. Rocky was drinking raw eggs every day. These guys were drinking raw "Jack." I knew I had to face some choices about who I wanted to be and where I wanted to end up. From that moment on, movies have always held a special place in my life.

While I was in the pager business, I would rent movies all the time from a video store in my neighborhood. I went there for the convenience; it was no palace. They had poor selection, and you often had to wait over a month for new releases, which just pissed me off. I thought, *This place needs to treat their customers better and get some*

91

damn movies in here. But what was amazing was that the chain was expanding. Pretty soon they had five stores around town. Every time I went into the video store, I'd say to myself, *I could do better than this. Someday I'm going to own one of these and do it right!*

This is what business is about. Look at a business and see what it is that you can do better. Put yourself in the customers' position and understand what they want. You will find out they want the same things you want. So give it to them.

The pager and cell phone business had been very good to me. I took on more responsibility and made more money than ever before. It's also where I met my first wife, Ann, who remains my best friend to this day.

Connecting with Ann was one of the biggest blessings of my life. Ann is the real deal. We were married for twelve years and have raised our two children together. Ann has never turned on me, even during and after the divorce. That is special. That's when you know someone has real class. She has stood by me through tough times. She's proved to me that my belief in people is right on. You just have to know which people to trust. Ann and I have remained close friends for over twenty-five years.

In business or in life, there's nothing worse than a bad partner or a bad wife. They will suck the life right out of you. So many people are afraid to be alone; they need partners. They think being alone is the scariest thing in the world. However, if you don't already know, there's something a lot scarier than that—it's being with the *wrong* person. Talk about a nightmare! This is a horror movie that doesn't end after a couple hours. With a bad partner, you live that horror flick 24-7. You never know when the ax is going to fall, but you can feel it up there dangling over your head. Don't settle for a half-assed partnership; go for an "all-the-way deal" or nothing at all. You'll be a lot better off.

Showtime

Ann and I opened our first video store on October 1988 in the middle of a strip mall in Phoenix. We started out small—about eight hundred square feet small—and carried fewer than four hundred titles. Compare that to the fifteen thousand movies Blockbuster carried at the time, we were pretty puny. But it's all we could do with the money we had.

This was to be the next big victory. We were broke, but it was a different kind of broke. We were broke, and we did not really care that we were broke; we were happy just to be chasing our dream. We found a passion, and we had a dream. We believed in ourselves, and we believed in our dream, so we went for it. As I wrote earlier, I would rather be broke doing something I believed in than make money while hating what I do. Ann believed this as well. Going for it never gave us much pause at all.

If you want to be in business for yourself, you have to make many, many sacrifices. If you are willing to go for it and are willing to make the sacrifices, you will never know a better life.

To bring in cash until we were able to crank up the business, I kept selling cell phones right out of the video store. I also worked at selling commercial real estate, whatever it took to pay the rent and keep the shelves stocked with current movie titles. We couldn't afford to hire any employees, so we worked ourselves nine to nine Monday through Sunday. These are the sacrifices you make when you are chasing your dreams; and if you do everything right, and if you focus on your passion, you just might make it. Better yet, even if you do not make it, at least you would have taken the chance and tried. It is far better to try and fail than to not have tried at all.

We had no life, but then again, we had a great life. Best life ever, and the biggest payday was still to come. We were punching our own clock, doing our own thing. I didn't mind the hours. I wasn't looking for a nine-to-five job. I was done with all of that, and I was never going to go back. All the money I could bring in, I pumped into the business. That money was like the blood and oxygen that was giving this baby of ours a chance to make it.

Our customers loved us. They knew us personally and always came back, except when we didn't have the movie they wanted. Or they were hit by one too many ads from the "big boys" like Blockbuster. Our service kicked butt, and we had more real passion for the business than any big corporation could even fake. But we still weren't cutting it. By May 1989, we were really in a hole, the bills were piling up, our house was in foreclosure, and there was not enough money coming in. We needed to make a break and take a big chance. We just couldn't get over the hump without a push. We were already all-in and we had gone for it, but now we had to go to the next level. We had to take even bigger leaps.

People told us to give it up. Friends and associates, they all seemed to be standing in line just to let us know it was impossible. Of course, I'd heard that tune before. Seems like you never run out of those kinds of people. I have been hearing that since the time I spent in Flint. In particular, when my high school counselor told me I was not "college material." They're like vultures circling. They can smell when you're vulnerable, and they're just waiting for you to prove them right. But I was used to being the underdog. I was used to being told I could not make it. I was used to being told I was in over my head. But there was one little secret that kept me going. Even though I was being told I could not make it, I was not listening. I never once bought into that kind of talk. I knew then, and I know now, that I can make it. I always do. I was Rocky running up the steps of the Philadelphia City Hall, punching those sides of beef. I was going to make it. One way or another, I was going to make it.

As they told us we could not compete and we would fail, Ann and I made a simple decision—don't listen to anybody but us.

I remember an Eleanor Roosevelt quote Grandpa Van shared with me when I was eight years old. "Mike! Nobody can make you feel inferior if you do not give them your permission." We were not giving our permission to the doubters. We were not listening to anybody but ourselves. At the time, and to this day, there was not a better voice than ours. Listen to your own voice; it is the best one there is, and it is always fighting for you.

One day, in walked Greg Price, who owned three video stores in Phoenix. Ann was working the counter and he spent twenty minutes telling her why we would never make it. Our location sucked, our inventory was too small, and Blockbuster was planning to put a store in right across the street. On the bright side . . . but there was no bright side!

Just what Ann needed to hear, right? She called me, tearfully upset, and told me about the whole failure trip that Greg had just laid on her. He was so sure we were going down the toilet that he'd convinced Ann. He was selling gloom and doom, and she bought it.

But I wasn't buying. I told Ann that Greg's words were just what we needed to fire us up, to spark us to success. Ann is no quitter. One thing I've always loved about Ann is that while she might get down, she doesn't stay down and she never ever quits. All she needed was some encouragement from me and she was ready to go right back at it again.

I ended up meeting Greg, and later on, we became partners in a store. To this day, Greg remains one of my best friends. He is a good man and a very good friend. What initially had appeared to be a doom and gloom turned into a cherished friendship.

Encouragement creates momentum. When I gave Ann a boost about how we were definitely going to make it, it got me pumped up too. I felt more passionate about pushing the store over the top now more than ever. Not only was I not ready to fold, I wanted to raise the stakes. And that's exactly what we did.

Go Big or Go Home

Sometimes in business, playing it safe is the most dangerous thing you can do. Professional sports teams lose more games than they win by playing it safe. I have watched several sports teams that get the lead and then they play to protect that lead. They go from playing to win to playing not to lose, and inevitably, in the final minutes they lose. Folks, you need to always play to win; never play not to lose. You gotta go big if you want to be big. If we stayed put, we were going down. We needed to grow if we were ever going to make it. Yes, we were strapped for cash, we were broke, but with such a small store, we were really in a bind when it came to current cash flow. Talk about a Catch-22 situation.

The only way to go forward was to go for broke. We had to risk being big-time just to survive. When the large end-cap store at our strip mall opened up, we knew we needed to be in it. The bigger space and better visibility from the street would mean we could stock more movies and draw more customers. We could totally see it happening. Problem was, we could barely pay our $800-a-month rent where we were. This new space was going for five times that.

Again the "no way" posse lined up to let us know that there was, well, no way. *"If you're barely making it where you are, why would you take on such a big challenge?"* They all wanted to know.

They couldn't deal with the risk, but I knew it was "do or die." It was clearly a "now or never" scenario. We were either going to grow and hit it big, or shrink away to nothing. Status quo was not an option. We couldn't stay put—we had to make a move. The only choice we had was whether to believe in ourselves or not. Henry Ford put it best when he said, "Tell yourself you can, or tell yourself you can't and whatever you choose, you'll always be right."

I told myself, "Go, go, go. Make it happen, and don't look back!" Ann was all-in—hell, she was less scared than I was.

We pulled out every last dime we could come up with. We managed to scrape together enough to get into this massive new space and to stock it with enough titles to at least look legit. Then we had to talk the property management company into letting us sign the lease. They knew we were extended to the max, especially since we were always last minute with rent. We weren't exactly your perfect picture of the ideal client you would want to anchor your strip mall.

But I pumped them up about our vision for the business; they felt the fire, and they saw our passion. They agreed! We put it all on the line and made it look as good as it could look, and in the end, they said yes. Game on! Now we had to make it work. I thought, *Shit, these guys really believe me. Oh, man, what have I done?*

We moved in on a Friday on June 1989. We were in such a jam for cash that we couldn't even afford to close while we moved the inventory over to the new place. It was hilarious and desperate—a total circus. We just hauled videos from the old store to the new one and took care of customers while we were at it. As we walked down the sidewalk to the new suite, we were stopped with the videos we were carrying so people could browse for something we'd already pulled off the shelves. They were literally looking in our hands to take a movie and check it out. I could not give them the movies fast enough.

If you didn't know any better, it might have looked like a going-out-of-business sale, but we weren't going anywhere but up.

Someone upstairs was looking out for us because a monsoon hit hard that weekend. In the video rental business, rain means money. People want to stay in, and their best bet, of course, is watching a movie. In Phoenix, the monsoon is notorious for showing up on its own time. You never really know when that rain is going to come. Sometimes it gets cloudy and humid, but the heavy weather just hangs around and rain never really happens. But that first weekend, the heavens were cooperating.

It poured down rain, and we hit a monster blast on the first day. By the end of the day, Saturday, we had our rent money made. We were on our way. We did more on that first day in the new store than our best week ever in the old store. We went for it, and we hit the ball out of the park on our first swing. We had been so afraid, even though we knew it was what we needed, and it was our only hope; we were scared big-time. *If we failed, we were toast. An important lesson that day to be sure: fear will hold you back, and if you give in to it, you will lose.*

Movie Momentum

When some people taste a little success, they put on the breaks. They feel lucky they got that far and they don't want to risk losing it. My head just doesn't work that way. As soon as we got that first store rocking, I wanted to open the next one, and then the next one, and then the next one after that.

What turns me on is that feeling of momentum, of flying right over anything that would stop you, not to mention that I had just proved all the doubters wrong. For everyone who said we could not, we just *did*. This is a huge reward and it is what drives us all to win.

I couldn't open enough stores. I loved it! We took the money we made off the stores we had and poured it back into the business in anticipation of the next grand opening. Ann said I was obsessed, but I loved what we were doing. As a result, our business exploded and so did the money.

When we would ink a new deal for another store, the team knew exactly what that meant—that we'd be up three nights straight stocking the shelves. That's how we rolled. In the seven years we owned the video stores, I slept more than fifty to a hundred nights in the stores themselves. How did I get the team to rise to that challenge? By stepping up myself! Nobody worked harder than Ann and I did. Our employees saw us push it, and suddenly they were willing to go above and beyond themselves. *You lead by example, not by fear or command. You will earn the team's respect by rolling up your own sleeves rather than by barking out orders. Respect is earned, it is not given, and never mistake a title as a reason to give respect.*

If you're going to be a leader, then you'd better get ready to set an example. It's exactly as Knute Rockne said, "One man practicing sportsmanship is better than a hundred teaching it."

Don't bother trying to expect hard work if you're not willing to put in the hours yourself. If you slack off, don't be surprised if your payroll is heavy with slackers. But if you go "balls to the wall," you can inspire others to do the same.

Believe in what you're doing and let your people see that. Let your team see you rolling up your sleeves and getting it done. Let them feel your passion and see you bleed from it. They won't respect you any less. If anything, they'll see that you're for real. I never wanted to be above our team. I didn't want the kind of respect that says, *You can't touch me. I'm better than you.*

I'm not better than anyone. I'm just excited about what I do, ready to work hard, and stubborn enough not to stop until I get where I want to go.

We built up the business to forty stores in Phoenix, Tucson, and Las Vegas. We were the biggest in Phoenix. Just to give you an idea, we went from buying three copies of a movie to buying three thousand for all of our stores on the really big titles. That's a fact—for *Lethal Weapon 3*, we bought over three thousand copies. We went from being some little store that no one had ever heard of to having Paramount Pictures do private screenings for our employees only. One of these private screenings was for *Leap of Faith*, what else? This was Paramount's way of saying thank you. They brought in BBQ from Honey Bears for three hundred people to boot.

Major Money in the Bank

For the first time, we had major money in the bank. We didn't really know what to do with it, so we started paying off everything we had. We owned a $1 million home outright. We paid off the loans on our cars, and we were 100 percent debt-free. I wanted to own everything free and clear.

It felt good for the ego to not owe anyone a red cent, but it really didn't make much business sense. We could have used that same cash to open new stores and would have made a lot more money than what we saved on interest. It cost about $100,000 to open a store, so that house could have paid for ten stores, which would have made us an average of $15,000 to $25,000 per store every month. Do the math. It's pretty obvious, but it took me a while to get it.

My grandfather taught me never to have debt; he himself never took out loans. Taking out a loan was not part of his mind-set. The idea that loans are dangerous went back to the depression era when banks could take back your house if you so much as missed one payment. Then again, they do this today. People back then only felt secure if they owned things outright. My grandfather wanted me to have that solidity in my life. However, times change, and if you want to be successful, you have to keep up. This world is one big credit card. The country lives on credit, but this is good because it stimulates the economy, and that is what makes the whole world tick.

I had to break out of that old mentality and learn to think bigger when it came to cash. That's what being an entrepreneur is all about. New situations bring new challenges. Every morning means facing something new. You have to figure out what the best move is today, not yesterday. Experience is great, but it doesn't answer all the questions. Want to be a know-it-all? Get into a different line of work. Being an entrepreneur means you're always facing the unknown, you're always learning as you go. It is on-the-job training. It's not a drag; it's what makes being in business exciting. Some people call that scary. I call it real life. I call it going for it. I call it being an entrepreneur.

The Fat Lady Sings

The video stores were the calling card to fame and fortune. They were a result of hard work, and the learning curve was huge. The stores worked because we worked. We were the best of the best, and when the dust settled, we sold the stores. We walked away with almost $10 million in cash. We sold to Video Update who outbid Blockbuster at the eleventh hour. There were no partners, no banks, no loans, and when we sold, we owed less than $100,000 to vendors, etc. Selling the business was the hardest thing I had ever done. The second hardest thing was writing a check to the IRS for $2 million that next April. Just imagine that! I kept the welfare line going for 3.8 seconds. Can you imagine writing a check to the IRS for that amount? Blows your mind, doesn't it?

We never ever wanted to sell. We had no choice; technology was coming full speed ahead, and the final doorstop was in place. With Video on Demand, the Dish Network, Redbox, Netflix, Direct TV, and better TV programming of more sports teams (D'Backs, Coyotes), we had a short fuse. We knew that we would end up where Hollywood Video and Blockbuster ended up—in bankruptcy. Our timing was perfect, and suddenly, against our will, we were out of the greatest business ever.

The video business taught me a lot about retail, it taught me a lot about people, it taught me a lot about life. And it showed me a firsthand look at winning, and winning big. We hated to sell, and as we said good-bye to the 394 employees, I cried a lot of mournful tears. The day they handed us a personal check for almost $10 million, I had very mixed feelings. I was like *"I cannot believe it!"* but I was also giving the keys away to the last six years of my life. The hardest part was the employees who fought and died for us, who put it on the line every day. "No! Not me, Chief Brody! I will never go into the water again!" and I will never sell out again.

The check in my hand was similar to the mixed emotions I experience when I would think about my mother-in-law driving over a cliff in my brand-new Cadillac. Selling out is not worth it, and it never will be. I could have been a video retailer forever, and we would be well beyond five thousand stores today if the market could have held. But it could not, and we had to move on. We were now out of the video business, and June 19, 1995, was both one of the saddest days and one of the happiest days of my life.

Even today, as I sit here writing about being broke but not broken, I would not change a thing. You always have to go for it or you will never make it. No matter how bad it gets, it will always get better. The end of the road is nothing more than the first step to a new road. *Believing* in yourself will make you a winner. Life is full of good and bad, and the way you see it is how you live it.

Chapter 9
No Safety Nets

A real entrepreneur is somebody who has no safety net underneath them.

—Henry Kravis

When the first video rental store was opened, I became my own boss, and I haven't punched a clock since. I looked at it as the ultimate straight commission sales position, but I wasn't just selling a product, I was selling everything about the business to customers, to employees, to vendors, to everyone. I was the salesman in chief. It didn't feel like too much, it felt like what I was born to do, it felt natural.

This is where the passion pays off. It was perfect. I loved movies and I loved what I was doing. It was exciting. You could feel the rush, and every day was a great day. Sure you had your daily fires, but the passion is a thing of beauty—it is the passion that lets you rise above it all. The theory of the sacrifices was for a greater good, and that greater good we could taste. You could see it, and you knew it was coming. On one hand, every day we asked ourselves, "Are we going to make it?" And on the other hand, we said, "No problem, do or die, baby!" This is where seeing yourself in the future pays off big-time. We knew, in spite of the constant pressures and threats of failure, that we would make it. We believed, and we also saw ourselves in the success seat. We saw ourselves at the finish line, and this is the most important key to believing. *You must see yourself there, in the future.* It is almost like a crystal ball moment. It is like weight control. If you are serious, you will see yourself thin. You will have your vision, and your vision will be your pursuit. The stronger your vision is, the stronger your pursuit will be, hence the stronger your commitment. If you do not see yourself thin and you do not know what the winning picture looks like, then you are shooting into the future blindly, hoping that you will make it! Nothing happens on hope. It is all about hard work.

As for me, I was done working for paychecks. I was all-in, and win or lose, I would fight the good fight. I would go for it. I figured I would rather go for it and fail than to not go for it at all. Once I tasted that level of reward and responsibility, I knew I was never going back. I would never work for anyone else again. This would scare the crap out of some people especially those who think a job brings security. They'd rather pull in a $50,000-a-year paycheck than take even a small risk to be an entrepreneur. There's this BS belief out there that's been pounded into our heads since school. The path to a "good" life ends at a "good" job with a "good" company. You're basically taught to follow the herd. You almost never hear anything about being an entrepreneur. College offers you one million different classes—hell, you can even take classes on bobsledding in the

Bahamas and analytic forward thinking for backward thinkers, but there is not one class on being an entrepreneur. Hmmm?

This mentality of *birth→ school→ work→ retire→ death* doesn't work for me. As Steven Tyler, the lead singer of Aerosmith and *American Idol* icon, once said, *"Life is a journey, not a destination."* Next time you visit the Hard Rock Hotel in Las Vegas, this is written right over the exit door. Tyler is right. If you follow the destination to the end, you will have never known what life is about. Make it a journey!

The idea that a job equals security is one of the biggest scams out there, and it should be reported to your local FBI post. I'd take a well-thought-out business venture any day of the week. At least with a business venture, your life is in your own hands. Just because someone is your boss, or they are the owner of your company, doesn't mean they have a clue as to what they are doing—or for that matter, what you are doing!

I hate to break it to you, but the world's full of idiots, and you just might be working for one or two. *Furthermore, a lot of the so-called safe jobs with "good" companies are on the chopping block. Mass layoffs, plant closings, company restructurings, overseas outsourcing are making people live in fear of losing their job from day to day. So tell me, where is the real risk? At the end of the day, are you really safe? Honestly? I think not.*

Also, big doesn't always mean better. No matter how big the company is, there is always a chance you'll walk in one morning, pour your coffee, go to your cubicle, and find a pink slip waiting for you. The company might be going under, your department might have been eliminated, or maybe you just pissed off the wrong person and office politics caught up with you.

In Flint, in the '50s, they thought Ford and GM were forever. Then the '70s came along and knocked those giants to their knees. Look at the financial sector today: Bear Stearns, Countrywide, Circuit City, Lionel, Drexel Burnham, Schwinn Bicycle, Woolworths, Bethlehem Steel, Sunbeam, Enron, Polaroid, Montgomery Wards (even Monkey Wards), and Mervyns—are all gone! This list also does not mention the dozens of banks and airlines that all folded. *POOF!* Here for a hundred years, then gone in a flash. It is going to get much worse. They're all dust now. Hell, even Mother's Cookies closed down after ninety years in business. Do you think the bakery foreman at Mother's thought she had a secure job a year ago? You bet she did. Everyone eats cookies, especially mothers! What happened? Now what? Where is my secure job?

Bottom line is, as an employee, your future is in the hands of someone else. They might be brilliant or they might be total morons, but they control your future. You just never really know. The good news is, if a company you work for goes down, you have someone to pin it on. That makes some people feel better, even though it does nothing for their bank account.

If you're in business for yourself and the company eats it, you can only look in the mirror. That scares the hell out of a lot of people. The true deal is that most of us want to blame someone or something. We are taught to look for excuses. You'd think they were making big bucks for all the excuses they would come up with. But guess what? Excuses don't pay a dividend. They just sap you of your strength and your ability to step up and rock the world.

I could say my home-building business failed because of the housing collapse and the economy, but ultimately, it was my responsibility to see that coming and be ready for it. I'm the guy at the top, so I'm the guy you blame. The toughest part of seeing my business go down was knowing there were people depending on the company and depending on me personally. That kind of pressure is too much for a lot of people. It was almost too much pressure for me. It put as much pressure on the trigger as anything else.

Being your own boss means taking total responsibility. You da man! Or da woman! You are it. That's true for whatever business you go into. I've owned gas stations, a chain of cigar stores, a print shop, a plumbing company, a video store chain, and a home-building company, and they have all given me the things I have always been hungry for—the chance to create, to lead, to succeed, to build and build and build, and to make money, lots of money.

Furthermore, a lot of so-called safe jobs with "good" companies are on the chopping block. Mass layoffs, plant closings, company restructurings, overseas outsourcing are making people live in fear of losing their job from day to day. So tell me, where is the real risk? At the end of the day, are you really safe? Honestly? I think not.

Born To Be a Business Owner

Even with all the ups and downs I've been through, all the glory and all the crap, there is no doubt in my mind that I'm meant to be a business owner. There is also no doubt that we can all be business owners. Of course, it's true that if I'd had a corporate gig all these years, I may never had filed one of the largest bankruptcies in Arizona history—and for sure, I wouldn't have had investors out to blow my head off. If you're going to go into business for yourself, you have to know what you're going to face. The pay can stink, the hours can run long, and the rewards can be slow to show up, and of course, you might not make it at all. Most don't.

There are no guarantees, but that's the beauty of it. It is your opportunity, perhaps for the first time in your life, maybe, to stop playing it safe, believe in yourself, and prove you can do it. Know this going in—you may be the biggest doubter, the only one who can hurt you is you and those silly voices in your own head, the voices that you put there. Once you've shut up those voices, no one can stop you. It does not matter what others think you can do. It does matter what you think you can do, and if you think you can do it, then you most likely can and will. But if you make the tragic mistake, the true deal killer, where you think you cannot do it, then you never will, and what's more, you should never ever try until you believe you can do it.

Throughout my entrepreneurial life, I've learned a lot about business and what it takes to make a business work. I also have learned what makes a business fail, which is more important. More than anything else, it comes down to personal effort, ability, belief, and passion—and that's exactly what I love about it! We ended up thriving in the video rental industry because we had a passion for it and we were focused on being successful no matter what. The only voices we listened to were the ones in our heads, telling us we could do it. I knew that whether we succeeded or failed, it was up to me. So I did what I had to do to make it work. Hard work alone doesn't make you successful. Still, it is the number one ingredient. Some of the toughest, nastiest, most demanding jobs in the world pay very little. But they all require hard work or you fail.

The rewards of owning my own businesses have far exceeded any downside. I have been, and in most cases with my family, on outrageous vacations all over the globe. This, including Chile, Argentina, Switzerland, China, Germany, Ireland, Austria, England, Scotland, Greece, Spain, France, Holland, Mexico, the Bahamas, and Hawaii, to name a few. I've owned eight airplanes, including three jets. I've owned three lake houses, as well as five $1 million-plus homes. I've had Jaguars, Mercedes, and a fleet of Cadillac Escalades to drive. I've been able to give my kids the very best education money can buy and a lifestyle that every parent wishes they could provide for their children. This is the good side. I can also assure I have eaten more Spam than you have and that I have had more process servers show up at my door than you can count.

Corporate jobs offer opportunities for some, no doubt about it, but it's still the slow road to success, and even if I had taken that route and slogged my way up the corporate ladder, I would only now (maybe) be approaching a level that paid enough to make Hawaii a travel vacation once a year. If I'd stayed in Flint, and kept working in the Hole, I'd be up for retirement right about now, with a little cabin in Northern Michigan waiting for me. Turns out, however, the hole was vaporized by GM and Chevrolet some years ago. It and has been replaced by fields of grass and concrete. No thanks! I'll go my own way and take my chances every time.

Sometimes you are on top of the world and other times the world is on top of you.
—Cam Newton, NFL quarterback

Filing for BK and feeling like the whole world crashed in on me was the huge downside in going for it. It was a risk I took—and I would take it again! I proved that to myself after my whole world was destroyed. There I was, bankrupt, broke, struggling to sustain the basic needs of life. I'd hit bottom, the gun was in my hand, and I was still looking for the bounce back when a friend contacted me and said he wanted to meet to discuss an offer he had for me.

He had been a close associate of mine and happened to be one of the richest guys in Arizona. I was definitely interested in hearing what he had to say. We met at his office, located in prime Arizona business real estate, at the Scottsdale Airpark, in his top-floor office suite with sweeping views of the big jets landing. The oversized office suite, the high ceilings, the pricey furnishings all made me feel nostalgic for the days, not so long removed, when I worked behind that kind of desk.

"Mike," he said, "I need someone to represent me in certain interests on behalf of the company. You are a very bright guy, and you know how to handle this stuff. I'll pay you $200,000 a year, and I'll give you $75,000 so you have some moving-around money. I'll put you on the payroll. I need you, and I am sure you need a break like this one. I need you to be available to fly to meetings for me and be my liaison—an ambassador, if you will. You'll represent the firm, evaluate proposals, and help make some market decisions. I know what you're capable of, and I could really use your talent on my team. Of course, you'll fly the CJ. We'll cover your expenses and provide you with full-coverage healthcare. What do you think?"

What did I think? Just a couple weeks earlier, I'd stuck a gun in my mouth and wondered if I even wanted to take another breath. It was the deepest, darkest pit I'd ever been in. But I'd pulled that 9mm out of my mouth and trashed the coke and the Jack Daniels and chose life. My kids needed me alive; suicide meant quitting, and I was no quitter.

Since then, I was starting to figure out that feeling like a loser was getting me nowhere. I wanted to get back in the game, to be Mike Roberts again. I realized my life wasn't over unless I said it was over. I was broke, but not broken. I was in charge. I had dug the hole; I would dig my way out.

Again I listened to him rattle the offer off. *"What do you think?"* *"What do you think?"* *"What do you think?"* It was like a broken record that played over and over in my mind. I think I am busted! I think I am broke! I think this is the best opportunity in the world for me. Well, wait a minute. What does this picture look like two years from now? Hmmm? I could not believe I was even thinking about it. There was nothing to contemplate taking the offer. I would do very well, and all my money problems were solved. I could go for it, just as I would be going for it for somebody else. Maybe I do it for a while till I get back on my feet? Then it hit me. I realized I could not do it. I could not take the offer. I guess I needed to do what I was built to do, and that was to go for it, go for it for me. I needed to prove to myself and nobody else I could do it. I could bounce back. Then right out of nowhere, a favorite hero's quote hit me right between the eyes.

It's not whether you got knocked down; it's whether you get back up.

—Vince Lombardi

I knew I had to get back up. Screw the money. I needed to be back in the game! Some people might think that this job was the perfect chance for me to get back on my feet. It was! I had filed bankruptcy and been cleaned out. So it was an incredible offer. Not only would it get me back in action, it would also put me in the cockpit of a corporate jet, my CJ2 in fact, good old 91 Alpha. Flying was and is one of the great passions in my life. It's my drug of choice. In some ways, the chance to fly was more exciting than the money, and getting health insurance again wasn't a bad deal either.

But the fact was I wanted to rebuild my life, not someone else's, and in my world, taking a job wasn't an option. I had made a promise to myself over twenty-five years earlier that I would never work for anyone but myself again. Never! So when my buddy said, "I'll put you on my payroll," I knew it was no deal. I haven't been on anyone else's payroll for over twenty-five years, and I wasn't about to now. That would have been much worse than bankruptcy for me—that would have been defeat.

I thanked him for a very generous offer, and I walked out of his office. I looked to the sky and said, "I sure hope you know what the hell you are doing?" I truly appreciated his offer, and his heart was in the right place, but I just had to turn him down. I did, however, offer to take the moving-around money.

This was to be one of my biggest moments ever in my life—the true moment where I was 1,000 percent believing in me. I was truly broke, and it was at that exact moment I realized I was not broken. I had the spirit to fight, and that was the best place for me to start. I had been knocked down, and I mean down, like I had been tackled and mauled by the entire Chicago Bears front line. Even though I was badly beaten and nearly broken, it was time to get back up. It was time to get back in the game.

Chapter 10

The Total Meltdown

My great concern is not whether you have failed, but whether you are content with your failure.

—Abraham Lincoln

Going for it and losing it all! Not exactly the plan. The risk was there. It's always there. That's the price—the ultimate price—the entrepreneur may pay. It was time to ante up. The market collapsed, and I was to be its carnage. A total financial meltdown. Bankruptcy! The Big BK. This is the price you risk for going for it. Then again, there are a lot of folks who did file and are filing BK, and they did not go for anything; they simply overleveraged themselves buying that new Toyota or they ran up their credit cards, and *Shazaam*, hello, BK. They took very little risk, and their upside was a pretty car. I went big—$131 million. I knew I was at risk, but I was all–in, and there was no OFF switch. I signed one personal guarantee after another. I had loans with nine different banks. I had heard stories that you get to a point where you do not have to sign personal guarantees with banks. I have never in my thirty years of bank borrowing been able to borrow any money without signing for it personally. Not even a $1,500 loan to buy a new TV. I tried, but that is not how it works with banks. Banks know that life is about trends, and when you trend down, they want to be covered. There is the fact that the big Wall Street lenders (GE, Goldman Sachs, Citibank, etc.) will do what is known as non-recourse lending, but they give low LTV (loan to values) and are well protected with the asset itself. They are actually the smart ones, because if they take back the property, they just go get the property and dispose of it. Why waste money with the PGs (personal guarantees)?

As for the real world, John Hancock was everywhere. After being on so many loans, what did it matter anymore? I figured what the hell, if I go down, I go down! I went down, and I was right, it did not matter. I never even flinched when a bank needed my personal guarantee. I was so far in, it simply would never make a difference. Never would, and in my case, it never did. I was actually very surprised that they even wanted my signature. For me, I figured, what is another pound to an elephant? The call would come in: "Mike, can you stop by the bank today and sign the loan docs?" "Sure, what time?" I almost never even asked how much. I had an idea, of course, but it did not matter. I was going to sign; I needed the money to keep building homes. When I did ask how much, it may sound like this: "Four million!" "Okay! I will be by later today! No problem." It could have been ten, fifteen, twenty million—it made no difference to me. I was all-in and there was no way out. Of course I cared, but what was I going to do? Refuse to sign? Then the loans would not happen and the house would not get built and everything would come comes to a screeching halt! There was no way I could say no, and if they were going to keep giving me the money, I was going to keep taking it. I was not dumb. At the time we were borrowing the money, the loans were sound.

It was like watching the movie with Johnny Depp, *Blow*. It was all happening fast, and the money just kept rolling in. Only this was legal. We were building and selling a lot of homes, and we had been doing it for several years. The market exploded and we jumped on board, head-first, all-in. Business accounts were everywhere with hundreds of thousands of dollars in each of them. Each community and each bank had its own accounts and they were full.

The accountants were keeping track, and they were doing mine and the company's financials. They had to provide banks with my net worth. What was I worth personally? Last tally was $46 million. My net worth was $46 million, and this was by real accountants who were doing their best calculations—calculations they could stand behind. I had a few million, but where was the $46 million I was worth? It was all in the land. *This is how it works. You want to know somebody's real worth, figure out what they have liquid. What is their liquidity? That's the number, and it is always lower than the paper numbers, I will assure you.*

The best part of all of this is that I could borrow the money and the machine could be fed. It was a feeding frenzy, and I was not alone. Every builder in town was feeding as well, and some had a much bigger appetite than I had. But the machine had now come to a screeching halt, and the piper was looking for the fat lady.

The entrepreneur's nightmare was now my reality. The venom was sweet, but the poison was now going to put me to death. There I sat in my bedroom with the 9mm in my hand. I was thinking of all the great moments, but they were distant memories now. The world was a dark, horrible place. The only positive thing was that I was still in control, and I could still make choices about me. Do I pull the trigger or not? Do I give up and give in, or do I fight? Yes! I had control of the gun. Where was everyone? All the people I had helped through the years, where were they now? In short, they were all fighting their own demons. Besides, I did not let them know I was alone in my horror. They all knew it, but what could they do?

The team gone, the banks gone, the money gone, everything was gone. This is the point where you find out what friends are all about, but it is also the point where you find out what you are all about, what you are truly made of. Do you pull the trigger, or do you fight? You can't blame friends, nor should you put them in a position where you have to depend on them. You have to be accountable for you. Each of us is exactly where we put ourselves. As I wallowed in self-pity, the Colt 9mm became my only friend. I wanted to blame friends, but that was just simply a mistake. They have their own lives, and they were not the ones who put me there. It was like what Mark Twain said: *"The world owes you nothing; it was here first."*

Mark was and is right. You have to step up and take charge and be accountable for yourself. You are where you are because you put yourself there. You made the decisions to be where you are. No one made you do it except you, so pony up and accept accountability for yourself.

It mattered very little at the time how much I cared about life. I had been so beaten that for the first time in my life I was nearly broken. I came within 1/16 inch of cashing it all in. The ultimate quit, but I could not quit. I could not do it to Hannah and David. I took an oath to be the best father I could be, and this was the deciding factor. I am not sure I could not have gone through with it, but the idea felt good. I hated life and all there was to it. This shitty world was kicking my ass and there was nowhere to turn, nowhere to run, nowhere to hide, so why not pull the trigger and game over? Free at last! I think most of us have all been to a point where we think the end looks better than the today and that was where I sat.

It is a very difficult period to explain to someone who has never experienced a total meltdown. It is a total meltdown to be sure. All parts of your life are affected by the meltdown. Your business, your life, your family, your friends, your moment by moment life—it is a total meltdown. You do not do one without the other. It is even harder when you are the CEO, the man in charge and living large, the fearless leader. The guy the team turns to and says, "Now what?" Well, on this day, I did not know "now what?" As a leader, you have to know "now what," and if you don't, then you should put the gun to your head. A leader makes a decision and enacts a plan. *Even if it is a bad plan, at least they act and they lead. If you are a leader, and we all are, you always have a plan B, a plan C, and more. You will also always have at least five backup plans.*

No matter what you do in your life, if you are in charge, then by all means be in charge. Take charge and execute. You may only be in charge of you, and if this is the case, then take charge of you. Again I identify two movies that drive this leadership thing home. The first is *U-571* where Harvey Keitel tells Matthew McConaughey, *"Don't ever tell the men you do not know, you are in charge and you are supposed to know, so don't ever say that again no matter what, especially if you don't know!"* and the second movie is *Battle LA* where Alan Eckhart tells Lieutenant Rodriguez, *"We need an answer, you are the leader, you are in charge, right or wrong, that call is yours, so make it, sir!"* Clearly the point is, if you lead, you need to lead. Bad or good, make a decision and lead—that is why you are the leader.

I was the leader, but I had nothing left to lead anymore. The troops were all gone, left to fend for themselves, while I sat there in my own little world. The harsh reality goes something like this: I was king, and now I was on the run.

Just twelve months prior, we had fifty employees, some two to three hundred homes under construction, and another one thousand two hundred lots in development. We also employed some four to five hundred subcontractors who were working in our various communities. Then the administrative support teams, the banks, the other vendors, lawyers, accountants, para's—hell, just para's. We easily touched two thousand five hundred people financially with our company. It started with me, and it ended with me. Two thousand five hundred people were now on the ropes. I wondered how many other guys were out there with a 9mm. *As I mentioned earlier, this kind of loss can make you think seriously about killing yourself. In this place, you can't see the whole picture. All that registers in your head is darkness and death.*

I knew Scott Coles had taken his own life because of the meltdown. Scott Coles was a very successful hard-money lender who took over a business his father started many years before him. Scott was a bigger fish than I was, but not by much. He was well-known and well-respected, having logged over twenty-five years in business. He made a lot of people tons of money. On a social note, he was well-known for hiring Hollywood stars for private parties. He paid $250,000 to have dinner with Donald Trump in New York. But now the dike had crumbled and all the money he had made for so many others, multitudes of times before, did not matter. He was now a casualty of the real estate meltdown. Multitudes of stories hit the newspapers.

The work was coming to an end, and he wanted an out. Scott was racing around town trying to raise money to cover some over extensions he made, and his numerous friends and associates turned him down flat. It was all crumbling and the world was closing in on him. Realizing it was over, he apparently gathered his family around for a Sunday party. After the party some hours later, he put on a tuxedo, lay down on his bed, and ended his life. It was over. He took his exit. He chose the suicide route. I liked Scott and felt bad for him, but it was his family that I felt the most empathy for. The pressure of having to live in his reality was more than he could bear.

I saw Scott two weeks before his death. I knew how he felt more than any other person in the world. You never know what you are capable of until you put that gun in your mouth, or in Scott's case, you lie down on your bed for that last breath. It seems so easy at that very moment to just pull the trigger, and it is all over. The pain stops. Everything goes away—unfortunately, you too go away, and your loved ones are thrust into a state of devastation that they may not recover from for years to come.

Scott had checked out nearly a year after I almost had my exit. I was back on my road to life when he cashed in. I think of all the things in life Scott will now miss, he will miss his children. This has to be so incredibly hard on his loving children. I look back now and I think how close I came. It has been over four years, and I am here and I am doing well. I am still broke, but I am not broken. I am writing this book to you today, and I am building a very successful self-storage company. I know that I am well on my way back. I am alive, and I am going to make it just fine. I always have, and I always will. But on those cold, lonely nights, I thought maybe not.

Reality has many faces, but for every minute of good it gives you, it can offer just as many bad. I guess it goes back to the old saying "You have to take the good with the bad." I was getting a helluva lot more bad than I bargained for.

The point is, however, I had made a bargain. I wanted to be an entrepreneur, and I knew the risk. Nowhere in the bargain did I ever agree to check out. Here is a big tip and never forget it: You are only as good as your next deal. Scott made his own deal, and I made mine.

The Public Failure

The hard part was facing the investors, people who had invested with me, figuring their money was safe, and even if I lost everything that had no impact on them, I made millions for some folks. There were a lot of people who made really good money with me and our company. But the last ones in, folks who placed their money in our communities at the height of the market, lost money. They wanted the big payday that I had given so many others before them. A lot of the investors were repeat investors who had made money in other communities. Everyone loved real estate; it was the golden child. They could not wait to invest. I was right there with them; I was all-in. I was making money, good money, and everyone wanted in. They were right to get in. Unfortunately, the meltdown was about to hit, and there was no stopping it.

We were all caught in the mix. I may have lost everything in the world as it seemed at the time, but I soon found I was rich in many other ways. I went from an audited net worth of $46 million to $150 in twelve months. I had money everywhere, and it was now gone. The bulk of the people were sure I hid money in the Cayman Islands. I have never ever been to the Cayman Islands, but it was widely held I had millions down there, and to this they were sure. The *Titanic* had hit an iceberg, and we were sinking fast. I kept burning through everything I had to make payroll and pay subs. I was burning through my personal-earned money and the company's money to pay for the short fall on the few homes we were closing. I was trying to do the right thing to right the ship. I felt exactly like the guys on the *Titanic*. I was going down with the ship, and the music played on. It never ever dawned on me we would not make it. We were unsinkable!

I felt bad about my own plight, but it was the investors I felt worse for. They believed in me, as I did. In fact, I still to this day continue to work with the investors to help them recoup their losses. I do not have to, but when I hit, they hit. I could have dealt with the meltdown a whole lot better if I had not had investors who lost money. That was by far the hardest part. We all knew it was a risk, but we did not believe it would ever happen. The company was invincible, and the investors were right there with us. They followed their fearless leader right into the ground. It was the misery that became my nightmare. It is a lot easier when you lose your own money than when you lose somebody else's money. It is the ultimate nightmare.

The investors were all different. It was very interesting to see how each handled it. Some wanted me shot and killed while others sincerely cared about me. It was all over the board. The hate calls and the attacks were as popular as the calls from others who wanted to see if they could help. There was one lady in particular who had invested in one of our communities; she was a friend of a friend who called me out of the blue to tell me that she had lost $50,000. I expected her to be mad. Instead, she said she was sad, but would be okay. She then asked about me: "Is there anything my husband and I can do to help you and your family?" She truly cared and wanted to know. It was one of the nicest things anyone could have done for me at that very moment. Then, on the very same day, I received a call from a friend who said to me, *"I trusted you with my investment, and you totally fucked me over. I need that money now, and I do not care if you rob a bank, I want my money by Friday."*

Most folks would say things like, "Hey, I knew it was a risk, it is not the first time I have lost money!" "I hope you will remember me on your next venture and give me some credit there!" or, "It is what it is." For sure the investor loss was by far the hardest of all experiences, and the hurt goes deep. Several investors thought I did not give a shit. The reality is I always care, and it destroys me when these losses happen. If I had one dream, it is that I would never have allowed a single investor in; we were doing extremely well and did not need investors. They allowed us to grow fast, and that turned out to be the downfall.

I firmly believe that no one wants to lose a single investor dollar. How do you face that? But it happens, and it has been happening for years. However, when it happens to you, it is clearly the worst feeling in the world. You cannot pick up your sticks and start over with a clean slate. You have to make it up to each and every one of them. There is no walking away from them. The court says you can walk away, but you still need to look at yourself in the mirror. I want to see a winner in the mirror, and the one way to do this is to help the investors to get some of their investment back. It is clearly one of the most motivating forces in my life today.

Many of them do not think I care, but just as many know I do care. It is the ones who do believe that drive me. I remember dreaming of hitting the lottery and the first thing I do is call the investors and say, "Come on down! We are having a party." The truth, however, is that the lottery is a pipe dream, so I will do what I always do. I will go to the go-to guy, who is me, and I will fix this thing. It is my obsession, and it is my drive.

You will never understand what it is like to lose anyone's money unless, of course, you do. It is a very cold, hard feeling, and it is a pain that runs deeper than filing BK.

The feeling of utter despair had gripped me, and my life was total shit. The filing of the BK is the deepest place any entrepreneur can ever go, and I was right there. It was pure hell, and there was no deal to be made with Satan. I could not sell my soul. The only thing I could do was take my own life, and that just was not the exit strategy I had in mind. It was time to get up and get my life back. It was time to win again. It was time to see and show what I was made of. It was time to fight another day. Surrender? No! Hell no! Not this warrior.

The warrior, however, would have a long road back. I hated everything in life there was to hate. I was busted, I was broke, and I lost the respect of many people. I was a hero, but now I was a monster. The simple truth was several wanted me dead. I was pure evil to many, and one of them may be out there somewhere just waiting to put one in me. I slept with the 9mm under my pillow because I never knew when I may need to use it to defend myself. It was the worst of times, and it was the time when being an entrepreneur was a hard pill to swallow.

I woke up every day wondering what the day would bring and why I was still here. I soon realized that it was time to crawl out of my self-imposed dungeon, put the gun away, and do what I do best. Build! It was time to start anew and make it all back for the investors, for my family, for my friends, and most importantly, for me. When I say make it all back, I do not mean the money. I mean the success.

People need me to win; it gives them something to believe in. I need to win because I have to show the world I can. I have to fight. I have to win. I have to give my best. And if for some reason I do not make it, I will always know I tried, I did not give up. I fought, I gave it my best, and to this, I have won.

You cannot quit and you can never give in. If you want to be a champion, a winner, no matter how bad it gets, you must keep going, you must live to fight another day. You must give your best and you must never surrender. We all need something to believe in. I honestly believe that the point where Scott and I have been is the lowest point you can reach in your life. It is the hardest place to recover from. It will either make a winner out of you or it will not. I pray that you do not ever reach this point, but if you do, remember one simple thing:

You may only be one person in this world, but to one person you may be the whole world.

Chapter 11
The Venom Was Sweet

It is fortune, not wisdom, that rules man's life.

—Cicero

The Wealth of It All

The good times of being an entrepreneur were and are amazing. I just rattled off the downside to being an entrepreneur, and in my case, it was a huge downside. In the case of Scott Coles, it was the ultimate price. Paid in full. There is, however, the upside, and when it is good, it is great—far better than the downside.

This is the part of the story you want to read, the part where the king wears his crown, the part of the story that makes you really think. The chance to answer the "what if" question. What would you do if you made $3 million a year? How would you live? What would you do? Would you be foolish? Would you be wise? Would you be tempted?

For just a moment, think about what you would do if you made $3 million a year. We know what the pro athletes do; they buy their mothers nice homes. I did that.

I'm about to share with you what I did. I would like you to think about what you would do, and be really honest with yourself. I did a lot of the things I never thought I would do. I bought my then wife a $117,000 engagement ring that I let her pick out. Yep! I just wrote a check and said, "Here you go, Ed. Thank you!"

You will never know what you will do until you get there, until you are at that precise moment and you have the open checkbook. You may think you will know, but you will not. It is a lot like riding in a space shuttle; you are pretty sure you know what it would be like, but it is beyond your wildest dreams. However, until you are actually strapped in the shuttle and you have lifted off, you do not know what it feels like. The power of money is unmatched. I know. I lived in that world. It will suck you in and hold you like a little baby, and the more insecure you are, the bigger that world becomes. The more you feed the monster, the hungrier it becomes. Once you get the thirst of the lifestyle of the rich, it becomes a hunger. It grips you like the claw of an eagle, and it never lets you go.

Being rich, for me, was an addiction, and the addiction was an uncontrollable obsession. Just like a heroin junkie needs a fix, so did I. I was part of the new rich. The new rich suffer the worst from the addiction. It is through their naivety they think they can control their addiction, and exactly like a heroin junkie, they cannot. You get to a point where you cannot go sixty seconds without spending money.

I have often thought that the rich need counseling much the same way a drug addict or an alcoholic needs counseling. It does not work that way for the rich. First, there are not enough of them out there, and the ones that are out there simply buy their way out and that is their therapy. Out comes the Centurion Card, known informally as the black card, issued by American Express. The card itself is made of anodized titanium. It was created just for the rich, catering to a more affluent customer segment. A variety of exclusive benefits is given to the rich with this card. American Express created the card line amid rumors and urban legends in the 1980s that it produced an ultra-exclusive black card for elite users who could purchase anything with it. American Express decided to make the urban legend real.

I remember the first time one of my very rich friends, a new rich friend, pulled one of those cards out. I thought, *Man, I have got to get one of those!* I did not even know what the Centurion Card was. I am willing to bet I am not alone. If you pull one of these cards out, American Express says, "Don't ask, just charge it." Need a Lamborghini? Just put it on the card. Funny part is, I am not sure a therapist would know how to process the Centurion Card, so how could they possibly process their client? Nope! The rich can bypass rich spending counseling. Charge it! I am all better now.

So being rich is fun?! It is almost like that story where you want to be careful what you wish for because you might just get it. I got my wish. It was hand-delivered by room service with a note that read, "Welcome to the American dream." Good luck?! Funny thing about the American dream: everybody wants it, and nobody wants you to have it. This goes back to the bank story and the umbrella. The bank will give you an umbrella until it starts raining, and then they want it back. I hit the American dream, and they wanted it back. I could taste it, I just could not keep it; my library book was overdue, and it needed to be returned.

The only people really happy that you hit are those who feel the money hit their bottom line. This was the biggest adjustment for me. I thought I had a whole world of cheerleaders—everyone was with me. I was so self-absorbed in my own world that I totally missed it at first. I was so busy patting my own back that I broke my arm. Yep! That was me, boy genius. I really thought I was all that and more.

This is what happens to us; we begin to think we are a whole helluva lot more important than we truly are. I truly thought I had it under control, but I did not. I was fooling myself and trying to fool everyone around me. Sure, there were some folks who wanted me to do well. Please don't let me get away with it for a single second; this world is filled with good people, very special people. It was me who changed. I thought the money bought me the right to be better than others. It also made me lazy. My grandpa Van taught me the value of a hard day's work and respecting others. He taught me that a good effort is the best effort and to always do your best and *always* help others. Money taught me to buy loyalty and to buy services— everything totally opposite of the valuable lessons I learned from my hero, Grandpa Van. I no longer had to work for loyalty and services. I could simply buy them. *How much? No problem! Do you take cash?* I did not pick up a hammer but called a carpenter. I never changed a flat. I was way beyond that. *Hello, AAA.* You can buy anything done for you, and the more money you have, the more you can buy. I justified it by working 24-7, but I chose the work. I could change a tire, but why? Well, because Grandpa Van would have changed the tire, and that man taught me about life, I understand now. It is not whether you can do the hard work or not. What matters is, are you willing to?

The American dream had come right up to me, and it was all mine. Yay, baby! Get on board; it is a whole new world out there. What do you think, folks? Are you ready to live the dream? Well, I suggest you read on and take a bite out of it. Before we go any further, I really need you one more time to ask yourself: if you were earning $3 million a year, what would your life be like?

Do not judge, or you too will be judged. For in the same way you judge others, you will be judged,
and with the measure you use, it will be measured to you.

—Matthew 7

The ride is about to begin, so strap in and let's get to it. You want to be rich? Do you want me to give you the secrets and then hook you in on an offer? Do you want me to take you to a clever website and have you plug in your credit card and then sign you up? I don't think so, not today. I will just give it to you here and now. You want to be rich? Then follow all the things that took me there. I promise you none of them involved luck. If you want to be rich, then you have to believe. You have to believe you can be rich. See yourself there and go make it happen.

You need to take chances and you will need to work hard. You must have a passion. You have to get up every day and say you can do it—and you better believe it. You have to work hard and you have to go the extra step. You need to start where others quit. You need to think big and think real big. If you want to win big, then you have to go big. No charge! This is all part of the book. You are paid in full!

There are no shortcuts, and there is no luck. It is simply you getting after it, giving it your best, and never letting up. If it looks like you are not going to make it, well then that is when you get mean—I mean downright angry. You take no prisoners, and you give it everything you got. You do not rely on others but yourself. You take responsibility every step of the way, you take the blame, and you take the credit. Only one person can do this, and that person is you. Donald Trump will tell you that it is all luck, Trump is full of shit. It is not luck, Donald worked his ass off and made good moves. He is a very bright businessman who possesses all the skills above. He works hard. He knows what he wants, and he goes right after it. He never gives up, and he never takes prisoners. Luck? Are you kidding me? If you depend on luck, put this book down and go stick your head in the sand. If you depend on hard work and if you are willing to think big and act big, then read on. I am about to share with you what life is like when you make $3 million a year.

And So the Ride Took Place

Our home-building company was off and running. We started with a 107 four-story condo projects in central Phoenix. It was a deal that was in foreclosure. I was able to convince the second lien holder, who was about to lose his investment, to pay off Wells Fargo and take over. Not that I really had to convince him as this was his plan. It was through our meetings that I realized he was a good man, and we could build the project together. He agreed, and he funded. We were off and running.

Sales were very slow at first, but the property was coming together nicely. We were hitting all our timetables, the cranes were swinging, and the nails were flying. We had over a hundred people on-site working at all times. It was very exciting. This was late 2003 and the economy was sputtering, but it was about to explode—and explode it did. We had no clue what was about to happen, and we were right in the heart of it all, Phoenix, Arizona, the epicenter for the housing boom and the housing failure.

Like wildfire, the investor frenzy hit, and it hit with a vengeance. Houses were being released to the public and sold within minutes. The lottery system was in full swing. We opened up Saratoga Springs, our newest community for presale. We were completely sold out in six hours. *Poof!* Gone! All with deposits and our first delivery was eighteen months away. People wanted to be my friend in the worst way. I was the CEO/owner of one of Arizona's fastest-growing home-building companies. They wanted me in their back pocket so they would be the first call when I released a new community or another phase for presale.

I went to social events where people I didn't even know walked up to me to say they had bought a home in one of my communities and loved it. They would thank me for letting them in. Soon I would figure out who got them in. It was all a daze to me. It was happening at the speed of light, but in the end, it would all be happening at the speed of dark. Every homebuilder in town was experiencing the same thing. I had so many friends that I could barely keep them straight. I was like a deity of sorts. It was actually quite sad, but of course, being the egomaniac that I was, I ate it up. I am surprised I did not let them kiss my ring. I am sure that people could not believe who I was becoming. This is where I want you to ask yourself again: "What would you be like if you made $3 million a year?"

With all the sales came the cash. The spicket was running out of control. Time to upgrade the Denali! Think about that? Upgrading the Denali? A Denali is a fine automobile, but it is not an Escalade. Not even close. Nothing drives like a Cadillac except another Cadillac, of course. It was time to upgrade everything. We had a show to run and a home to build. I was about to upgrade my life to a point that was unbelievable. I was ready, but unfortunately, the rest of the world was not.

After I snatched an Escalade off the lot, I decided I also needed a big Hummer, and it was another couple of weeks before I grabbed one of those cute little XLRs. I was all-in. Next I met my good friend Ed Marshall of E.G. Marshall's Jewelry. You know you are in big trouble when you have a jeweler as a good friend. Ed took me into his office and always took my call no matter what. Ed is, without a doubt, one of the best people on this planet. I like Ed a whole bunch, haven't seen him in a long time, but I love him to death. I haven't exactly been buying jewelry lately. Ed helped me into a Rolex—not just any Rolex, a Gold Presidential. I totally hated jewelry my whole life, never wore it. I had never worn a watch in my whole life, which was of course until I wore a Rolex. Now that is a watch. It came in handy when I filed BK; it fetched $5,200 for the trustee. Right off my wrist and straight to the auction block it went. What can I buy next? Hmmm?

Of course I needed a big house. I found it! Tom VanWelden, the CEO/chairman of the board for Allied Waste, founding partner and one of the absolute best guys you will ever meet, had his estate on the market. It was a gorgeous almost-seven-acre horse property in Scottsdale—six horse pastures and matching stables complete with fully operational, state-of-the-art tennis and basketball courts. It even came with a tree house in the one-hundred-year-old sycamore tree. Thirteen thousand square feet of prime Scottsdale real estate and house! I was so over the top it was sickening. I was living like a king. I was still Mike Roberts from Flint, Michigan, but I just had money now—and lots of it. I had forgotten that you can take Mike out of Flint but you can't take Flint out of Mike.

Of course, a fella needs airplanes, or at least a couple of them. Of my many accomplishments in life, being a pilot is top on my list, but second only to being a father. I love to fly, and I am very good at it. I am a very safe pilot who took flying very serious. I was able to acquire a CJ2 (Citation Jet 2) from my good friend and investment partner Reggie Fowler. Reggie is part-owner of the Minnesota Vikings. Reggie is himself a very good pilot. He upgraded to the CJ3 and was kind enough to let me lease his CJ2 9-1 Alpha. It was a gem of a plane. We took it everywhere—fishing to Alaska, Christmas vacation to Atlantis, back to one of our vacation homes in Traverse City, Michigan, or Lake Manawa, Iowa, or skiing at the Canyons in Park City. We were rock stars. Just imagine you have your own private jet and you just get in it and go. It was like my car. I could be fishing in the Kenai in six and a half hours. We would grab our friends and go hop on the bird and off to Las Vegas we went. When we arrived in Las Vegas, we were booked at the Bellagio, the Venetian, the Palazzo, or the Four Seasons. We were whisked into the VIP entrances and taken up to the nicest suites. We were royalty. That is how the rich are treated. The rich have all their special entrances and exits to life. Every side door is their portal to the stars.

When we could not fly ourselves, we hopped on board the commercial guys and off to Europe we went all first class. Santorini, Athens, Rome, Zurich, Munich, London, Dublin—all the places where we could buy Prada. As for other travels, we saw parts of Hawaii most do not even know exist. We stayed on Lanai and Kauai when we traveled to the islands, no Waikiki for us. China, Switzerland, Germany, Austria—we saw the world.

Sports? Super Bowls, Stanley Cups, World Series. Reggie Fowler was very gracious, and he allowed us to join him in the owner's box for games. He even provided us field passes. I took my two children down on the field for a couple of Vikings games. We stood between the players and the cheerleaders on the side lines during the games. It was spectacular! You felt as if you were part of the action; I was ready to run a play in. I think that was without doubt one of the greatest sports moments in my long line of great sports moments. All the good seats—no nosebleeds for us. NHL Hockey, right on the glass and putting our drinks on the top of the dugout for the World Series, forty-yard seats for the Super Bowl. One Super Bowl, I was actually in a suite—my suite.

The suites were way over the top, and we had VIP suites for all the sports. The Coyotes, the Diamondbacks, the Cardinals, but best of all suites was for the Suns. The Suns suite was actually very extra sweet. It was way over the top. It seated seventy-two people. It was three suites combined, $400,000 per year. This did not include food or drinks; however, it did include our own private bartender. Abercrombie and Kent went bankrupt, and when they did, their over-the-top suite opened up and we were in. All in! Wood floors, granite countertops, and a whole shitload of TVs, special lighting—it was the suite that most never see, not even the suite holders themselves. It was all over the top—too far over the top.

Being rich has a whole different meaning, and you are treated differently. You should try it sometime. People treat you different; they treat you special. It is sad, very sad.

What would you do if you made $3 million a year? I did things I never thought I could do. You even tip big. You start tipping people $20 just for handing you a valet ticket, and if they are real good, you give them a hundred—everyday people, like bellman or valets, maybe the guy who fetches your car when you taxi your plane up.

We jumped in 91 Alpha, our plane, the CJ2, and flew to Atlantis for our Christmas vacation. We stayed at the luxurious Atlantis in their very private section known as the Cove. It is another area for the rich and famous. It is the best of the best; it is total upscale, and it is very private. There you tip a hundred as routine. Leaving a twenty in their palm is an insult, but they will take it. While staying at the Cove, we made new friends. I actually sat in the hot tub with Robin Williams, not that Robin would know me from a mole on a horse's ass, but we chatted. I was there, and he was telling all of us jokes; that guy is truly funny. He spent an hour with us. It was like we were having our own private Robin Williams show right there in the hot tub at the Cove. Robin was very gracious and polite to everyone. He asked all of our names and where we were from. When we went down to the beach, every day, of course the private beach, there was Ray Liotta. Ray was a tanning fool. I love that guy. Ray was going through some sort of ordeal at the time, so we really did not get in a whole lot of chatting with him. Then we walked up to the cabanas where Magic Johnson and his wife, Cookie, had their own. We sat up there and talked with Magic and Cookie for a couple of hours. Magic even gave me his cell phone number. I never tried to call it, but what the hell, he gave it to me. Magic took pictures with our children, and those very pictures sit on my desk today—one thing that the auctioneer did not take.

Magic and I were at Michigan State at the same time. We were both making an impact at MSU. Magic was winning a national championship, and I was trying to survive math. Magic's accomplishments are well noted, and mine are still a bit of a mystery.

It turns out being rich was the best thing going, and it was taking charge of my life. I could not even function if I did not buy something. My monthly nut was two hundred grand and I still had to keep up. There was not a better way to live. I was lost. I was so far gone that I no longer knew who I was, and the beast just kept eating me up and spitting me out. As I wallowed in the cesspool of the happiness that I kept searching for, I wondered what would ever become of me. The world melted down and it was about to take me right with it. The OFF switch was coming and it was not going to be very forgiving. I was too far in and I had thought I was really royalty. I was the godfather of sorts. I just did not realize I would someday, very soon, find myself again. The hard way!

Most of the people that have made it all...then lost it all did so because they failed to identify where the finish line was.

I never ever realized there was a finish line until one was made for me. The big producer in the sky flipped the OFF switch for the housing market, the whole world collapsed, and along with it was me. I was not a victim. I was pure carnage, plain and simple. It was a helluva ride, and more spectacular than anyone could ever imagine. We were rock stars, it was the best of times, but the price was heavy and I became lost in it all. I changed, and I changed for the worst.

I got a big break, the meltdown brought me back to reality—and I found my life again. *The ride was over and I had lost everything*—so I thought, but I had not. I had not lost me but I was close. I realized I had me back, and with me, anything is possible. I could win; all I had to do was what I have always done. I needed to believe in me, and with that little secret, I could pull through this and ride again another day. Only this time the ride would be different. It would be real.

I have discovered what is truly important to me. Life is truly important to me. I am able to breathe again. They say you learn from your experiences and what does not kill you only makes you stronger. I agree! I am stronger. I am stronger than Iron Man and Captain America combined. I lived the life of royalty. The ride was unbelievable, but knowing who I am again is even better. Feeling my life come back to me and stopping to smell the roses or hear the birds sing has helped me to appreciate all the glory there is. I am alive! I was beat hard and ready to surrender, but I never ever got to that last little point where I said, "Mike, time to give up." I never ever hit that one little point where you look down and put your finger on the trigger and say, "I am broken"—game over! I am broke but I am not broken, and I will never be broken.

So what would you do if you made $3 million a year? How would you live?

Chapter 12
The Backstory and the Bottom Story

In this world it is not what we take up, but what we give up, that makes us rich.
—Henry Ward Beecher

The backstory is the story that is so often overlooked. This is the part where you make the sacrifices, you work the long hours, eat Spam, and watch reruns of *Family Feud* because you cannot afford to do anything but work. You work hard to build your kingdom, yourself, or your company. Your family thinks you are a hermit, and they want to know what they have to do to be part of your life. You are wound-tight and everything that happens impacts you like nothing before. This is the little part where the entrepreneur has to make the really big sacrifices. This is the backstory—the early years, the years when you have special friends, the friends who really stick

135

with you. It is said, *"A friend is a friend who knows everything about you and still likes you."* That is a true friend.

The hours are shit, the pay even worse, and the sacrifices are unreal, but knowing all this, you march forward. You tell yourself the rewards will come, and if you give it everything you got and if you never give up, they will come. I will caution one thought; I have discovered that *we are judged more for our rewards than we are our sacrifices.* The journey to making it is often better than making it. The rewards and the taste of each victory are more delectable on the way as opposed to when you have arrived. It is the backstory that really earns you the right to celebrate and enjoy your victory. It is also the backstory that people rarely see; they just think you were born a king. I once had a casual acquaintance sum it up perfectly when he told me, "I was an overnight sensation, it just took ten years."

This backstory is often neglected and overshadowed by what you see and hear when you are on top. When I started the company, I was flat broke. I had nothing but a will to be something, to build something. I had one resource, and that one resource was me. That resource grew, it believed, and it became confident that it could succeed. It is here, however, that it all began with just me.

I worked around the clock always taking shit and eating more. I put up with every guy in town wanting to own me and tell me how I would fail. I would never make it as a home builder. People look down on you when you are on the bottom as if they are so much better than you. It is a harsh world. It is almost like being a fat kid in school and the other kids are teasing you. You feel so demoralized that some days the only way to go on is to tell yourself you have to go on. You learn to talk to yourself because nobody else will listen. You choose to be an entrepreneur and build your own business, but you have nothing, so what gives you the right? Well, nothing gives you the right, but you must try anyway. You must go on, and you must realize that some people do not see you any better than a piece of dirt under their feet. It is equally amazing how differently those same folks treat you when you have made it. I can even remember several wanting to take credit.

As I began my journey alone, I found my first cheerleader, Kristina. Kristina was a godsend because she believed in me and wanted to help however she could. She offered much of her time and was instrumental in our growth. She gave me the go power, and that go power made it all happen. She would attend many meetings and offered insight to the plan. She was as broke as I was, but she had the spirit. This is not to say that I had no other support. My mom, my children, my former wife Ann, and my sisters were right there behind me. Their support and belief in me were paramount, and without them, I could have never made it. Let's say without them, I may have chosen never to continue on as an entrepreneur. You need a support team, and I had that for sure.

I founded a company that would build and develop over some three thousand homes and later was responsible for the livelihoods of some two thousand five hundred people—it all began with one simple transaction. That first transaction was opening up the office. I was extremely fortunate as I was quickly able to utilize an office in every city we were thinking of working in. My most utilized office was the hood of my green Denali. If the office was dusty or out of gas, I would go to my next favorite office: the Denny's on Deer Valley and the Seventeenth. This office was great because they had lots of water and plenty of coffee. Sometimes I would have office meetings at my Scottsdale office, Village Inn on Scottsdale Road. Yes, I was really moving now, offices all over the city. I remember when folks would say, "Where is your office at?" I would say, "Where do you want it at?" They would say, "No! Really?" I would say, "Yes! Really!" I could not afford to meet at the more upscale restaurants; they did not appreciate coffee and water orders the way Denny's and the Cracker Barrel did. I wanted to sometimes meet at my house, but I was afraid the landlord would show up with the eviction notice in the middle of a meeting. This is the backstory. This is the story that is undersold. It is the glitz story that is sold. The rich guy with the fleet of cars, the big house, and the airplane. Now that story sells. You ever notice when someone tells you a story about someone, and if that someone has a lot of money, that is how the story starts? It is like you get their resume based upon their wealth. We all knew Steve Jobs, the founder of Apple and one of the leading geniuses in the tech world—actually, I would say the world at large. His backstory is the best. He built his first MAC in his garage, and at the same time, he dropped out of college. Steve figured it out as far as college was concerned; he did not like what they made him take, so he dropped out but he kept going. He just picked classes he liked and showed up; he simply dropped in and grabbed a seat. He went to a class on calligraphy and fell in love with it. It was in this class he created the unique fonts that are in use today on all computers. The Apple backstory began in a garage and a small college classroom that he dropped in on for fun.

The backstory is the story of tremendous sacrifice. Most folks do not see the backstory, but they see the today story. If you want to be an entrepreneur, you need to understand the backstory, and if you really want to experience the truly amazing entrepreneurial fight, then you go from the backstory to the bottom story. The story of where the entrepreneur who faces utter defeat puts the gun in his mouth and, for a second, gives up. The bottom story is a hard story, and it goes beyond sacrifice; it goes right to the heart of the beast, the very beast that is about to rip your life right away from you. The bottom story trumps the backstory. Most backstories are the history of a company and the sacrifices it made, or the sacrifice its founders made, but the bottom story is the story that is unbearable. The real bottom is upon them, but somehow they rise above and they fight another day. They fight another day not knowing if they will win, but they fight nonetheless. It is all they have left—to fight.

After this backstory, I am going to take you to the bottom story and the journey will be horrifying.

The Backstory in Layman's Terms

This backstory is often neglected and overshadowed by what you see and hear. Sure, you see me park my Mercedes outside. You saw my big home at last year's Christmas party. I'm sure all these flashy icons of luxury conjure up some idealized thoughts about my life. However, what you don't see is the backstory.

ANOTHER ENTREPRENEUR'S BACKSTORY

I started this company twelve years ago. At that time, I lived in a three-hundred-square-foot studio apartment for three years. My entire living space was converted into an office so I could put forth 100% effort into building a company, which, by the way, would eventually employ you. My diet consisted of Ramen Pride noodles because every dollar I spent went back into this company. I drove a rusty Toyota Corolla with a defective transmission. I didn't have time to date. Oftentimes, I stayed home on weekends, while my friends went out drinking and partying. In fact, I was married to my business—hard work, discipline, and sacrifice. Meanwhile, my friends got jobs. They worked forty hours a week and made a modest $50K a year and spent every dime they earned. They drove flashy cars and lived in expensive homes and wore fancy designer clothes. Instead of hitting the Nordstrom's for the latest hot fashion item, I was trolling through the Goodwill store extracting any clothing item that didn't look like it was birthed in the '70s. My friends refinanced their mortgages and lived a life of luxury. I, however, did not. I put my time, my money, and my life into a business with a vision that eventually, someday, I too will be able to afford these luxuries my friends supposedly had. So while you physically arrive at the office at 9:00 a.m., mentally check in at about noon, and then leave at 5:00 p.m., I don't. There is no OFF button for me. When you leave the office, you are done and you have a weekend all to yourself. I unfortunately do not have the freedom. I eat, live, and breathe this company every minute of the day. There is no rest. There is no weekend. There

139

is no happy hour. Every day this business is attached to me like a one-day-old baby. You, of course, only see the fruits of that garden—the nice house, the Mercedes, the vacations. You never realize the backstory and the sacrifices I've made. Now, the economy is falling apart and I, the guy that made all the right decisions and saved his money, have to bail out all the people who didn't. The people that overspent their paychecks suddenly feel entitled to the same luxuries that I earned and sacrificed a decade of my life for. Yes, business ownership has its benefits, but the price I've paid is steep and not without wounds. Unfortunately, the cost of running this business, and employing you, is starting to eclipse the threshold of marginal benefit.

This is the backstory. Like so many backstories, this author is a little bitter, but he makes several good points. The most important point is that there is no OFF switch. When you are an entrepreneur starting your own business, there is no OFF switch, and as long as you own the business, you will never find an OFF switch. The good news is that this is what a true entrepreneur thrives on, and this true entrepreneur could be you, probably is. The entrepreneur loves it just this way. These sacrifices are the part we call earning your stripes; after all, owning your own business is like having a baby, and you just do not walk away. You do not look for the OFF switch, and if you did, there is no way to turn it off.

I also would suggest that we all bear one thing in mind: as in the backstory above, the entrepreneur makes many sacrifices, as did this author. They make them for the greater good and glory—that is, their greater good and their greater glory. It was his or her decision to make those sacrifices. It was a risk, but it was still their risk, and they choose it. Nobody made them choose it, so if they are looking for sympathy, they came to the wrong reader. Speaking of sympathy, my grandpa Van always told me where I could find sympathy. He said, *"If you look in the dictionary, you will find* sympathy *right there between* shit *and* syphilis." There is a lot of truth in that. With this being said, being an entrepreneur is a road paved with hard work and sacrifice, and it is a choice that we all make.

As for backstories, there are many great ones and a few that need to be remembered here.

Michael Dell, born February 1965, started the road to success out of his University of Texas dorm room with just $1,000 and an idea in 1984. Michael wanted to provide a service. Today Michael Dell is both chairman and CEO of his company with a net worth of over $30 billion. Dell sells directly to the customer so as to avoid middleman markups.

Ben Cohen and Jerry Greenfield were childhood friends born four days apart in Brooklyn, New York, in 1951. You could say that ice cream runs in their veins. During his senior year of high school, Ben drove an ice cream truck. After high school, he attended and dropped out of various colleges in the Northeast, eventually leaving his studies altogether to teach pottery on a working farm in New York's Adirondack region, where he also dabbled in making ice cream.

Jerry started on a more traditional path. After graduating high school, he attended Oberlin College to study medicine. Jerry worked as an ice cream scooper in the school's cafeteria. Upon graduating, Jerry returned to New York to work as a lab technician while applying to medical school without success. During his lab tech days, he shared a Manhattan apartment with Ben. After moving to North Carolina for a few years, Jerry reunited with Ben in Saratoga Springs, New York, and they decided to go into the food business together. At first the pair thought about making bagels but decided the necessary equipment was too expensive. Instead, they settled on ice cream. This is Ben and Jerry's backstory.

Disney is one of the most recognized brands in the world today, but few know much about the man behind the Magic Kingdom, not to mention the hundreds of animated cartoons, countless feature films, and endless toys that bear his name. An influential innovator and entrepreneur in the mid-twentieth century, Walt Disney went from sketching a rabbit (yes, a rabbit) to running a multibillion-dollar empire. Many who know me well know that Walt Disney is my number one hero. Number two is Henry Ford, closely followed by Vince Lombardi. Walt was the true entrepreneur who knew more about the bottom story than the backstory. Walt filed bankruptcy seven times, yet he rose and never gave up. At the time of this writing, Disney will eclipse 40 billion dollars in annual revenues. I will write more about Walt and the mouse as we go—hell, I will even mention Oswald, the little rabbit that almost did him in.

Henry Ford's marriage to Clara Bryant in 1888 required him to get a better-paying job. In 1891, he started as an engineer for Edison Illuminating Company and was promptly promoted to chief engineer. The job required Ford to be on call twenty-four hours a day. In his on-call time, he began to experiment with internal combustion engines and created the Quadricycle, the first "horseless carriage," powered by gasoline and riding on four bicycle wheels. This invention led to the founding of Ford Motor Company.

Henry Ford made several attempts to establish his company. In 1903, with $28,000, eleven men, and Ford as vice president and chief engineer, Ford Motor Company was incorporated. They produced three cars a day and had up to three men working on each. In 1908, the company produced the famous Model T, a reliable and affordable vehicle for the mass market. Ford drove and raced this vehicle at every opportunity to prove how reliable it was. By 1918, half of all cars in the United States were a Model T. Just imagine Henry's backstory. He never had a dime, but he had a dream and convinced others to believe in his dream.

At age twenty, Debbi Fields was a housewife with no business experience, but she had a great chocolate chip cookie recipe and a dream. Today, Mrs. Fields Cookies is one of the world's most recognizable dessert franchises, with over six hundred stores in the United States and ten other countries.

Microsoft Corp. cofounder Bill Gates is perhaps the most famous entrepreneur of this era. William Gates III was born in 1955. The son of an attorney and a teacher, Gates grew up in Seattle with his two sisters. He began dabbling in computer programming at age thirteen and sold his first program to a school for about $4,000. As a teenager, he befriended Paul Allen, and the two both left Seattle to attend Harvard University. While at Harvard, they formed a company specializing in computer software, which they named Microsoft. They trademarked the name in 1976. Gates did not finish his education at Harvard. He dropped out in his junior year to devote himself to Microsoft.

They all have backstories. They are all entrepreneurs who fought the odds and won; they also believed in themselves and their products. They are and were visionaries. They never gave up.

The backstories are very exciting. All the great entrepreneurs had and have them. Ray Kroc with McDonald's, Herb Kelleher with Southwest Airlines, Steve Jobs, P. T. Barnum, Thomas Edison, John Rockefeller, J.P. Morgan, Ralph Lauren, Levi Strauss, Estee Lauder, and yes, even Sam Walton. The list grows every day.

I could share with you my very own backstory, but it is the bottom story that elevates things. The bottom story goes beyond the sacrifices. I understand what it means to go without and what it means to make sacrifices, but what I did not understand was what it was like to ask yourself if you really want to keep on fighting and keep on living.

Life started as a backstory. It was all good; being broke was okay. I was born that way, and that was the way it was. When you grow up like most people, you are living the typical dream, one pay check to the next. Our home was no different. Mom faced all kinds of struggles, but with four small children and Dad gone, it presented a pretty ugly situation. Mom was a warrior nonetheless; she never held back from giving it her best. Mom was an expert at sacrifices. I remember Mom always made sure we all had good shoes. I never understood why it was so important to have nice shoes. I could be wearing rags but the shoes must be good. Then one day Mom told me a very important story about shoes. Mom said that you could tell a lot about a person by their shoes. She said that if their shoes were not well cared for or cheap, they would be the same themselves. If they did not care about their shoes, they would not care about much else, she reasoned. A bad pair of shoes showed a lack of self-respect or one's pride in themselves. She would say it took more than a nice dress; it also took a fine pair of well-kept shoes. With men, it was even more important, she argued; if a businessman wears unpolished shoes or cheap scuffed shoes, he was not a very good person and, most likely, not a very good business person. Mom always believed you go the distance and the shoes showed the distance. I later reasoned that the shoes were clearly a sign of going the extra step.

It was always a top priority with Mom, this whole idea of shoes. The following is the very example that led me to tears. I was watching Mom one morning as she was cutting out a piece of cardboard. As she finished cutting the cardboard, she put the piece in the bottom of her shoe as the soles had worn through. Mom never said a word nor did she know I saw her do it. I looked later as she sat down and you could see the bottom of her shoe and the cardboard coming right through. I would use the same cardboard trick later in my life. Mom made tons of sacrifices, and she never said a word about them. She made sacrifices one right after the other, but as long as her children had new shoes, she never saw it as a sacrifice. This is the very lesson she taught me that I soon realized would be my guide through life. I was living the backstory, and that is exactly how we were raised. It was the bottom story that I was not trained for.

I think what made life so interesting was that I had spent my whole life living the backstory, one sacrifice after another, never even realizing that we were making sacrifices; it was more like we were simply doing what we needed to do to get along, yet I hit the big time. Yes! This was exactly what made it all so interesting. I was well on my way to riches, and I was headed for the today story—the story of success and riches. I was alive and fine in the land of opportunity. I was living the American dream. The big houses, the fancy cars, the fat bank accounts, the airplanes—it was all a dream and that little backstory in Flint was a very distant past. I had earned my wings, I had paid the price, I had rallied to the top—I had paid my dues. So I thought! Little did I know that I still had to pay more. The devil never told me the price I was about to pay. I had lived and experienced the backstory, but now it was time for the bottom story, and nothing in the world could have ever prepared me for the bottom story.

Life had beaten me down so bad I was ready to die. I wanted to die. I dreamed that I would get cancer and everyone would just let me die and feel sorry for me. Poor Mike! I had had enough. I was reaching deep in my soul begging for it all to stop. "Let me off up ahead," the sign read, but up ahead never came and I could not get off. I kept looking for the answers. I kept asking what happened. Every day seemed worse than the day before and even worse than the one before that one. There was nothing positive, and bad news was coming in so fast that if I got any good news, I would not be able to recognize it. Bad news was piling up like dirty dishes in the sink. When the courts and creditors were not on me, it was the investors' turn. I was the mud of the world, and my name, a name I had spent my whole life building, was pure shit. The fight was leaving me, and it was on the 5:10 out of town. There was no longer a battle to win but a fight to survive, and I was looking for just one reason to go on one more day—one simple reason to believe that tomorrow could be a better day. There was no room to hate myself because the dance card was all full up with those people who wanted me dead. It did not matter that the whole country and the world was on a meltdown. I was the bad guy. I was living the entrepreneur's worst nightmare.

The troops followed me into battle and we were slaughtered. I knew how Custer felt at the Little Big Horn. I could only think of the horrific battles. Waterloo, Battle of Cannae with Hannibal, Battle of Gallipoli, Battle of Gettysburg, Napoleon's invasion of Russia—all pure disasters that all began so well. I had faced the ultimate death and I had no army left. I was bankrupt, I was broke, and I was almost without hope. I was about to be broken. *I nuzzled the 9mm, and I knew I had hit rock bottom. I was now living the bottom story. The glory of the backstory was now gone, and I was at a point as low as I could go. I was at the bottom, and I was searching for the last glimmer of hope, that one little spark that would put the Colt away and tell me to stand up. It was like watching a Hollywood movie and the good guy was lying on the canvas, and he was not moving. The crowd was in a hush, and they all looked on in horror. Again there is still no movement and the crowd settles back with their mouths open and their hands over their eyes. The lights dim and the body still lays there lifeless. You say to yourself that the fight has left him and he is gone. You look for the sheet to put over the body.

Then just at that moment, you see a finger twitch and pretty soon you see it twitch again. You hold up on the sheet as you are not sure if that was a twitch or if your eyes are playing tricks on you. But there it is again—it is a twitch!

You have hit bottom and the whole world is caving in on you. You were on top of the world and now the world is on top of you. The will to fight and the will to live is gone and your heart has lost itself, but you are a fighter, and for reasons you may never know, you know you have to get off that canvas and fight. You just need to believe; while you do not know what the battle will be and for what you will fight, you tell yourself you can't give up. You need to find one reason to believe, one reason to hope, then you need to build on that hope, that belief, and find the reason to look for one more hope. You need to get up off the canvas and learn to live again. You need to get up and fight again. You cannot give up because even though you've hit rock bottom, you know you are an entrepreneur and you have to go get it done once more. You may have lost everything, but you still have you, and no matter how bad it gets, at least you are alive—and that is the place to start. It is not the place to stop.

The backstory is a good place to start, but the backstory is nothing when compared to the bottom story. Most people start with a backstory, and it is often their choice. But for the bottom story, nobody chooses that. If you ever have to live it, it is pure hell. The bottom story is where you truly can tell yourself, if it does not kill you, it will make you stronger. It is strong, and you should avoid it at all cost. You don't brag about the bottom story; you fight with everything in you to avoid it. *The backstory builds character where the bottom story teaches you survival.* After the backstory, you are glad to be at the today story, but after the bottom story, you are just glad to be alive and have survived your darkest hour.

I hit bottom, and I have never ever in my life so badly wanted to die; I just wanted it all to be over. The world had beaten me and tortured me, and I just wanted off. There was only one OFF switch and it was permanent. I just could not pull that switch. I wanted it all to stop and it would not. I finally realized that I would have to fight it and that it would be the absolute biggest fight of my life ever.

This is the moment where you realize you have to do it and you have to fight. I fought it and I won. I was broke but I was not broken. *Round 1: Mike 1, Bottom Story 0.*

147

Chapter 13
Time to Fight

Only a man who knows what it is like to be defeated can reach down to the bottom
of his soul and come up with the extra ounce of power it takes to win.

—Muhammad Ali

You have experienced the harshest of realities and the world is against you. As you search for the answers, you find none, so you have to rebuild. You figure out that quitting does not work, no matter how close you come to the end, to that moment where checking out seems to be the answer, you don't. You go forward.

Going forward is a very hard thing to do when you have been down for so long. You have to start rebuilding, and rebuilding starts by rebuilding you. In order to start rebuilding you, you have to start thinking of the good things in life. You slowly build yourself up, and you realize you can only focus on the positives if you are going to win again. You will never think of the good things in life if you allow yourself to be beat down. If you beat yourself down or allow others to beat you down, you cannot rise. This is where you need to remember Grandpa Van's words: *"You must give your permission to feel inferior, so don't give it."* I knew I had been giving my permission plenty; I was the hero, but now I was the monster—the fall guy. And being the fall guy comes with the territory. You want to be an entrepreneur, then you get the good with the bad, or if you play with the bull, you will get the horns.

As you grow forward and you start your journey to life again, you must remember that you may not even know where your journey will go. You just know you have got to go forward and anything positive is a start in the right direction. *"You don't have to see the whole staircase, just take the first step"* (Martin Luther King Jr.). This idea of starting over or crawling out of the pit to find your life again is critical. You may not even know where you are going; you just know you have got to go. It reminds you of Tom Petty's "Learning to Fly."

> *Well, some say life will beat you down*
> *Break your heart, steal your crown*
> *So I've started out for God knows where*
> *I guess I'll know when I get there*
> *I'm learning to fly*

You are learning to fly. You have been beat down, you have lost your crown, and make no mistake, you will know when you get to wherever it is you arrive.

You have to look in the mirror and believe in yourself. You have to quit focusing on self-pity or the attacks of others. You have to trust in your own judgment of who you are. You must learn to value only your opinion when it comes to evaluating the type of person you are. You have to rise above and remember the things that make you good. You have to see the good and remember the good that rests in your heart and in your soul. I knew this was to be my only way back to life, the successful business life, I once had. More importantly, it was my fight back to life. I would focus on the successes that I had achieved before and remember them. I would use them as my step board to resurrecting myself. I had to look back at those things that allowed me to say, "Mike, you are a good guy. You are not a monster." This was my first step. We have all been there at one time or another, but I had clearly been to the bottom, and I needed a reason to believe. At this point, I realized I was the only one who could give me a reason.

This realization is a very important part of the survival and recovery of your life and believing in who you are. To better understand this thinking, you turn to yourself and search for the things that make you good. Once you find them, then you repeat them over and over. You quit feeling sorry for yourself. You look for inspirations or words that can help you rise up. You quit questioning yourself. You accept that you can win and that you need to win. You look at yourself and say you will do this. You begin by taking baby steps on your road to recovery. To aid in this, inspirational words are the best—quotes, sayings, success stories, or motivational words. I even would write poetry to help with this rebuilding. In short, you have to rebuild your mental attitude. You start looking at things that are worse or harder times for others and be thankful that you are better off. Everyone has problems, and maybe yours are not so bad. Bottom line, you are still breathing. I used Post-its on the wall to remind me I was and am a winner, and that no matter how bad it is, it will get better. I started my day by thanking the world for allowing me another day in it. I watched the birds fly and the sun shine and I screamed, *I AM HERE! THANK YOU, LORD!*

You also have to make the biggest adjustment in your life; you have to not be afraid anymore. You have to defeat your fears. I have experienced pure horror, so I say to myself, "What else can I fear?" "NOTHING!" As for the bad, I say to myself, "What is another pound to an elephant? Or another bucket of water to the ocean?" Screw it, there is nothing left to lose, so now let's go forward and kick fear to the street as it will never serve you well.

When it comes to fear, I have a favorite writing:

Our Deepest Fear
By Marianne Williamson

Our deepest fear is not that we are inadequate.
Our deepest fear is that we are powerful beyond measure.
It is our light, not our darkness that most frightens us.
You're playing small does not serve the world.
There is nothing enlightened about shrinking
So that other people won't feel insecure around you.
We were all meant to shine, as children do.
It's not just in some of us; it's in everyone.
And as we let our own light shine,
We unconsciously give other people permission to do the same
As we are liberated from our own fear,
Our presence automatically liberates others.

This guides me through many a battle with fear. Not only must we defeat our fears, but we must also use them to help others. This teaches us to not give into our fears but use them to be better, to shine, and to let others shine because we shine.

I was beating my fears, and I again believed in me. I was no longer feeling sorry for myself, and it was time to take the battle to the streets. I know that as you read along, you can remember a time in your life when it totally sucked and you felt like the world was coming to an end. Maybe that time is right now. It hurts, and it hurts bad. It seems like no matter what you try, it does not get better. I have been there and I have spent years fighting. I am here to tell you that you can win and it will get better. I can prove it.

As I began my recovery from economic disaster, I started a self-storage company, Sure Storage USA. It was to be my lifeline, my way back to reality and to success. It was no longer about the money. It was about building another winning formula. It was about winning and being a winner. I did not give a rat's ass about the money. I wanted to help people. I wanted people to believe in themselves, and if they saw that I could come back, then maybe they would come back, or they would at least lunge forward, take a chance on themselves, and take the risk that they might be afraid to otherwise take. I wanted people to believe we could win again. I wanted people to believe in themselves, and if they saw me do it, then they could do it. I wanted to build a company and build families. Owning a big house no longer interested me. I needed to fulfill a dream. I needed to rally for the troops. My success was driven by the will to succeed and not economic gain. However, economic gain is the barometer to success. We use economic gain as the way to keep score. Sure I want to make others money, but I wanted more than anything to build dreams, not bank accounts. If you build dreams, then bank accounts will come. My meltdown was the best thing that ever happened to me, and I just did not know it at the time. I was born again, and just weeks earlier, I wanted to quit.

My priorities became clearer than ever. My family and friends dominated my landscape, and the need to help them was the number one force in my life. I put my family's and friends' names on Post-its and then put them on the wall by my desk. I looked at their names and I decided I would do this for them. I was not a quitter. I was driven with a fever. I was clearer than I had ever been in my whole life. I was like the Blues Brothers. I was on a mission from God. But it was not God who needed me; it was my family and my friends. The fever was out of control, and I would do whatever I needed to do to protect and help them. My own needs were irrelevant.

I no longer was defeated, but I had now become a warrior. I was on my way back because I had been to the bottom and I had been to the devil's parlor, and I knew my greatest fight was ahead of me. I knew I could handle the challenge; there was nothing that could be thrown at me now that I could not handle. Yes! I was a warrior and I would not stop. I was no longer afraid.

I made a simple deal with myself. I promised that no matter what I did, as long as I could make a difference in at least one person, then I would fight, and so here and now, this fight rages on. As I started out here, I needed to think of the good guy and kill the monster. The good guy assured me I could fight, and I needed to quit accepting the bad side. The dark side was going to undo me, but the side of the light would save me, and it was up to me to now do that.

I revisited numerous experiences of my life in which I had accomplished good, or more specifically, in which I had helped others. I focused on it daily. Helping others was and is the one thing in my life that I have always found extremely rewarding. We all have a little button inside of us that wants us to help others, and when we do good deeds for others, we feel good about ourselves. To find that good feeling was the key I needed, so I could start to rebuild the positive life I so desperately wanted back. I began to write some of these things down so I could review them again and again on a daily basis. The next step to fixing me was to believe in me and how I felt about me as opposed to how others felt about me. I became solely focused on me and how I saw me, and I refused to let anyone's opinion of me impact my own opinion of me. I refused to listen— unless, of course, I liked it. It sounds conceited, but it is not. The times had become desperate, and in spite of everything, I still trusted and valued myself. So to the events that made me the proudest, I traveled. The trip was all in my mind, but it was my mind that would save me.

The Heart of a Lion

Ironically there was one letter given to me by a good friend who I had helped, and this very letter was to help me. I had a friend who was very dear to me who had passed on. Fortunately, or unfortunately, for him, it was before the collapse of the housing market and, ultimately, the company he helped to build. Before he passed, we spent time talking and laughing. Just hours before his death, he wrote me a very wonderful letter that he had his wife give to me after he died. It was this letter that I read a hundred times that pulled me through my own moment of despair. As I helped him, he in turn helped me. The following story I never thought I would tell, but I know my friend would want it told, because it may just help you to help someone else, and if it does, then my friend will smile down upon us both.

I first met Scott Simkins when he was hired by our VP of construction, Bart Shea. Bart told me we were lucky to have Scott, and I later found out just how right Bart was. Bart was our second employee and Scott was to be our third. Scott was a good balance for Bart as they had worked together before. Bart did not take any shit, and he was all about getting the job done. Scott calmed Bart and helped him in a way nobody else could. Scott reminded me of a barnyard animal that slept near the prized stallion just to calm the stallion. Scott was a whole of lot more than a barnyard animal. He was amazing in his own right, and while I initially thought he was there to calm the stallion, I found out his talents were magnanimous. Scott was very special. He never tried to be special; it was just how Scott was built. Scott was a big man, in pretty good shape—when I say big, I mean tall. Scott was a gentle giant with a teddy bear quality to him that was all his own. In my years of working with Scott, I never saw him lose his temper or raise his voice. You could drive a Mack truck through Scott's front room and he would offer you a beer. Scott was a patient man who always took his time to see all sides. He had an uncanny ability to look at things logically and not focus on them personally. He never played devil's advocate, but he did bring to light the pros and cons. He always stayed the course, and his motives were simple and honest.

Scott battled cancer for about ten years before I met him. He fought it on three different occasions. Scott was, however, at the moment of joining the team cancer-free. Little did I know, I would get to go through his fourth and final episode with him. I guess I should not say *with him* because his battle was all his.

Scott had won his previous battles, but this time the cancer was back with a vengeance. Scott never lost his spirit, and he thought he would beat it again as he had done three times before. Scott came into my office and told me it was back and my heart sank. He said he needed to stay and work as it was his salvation. I told him whatever he needed take. Scott worked faithfully for a little while, but then the pain and the treatments wore him down and he needed to go home. They might have worn down his body but not his spirit. It was agreed that he would start working from home. We bought him a laptop and home he went. This worked for a while, but this too became very hard. The pain was overwhelming and he could never get comfortable. Like most cancer patients, he had good days and bad days. Scott figured he had cancer and it did not have him.

We would talk about his family and how much he knew they were hurting. This was a pain that he could not describe, and it hurt more than the cancer. I would sit there and think Scott's whole world has changed and his dreams are fading like a light as it goes off into the distance.

Scott's wife, Martha, and his two children were a great support system for him. His daughter, Elizabeth, who was now a teenager, had grown up her whole life with her father having cancer. He would beat it, and then it would return. I remember one day as I sat with Scott in his bedroom and he told me this. I thought how sad to think that his little girl has never known him without cancer and now she was off to high school. Scott spoke of her getting married someday. He had all these model cars and trains that lined his bedroom wall near the ceiling. He loved cars, especially the cars of the '70s. He was working on restoring his GTO in his garage. A real beauty! He wanted to give it to his son, Andrew. This made him happy, and he found solace.

We would also talk about him getting back to work and getting the city to pass our permits so we could build more homes. Scott was a great guy and he always worried about the work. Scott and I would talk about all the team members; he always wanted to know how they were doing. He would ask me about each and every one. As he lay there dying, he was more worried about the team and how they were doing. As he lay there in bed suffering in pain, he would only concern himself with the happiness of others. I thought he might come back—after all, he had three times before—but then I looked at him and thought this could be the last fight, and as it turned out, it was. I don't think Scott truly knew himself.

Before Scott became really sick, I had kept him on the payroll while he worked from home and even when he could not work anymore. They had just bought a new home and his income was critical. I thought as the owner of the company I could not allow Scott to lose his paycheck. I felt since he was fighting for his life, he should not have to worry about his income. I made a promise to myself that no matter what, he would not miss a paycheck. Scott was ill for many, many months. I believe he probably fought it all told eighteen months or more.

One day my CFO came to me and explained how Scott was killing our profitability and our budgets with his payroll cost. He advised that the best thing for the company to do was to give Scott a settlement. A onetime payoff and we could charge it against earnings and write it down. I thought to myself, *You cold jerk. Really? A settlement? What is a fair number for someone who is about to die? Should we throw in the incredible Ginsu knives as a bonus?* I refused to hear another word of it. I was crystal clear that while Scott was fighting for his life, he would not be fighting for his family to keep their home. It is only money, and I will pay it personally, which I did on several occasions. My CFO left in disappointment. Here is the best part: a few weeks later when we were giving employee bonuses, he left Scott out. I immediately changed that. Not only did we give Scott that bonus, he never missed another one as well. I do not believe many companies would have gone on as long as we did. Then again, I was not nor have I ever been most companies. I take the time to care about the team and not categorize them into a statistical formula for terminating them or paying them off.

It was very simple for me. If I were dying, I would want to know I could count on the company, I had given my heart to help me, and I was not about to let Scott down.

As Scott's battle raged on, we would continue to talk and talk and talk. He shared with me a lot of things, and I with him. Scott was no longer an employee but a friend. Scott was so happy we kept him on the payroll. He never missed a chance to say thank you. Scott said it was my coming to talk with him that made it all special. Scott helped me more than he ever knew; it was when I encountered my own fight to live did it come full circle. It was these talks and the fact that I could help Scott that made me a true believer.

Doing the right thing was the right thing to do, and no matter what, if you help someone someday, you will be rewarded. This reward was now coming. I was in need of believing in the good me, and it was this thing that we all did for Scott as the cancer took him that made me realize we were good and that I could be proud of what I did. This is not a moment to say I was a saint. I am not. In fact, I am very far from it. I knew that I cared deeply for this man and I needed to do something, and I did. It was the knowledge of what I did that I was now calling on to get me through this time. As I said at the outset, I needed to believe in the good me, and the way to do that was to remember my moments of good. Those moments where I helped and for which I was very proud. This was one of those moments.

I spent many a time in Scott's bedroom speaking with him as he was confined to his bed. Little did I know later in my life these conversations would become more important than I ever imagined. As I was looking for the answers to my own living hell, I started to think of Scott, what he went through and that he was now gone. I told myself I had no right to spend another minute not being eternally grateful. It was these thoughts and the letter he wrote me that was to be my own rescue.

Scott was gone, but his heart lived on, and his love lived in me. It was Scott's way of helping me, and that was truly one thing he wanted to do. He told me he wanted to help me for all I had done for him. I assured him someday, someway, somehow he would, and even at that moment, we did not know how but that he would. Today I got my answer.

Remember Bart? Well, Bart was to Scott everything Scott was to Bart. They were the best of friends, and it was Bart who saw Scott at his home as well. Bart stopped by often to chat with his best friend. Bart, too, is a hero as was Scott. Bart had a way of kicking Scott in the butt and telling him he needed him to get back to work; this was important to Scott as Bart made him feel needed and wanted to get back to it. I think deep down Bart believed Scott would be back, and if he did not, he wanted Scott to believe it. Bart is a very special guy, and he always puts his friends ahead of himself.

Scott on his fourth and final battle never did get back to work. He tried but he was called to a more important assignment. When I attended the funeral, I was so glad to see all those who had attended. There was a celebration afterward at Scott's home, and it was there that Martha handed me the letter—the one that Scott had written for me as his candle was going out. It was this letter that I have read several times, and each time, I shed yet another tear. I had never had a friend die and take the time to write me a letter of his thoughts about me, his final thoughts. If I had any doubts about my help or the hero Scott was, this letter erased all of them.

The Letter of a Friend as He Says Good-bye

Dear Mike,

I am without words to show you gratitude enough for your support during my illness. I apologize if this letter seems poorly written, but it is getting harder to steady my hand. I thought I would update you of my condition as well as express my thanks. The birthday card you brought me was very nice. It seems hard to believe? Another birthday!

I want to thank you for the many times you came to visit and sit with me. Thank you for giving up your time to be with me. I am really grateful for everything that you have done for me during my illness. I also appreciate all the cards and e-mails from the team. The whole team has been amazing. I think about each one of them throughout the day and hope they are doing well. I love the company and that has been the hardest thing during my illness to not be there and see my work through. Mike, you have made the company into a unique company that cares about its employees and has always found ways to keep morale high.

In the beginning, I was always amazed at your positive energy and the way that the company and all of us benefited. It made coming to work fun, even though the company has grown, you still care about all of us.

I want to thank you again for your continued support. It has really kept stability in our uncertain house. Without the paycheck, I do not know how we would have ever made it.

Mike, it has been an honor to know you. Some people prove to be memorable characters that you always remember and you are one of those. I am a firm believer in capitalism and entrepreneurialism. Without guys like you who are willing to take chances the whole system would not work. My father was the opposite, a good man but so conservative that he would take no chances, but he did manage a pretty good stock portfolio that provides well for his retirement. As for me, remember the grasshopper and the ant? I'm the grasshopper.

As for my condition, today as yesterday have been rough days. I tell folks I have good days and bad days but bad days seem to be the norm. The pain controls me. Each position I put myself into takes a while to where I can adjust to it. The increased medication has made me extremely dizzy. I lay down and my arms and feet cramp, while my legs and feet swell when standing which I rarely do anymore because I can't. The blister on my foot is about the size of a potato and everyone who sees it wants to pop it except for the nurses who are afraid of infection. I no longer have the strength to get out of bed. The old saying "I've fallen and I can't get up" has a whole new meaning. The past week was the worst as I did not get up for three days, slept for two straight and went through Morphine withdrawals for two more while shaking and sweating.

I hope all of this does not depress you. Don't feel sorry for me. There are plenty of people that are far worse off than me. My attitude and sense of humor are still carrying me through. I am not sure how much longer I will make it but then are any of us sure? We are only here for a short time anyway and I am pretty content in my family and at ease with myself.

It seems to get rougher each day. I am worried about Lizzy and Andrew. They are my happiness and I want them to be ok. Martha is a very good mother and she will do a good job. I think about their wedding days and their families. If I had a wish, it is that I could be there to see them with their families. God has given me such a great gift with two beautiful children and a loving wife. I love them so much I hope my loss only helps them in some way. God will see to it. I was not as religious as I could have been, but I have spent a lot a time lately understanding God and it has helped me to be strong. I need to be strong for my family.

I do not know what my family and I would have done without your help during my illness this last year. It is the greatest act of support that anyone has ever shown me. God bless you and your family and thank you for unselfish kindness.

I keep feeling a deep sense of gratitude to you that humbles me, sometimes makes me feel unworthy and causes me to wonder why someone else would be so charitable to me. I have had many conversations with God during my illness mostly asking him to take the pain and give me the strength to go on. Now I know that he has answered me through you. He has come to you and asked you to act on his behalf. For this unselfish act, he will reward you and I cannot stop feeling the need to show my appreciation.

I said yesterday to consider me as a small tree that has just been through a drought, all the leaves died off and now they are slowly growing back. I'll be fine.

You are in my prayers,

Scott

These were to be the last words to me from Scott. A few days later, he was gone. There was an overwhelming emptiness as a piece of all us died with Scott. I would like to quote some verse and tell you that it is a celebration and he has gone to a better place, but right now I cannot. I know he looks down on us, and I know he watches over Lizzy, Andrew, and Martha—his true loves—and I am also sure he takes a look at that GTO.

When Martha gave me this letter, I read it and cried. I knew he was gone and I would miss our talks. Scott never wanted anything; he just wanted others to be happy. God called back one of his angels.

As for the letter, it was to be my saving grace. I read Scott's letter over and over again. God was now working through Scott and he was bringing me back to life. I had been saved and now it was time to fight. I used the letter to give me strength and to remember that I was a good person. I had to make a decision to fight or continue to wallow in self-pity. Thanks to Scott and this letter, I took the first step and the fight was mine to win, and win it I would. I was broke but I was not broken. Scott, I love you, my friend. Thank you for helping me.

Chapter 14
One More Day

A man of sense is never discouraged by difficulties; he redoubles his industry and his diligence, he perseveres, and infallibly prevails at last.

—Lord Chesterfield

The rebuilding process had begun. The first step had been taken. The importance of realizing that I had to win—and in order to do that, I must believe in myself, even if others do not—had special meaning. It is not that others doubted me or did not believe in me; it was more that I had to prove it up again. I had been beat down hard, and the simple reality is that most never recover from what I had experienced. In fact, most quit or fade away to wherever it is that they fade away to. I could not fade away. I had to do it again. I had to stand up and make a stand. I had to fight, and the fight of my life was now upon me. I wanted to check out, and I wanted to quit. I can remember asking myself, *How do I get off this bus?* I wanted out, but there was no out. Then it hit me like a ton of bricks. I now realized that "out" meant winning again. So it was time, and now I was on the first phase of the return. I also knew there were more bumps ahead. But it was okay. Because I knew no matter what I faced, I could make it. I knew whatever challenges I faced were now opportunities. My whole mind-set was changing and the winner was returning. Those dark moments with the 9mm were long gone.

I had two very important parts of this equation. I had to believe in me again. I did this by remembering I was a good person who had always done well by knowing and trusting in my character. And I would do well again. I had to understand that I was not a monster. The second most crucial step, by far the most important, was to think of those who needed me to rebuild myself and win. I had to do and give my best for those who expected me to do exactly that. My family was the next big part of my score card. My two children, Hannah and David, and my mother were the three people who needed me to win. I kept thinking that I may be one person in this world, but to my children and my mom, I was their world. It was my two children who had saved me from death, and now they were the reasons I would fight and not lie down on the field of battle watching the world go by. I stepped back onto the battlefield because I needed my children to need me. I needed them to see their father as the warrior he was, as the warrior they had always known. My mother had always taught me to look forward; she had always taught me to give my best, so she too needed to see me fight and to be the warrior that she had always known. There was no quitter in me. So the second step was the need to succeed for those who believed in me and needed me to fight. Even if I fought and lost, at least I fought. It would be my fight that

163

would give others strength, and better yet, it would let them believe in hopes and dreams, theirs as well as mine. I knew it was far better to try and fail than to not try at all. What good is a prizefighter if he does not even get into the ring?

The next step after this, of course, would be to get others to believe. However, working on myself had a lot left to do, so I kept working on myself.

If you hear a voice within you say "You cannot paint,"
then by all means paint, and that voice will be silenced.
—Vincent Van Gogh

The number one reason we fail is because we tell ourselves we will fail. Life and winning is a very simple formula, and it all starts by telling yourself you can do it. You can win. It is very simple this way. Either you can or you can't, and whatever you choose, you are right. I have my whole life rallied to success simply by believing "I can do it." I had approached everything as "It can be done," but after being beat down so bad, I had started to question this. The war had taken its toll. I knew internally I needed to believe in me and to believe without a doubt. I knew I needed to be an "I can" person. I had always been an "I can" person my whole life. Winning is everything, and it all starts with *cans*. Success comes in *cans*, not *can'ts*. The second you tell yourself you can't, you have lost.

I had known my whole life that the reason I was successful was because I knew I could do anything I put my mind to. Now I needed my own magic formula more than anything in my life. I mentioned earlier I greatly admired Walt Disney. This is because no matter what Walt experienced, seven bankruptcies, for instance, he never gave up. More importantly, he never gave up on himself, he always believed in himself, and he always knew he could do it. Henry Ford had the same magic as he built his cars. Henry Ford and Walt Disney were the ultimate "I can" guys, none better than these two.

Each morning, instead of saying, "I am a has-been," I learned to say, "I am a will-be." I began to believe in me, and I used my every thought to convince myself it was all up to me. I accepted that the beating I took would only serve to make me stronger. I made it my creed to fight forward and use the beating to my advantage. *"In order to get from what was to what will be, you must go through what is."* I knew that going through *"what is"* was the only way. At an early age, my mother taught me a very important lesson. You move forward and you do not use the past as a crutch. *You don't look back at misfortune but you look forward to opportunity.* There is no quitting. The best way to believe in you is twofold. First, remember your previous accomplishments. But there is only so much value to living in your past. Second, all new victories are valuable and needed. Because the small successes lead to big successes. I found even if the little victories were very little and I was the only one who recognized these victories, they were still victories—winning creates momentum in the right direction. I got in the habit of telling myself, "I can," but now I had learned to say more; I learned to say, "I am," as in, "I am doing it."

The little victories were starting to come to life. I had a winning attitude again. I believed that I could do it. I believed in me, and I believed I could win.

Eventually, I reasoned with myself that if I could get one other person to believe in me, then that would be two, and a third would be three, and pretty soon, the belief of others, as well as myself believing in me, would be the magic I would need. Winning the belief of others would be crucial to the rebuilding. With the help of others, you gain confidence, and the dream begins to grow. I was not looking for a flash mob, just a couple of believers. I have always found that when others believe in me, it is easy for me to do well. It is easy to let yourself down but almost impossible to fail when others believe in you. A good success platform requires believers, and the more believers, the better your platform will be. As always, I turned to myself, and it became very clear to me that if I believed in myself, there would come a day when others would have no choice but to believe in me. I would use this power of belief to create momentum.

Momentum is the most powerful force in the world. However, momentum left to its own accord will go the wrong direction. Success is always the result of building momentum, that is, of building positive momentum. How many times have you heard a coach say, "We need to build some momentum"? The coach knows that they have to get things going in the positive direction. The way to win the game is to build positive momentum and to continue building. I knew I needed positive momentum, so I turned to the small victories to start building momentum. It is equated to the idea of baby steps.

If you want to be victorious, you must almost invariably always start with baby steps. For instance, if you are to go on a diet, you would lay out a plan that would start with you telling (or convincing) yourself you can lose weight. Hence, you have to start your plan by believing in yourself. It needs to be a plan that works. The following plan is exactly how it *does not* work, but it is a great example. I am going to lose twenty pounds by Friday. The Plan: no eating and then I will couple it with working out six hours a day. This, I guess, they would call a crash diet. We all know that crash diets don't work, and if they do work, they don't last. The truth is that diets are a lot like life. Successful diets are a result of careful planning and small daily victories. For example, two pounds a week as your goal based upon baby steps of attending the gym three to four times per week along with proper nutrition all executed and maintained on a daily basis. This plan will provide the best results as opposed to the ever-popular crash—*all at once*—diet, which provides quick results and an even quicker failure.

You create a plan to rebuild yourself and you take baby steps. First, you believe you can rebuild yourself and then you create a plan. Your plan is a product of baby steps or small victories and then you get others to believe in your plan. They see the victories and they acknowledge your successes; again, this is like the diet when someone notices you have lost weight. It feels good and you build on these positive comments, on the positive input of others who see your successes. Hence, you are creating two things: believers in you and confidence in you.

See how life is like a diet plan? They both require believing in you, taking baby steps to success, or in this case, small victories leading up to and the support or belief of others. It is a simple plan, but it is the plan. It requires both you and others believing in your plan because the more others believe in your plan, the more they will build you up as to believing in your plan. Just as you convince them, they unknowingly convince you.

I started to pile on small victories—little ones, but they were huge to me. I started working harder and making more meetings. My day began at seven instead of eight. It went until six instead of five. I felt more active and more useful. I could feel the time that I was using was also becoming more productive. I could feel the confidence in myself again, and I could see it in the eyes of others around me. I knew I was getting stronger because I could see that others felt my strength returning. I was building momentum and confidence and this was due to my own belief and the belief of others.

I set little goals like reaching out to at least five people a day with my plan. Pretty soon the number became eight, and then it was ten. I could really feel the momentum building, and it was all positive. Positive things were happening, and I was feeling good about who I was. That monster guy I spoke of earlier was leaving, and he was well on his way out of town. As I realized that people were starting to believe in me, it allowed me to kill the monster and bring out the good guy that I had always known about—the winner that always believed in himself. I was on a roll. The good was outweighing the bad, at least in my mind. I was still fighting many, many demons, but the victories were letting me know that I could win, and with each victory, I was experiencing fewer defeats.

The bad times were still on my doorstep, and it seemed like every time I would take one step forward, something would come along and drag me back. A crystal-clear example is as follows. I filed bankruptcy, but that does not matter to the IRS. They are exempt from the bankruptcy plan. The IRS has amazing tentacles, and they were after me. I literally had losses of $2.7 million, but they only apply to my personal income taxes, not the other IRS items. For instance, as the company was crashing, we missed paying two different pay period payroll taxes of about $35 grand. As we filed bankruptcy, they only put these on hold. Once all the dust settled, four years later, here they came, but as we all know, penalties and interest were involved and the liability had grown to almost $85 grand at this point. Ouch! I tried the "Hey! I filed bankruptcy," but of course, they said, "And your point is?" I later discovered that since I was an LLC, I was personally responsible, but had I been a corporation (S Corp or C Corp, for instance), I would not be held liable. This is one of those cases where being an LLC is a bad decision.

For those of you who think you are protected by LLCs, think again. The average American believes you form an LLC to protect yourself and your assets. *Wrong!* The bankruptcy court rips through your LLCs like water through a screen door. They stepped in and took over all my possessions and positions; in short, they became me. The widely held belief of being protected by LLCs went right out the window. Furthermore, creditors can rip through them almost as fast as the bankruptcy court, a few more filings is all.

LLCs are being destroyed every day, and their ease of entry for creditors and courts is coming faster and faster and easier and easier.

I suggest you use LLCs if you want the tax breaks and the pass-throughs, but if you are looking as a way to shelter assets or to protect yourself from creditors, this is clearly the wrong instrument. Don't listen to me, though; I am just speaking from experience. I have engaged some thirty-five attorneys in the last ten years and I can assure you opinions, especially theirs, vary.

The point of this whole IRS meltdown story is to let you know two things. First, the IRS has their methods, and second, even though they were auditing me and going through all my stuff for four years after my bankruptcy, they never let up. I simply said, "What more can they do?" I have my spirit and I am going to win this thing. The IRS was a distraction that could not bring me down. I had to make a decision to let the IRS destroy me or to fight on. I chose to fight on. I fought on by believing in me and by focusing on my other small but more important daily victories. I could no longer allow the setbacks to be setbacks. They were diversions that I quickly extinguished. I dealt with them and continue to deal with them, but I could not let them get in the way of my victories.

I was winning, and the setbacks became more like speed bumps. Hit 'em and move on. Slow down a little bit, go over them, and keep going. Another key ingredient to success or rebuilding me and by far my favorite was the idea of "one more day." I started to tell myself I was one day closer to success. I made a pact with myself and started each morning with "Hold on for one more day." I ended each day with "We made it one more day." It became my drug of choice, this whole idea of "one more day." It was working, and I was winning.

As for drugs and alcohol, I turned against them both. I had reflected in my life all of my weak or down moments, and they all involved drugs and alcohol. I then looked at all my successes and none of them involved drugs and alcohol. They had to go and go they went. I am not born again or AA or any of that stuff. I just made a conscious, responsible decision that there was nothing more important in my life than my children and my family; they deserved my best. And the only way I could deliver my best to them and for them was by completely avoiding the distractions created by drugs and alcohol. I was not an alcoholic or a drug addict. I simply needed all my skills with me, and they were not when I drank. The guy who sat in his bedroom and thought about quitting the hard way would have never been there had he not decided to give in to the drink that led him to give in to his weaknesses. The answer is not in the bottom of the bottle but in the top of your mind.

The idea of being my best tied in directly with the idea of not allowing setbacks to derail me, just as I could not be derailed by alcohol. The IRS, while unfortunate, was not going to stop me from finding my victories, nor was alcohol.

It was a painful exercise, but I had to focus on the positives and rebuild. I was now becoming a machine. As the IRS was in pursuit, so was the State of Arizona. Several of the investors who had lost their money in the various properties wanted money back. Forget that I had filed bankruptcy; they still wanted something. They turned to the State of Arizona for help, and they got it. The State pursued two other fellas as well as me. In a civil agreement, we agreed to pay back the investors. This could have been a major setback, but it was not, as the best deal for the investor was any plan that returns them their money. As for me? I never quite figured out how I was supposed to get my money back. I simply said I will do my best and someday we will make good on it, but for now, I had to focus on the victories and grow forward. I could not allow the setbacks to derail the success plan. I must stay focused on the victories. Now, more than ever, I had a whole bunch of cheerleaders as the investors wanted me to win so they could win. We all wanted our money back.

The Daily's

I was in full swing and the victories were rolling in, and the true believers were starting to add up. Pretty soon, we had a team and we were on the go again.

As an owner, a CEO, a manager, a partner, an employer, a teammate—whatever my role—it has always been important for me to be a good communicator. I have subscribed to two very simple philosophies. The first is to be a good communicator with whom you work, keeping them informed at all times, or to the best of your ability. I have never been big on secrets or isolating team members from the activities of the company, good or bad. The second philosophy that I strongly subscribe to is the idea of *"Catching somebody doing something right."* I truly believe in this principle. When I catch someone in the act of doing something right, I praise them and I reward them, and I do it publicly. I do not believe in catching somebody doing something wrong.

As a part of being a good communicator, I would stay in contact with the team on a daily basis. I would do so through any means possible—fax, telephone, personal visits, e-mails, blogs, carrier pigeons, whatever it takes. These actions are signs to your team that they are a part of the company. They will work harder when they feel connected and know their hard work is being appreciated. They want and deserve ownership, even if it is in the form of being on the team. I would rather be a part of a team, even a losing team, which communicates regularly than a team that rarely ever communicates. Communicating gives you a chance to praise and reward; it is an opportunity that you should never miss.

As a result of communicating with the team, the Daily's were created. They are one of the most remarkable things that happened and became the real life changer for me. The Daily is an e-mail that is sent out to the team each and every morning to share with them the activities of myself and the company, which is almost always the same thing. These kept them in the loop and they knew exactly where we were positioned at all times. In the beginning, the Daily's were going out to the team only, the next thing I knew, I was receiving requests from various team members to forward them to their friends and family. The requests were due to the positive, upbeat messages of the Daily's. Before I knew it, the team members were asking if I could add their friends and family to The Daily's recipient list. I agreed, and the list of recipients grew. Then those folks were forwarding them on and they were asking if their friends could be added, and before long, we had one thousand people receiving the Daily's. Readers were posting them at their workplace, putting them on Facebook or their web pages. To this day, they continue to send them to their family and friends. At one point, one of the Daily's was delivered to over fifty thousand people.

The other reason I created the Daily's was for me. I write the Daily's each morning and this added purpose to my life. It was great therapy. They were helping me communicate, and the recovery was in full bloom. I would share positive stories of success, and these stories motivated me as well as the readers. I soon realized that the rules for successful businesses were very similar to some of the rules or theories for a successful life and home as well. I knew the Daily's were helping us all, as evidenced by the tremendous positive reader responses I received. There were several times I considered making the Daily's weekly or passing off the torch. But each time I considered a change, someone would write in to tell me how much the Daily's impacted their life.

There are many work practices that help us all as we perform in the world of success and the world of business. The Daily's focus is on certain successful business practices and disciplines—rules of business that I had discovered after working for over forty years and being in business nearly thirty years for myself. Little rules like "Praise in public, criticize in private," or, "Lead by example, not by word of mouth."

The Daily's take much work and consume at least an hour every morning. However, they are the best work of my day. As part of my comeback, and at the heart of the Daily's, I follow a simple rule that allows me to give my best every day: *"As long as I can make a difference in at least one person each day, then I will continue and I will work effortlessly to this end."* I have never failed this goal, or outcome, as my good friend Dan calls them. To this day, I receive at least one response (often several responses) every single day, and 99 percent of them are positive and filled with gratitude.

I was now putting my true talents to work. I was helping people again. This was at the same time helping me to move to the next level in life. I had purpose again, and I had believers. More importantly, my doubts had disappeared and I was well on my way back. Just imagine a few years earlier I sat on my bed and thought it was time to check out. I honestly knew I could never have pulled that trigger, but between the Jack and the ration of hate coming my way, it was an alternative that had much appeal. Now, looking back, I believe it was a test, and I had passed. It was time to get after it, so get after I did. This test gave true meaning to the saying "What does not kill you will only make you stronger." I was as strong as they came. I could whoop Arnold at this point.

While life was on a great upswing, I was not out of the woods yet, not by a long shot. But at least I was back on my mount, and I was saddled up, ready to go onto the field of battle and fight. It felt good, and winning was now the plan. I was leaving survival. I got stronger each day. The Daily's were a big part of it. Still, the reality of knowing that there were people who needed me to win remained paramount to my victories. I figured if I wanted to be a failure that was my choice. But if I wanted my family and friends to see me be a failure, well, that would never do. I again reached into my bag of tricks and employed a critical philosophy. Even if *I failed, I would at least try as it is far better to try and fail than to not try at all.* I was alive and the dogs were barking again.

There was no going backward at this point, and it was time to keep the oars in the water at all times. The second you pull the oars out of the water and rest, you will drift backward. The fight was now in full force and the oars needed to be working at all times. The victories were getting a little bigger with each new conquest. I had accepted that the one guiding force that had carried me through my entire life would need to become bigger and better than ever. That force was me. I once read that you must put your future in good hands—yours. So I did! Although I knew I needed the help and support of others, I also knew it was still up to me. Win, lose, or draw, I was the guy who was accountable.

If you are, as I am, in the fight of your life, then by all means, take charge and be the reason you succeed or fail, but at least be the reason. We all need the help and support of others, but at the end of the day, it is up to us to each drive our own bus, and if you tell yourself you can, then you will. This is why believing is so important, and believing in you is where it all starts.

By the time I hit rock bottom and really felt what it was like to come to the end of the world, it was precisely at that point I knew there was nowhere but up. It was like an alcoholic or a drug addict who hits bottom. But instead of finding a way to go past bottom, you have to wake up and rally. Most don't wake up; most go right past bottom and keep on going. My crash was not the crash of the alcoholic—in fact, quite the opposite. I had the hardest crash an entrepreneur can crash—total financial failure. Looking back, I think it would have been easier to be an alcoholic who had money.

Entrepreneurs live to succeed financially and philanthropically. Entrepreneurs are admired and known as risk takers who succeed because they do take risk. They think BIG! They see the big picture and know they can accomplish anything they set their entrepreneurial minds to. *What most consider risk they view as everyday business; in fact, they do not even see the risk.* To them, it is business as usual. To me, however, business as usual was a total disaster, and the victories were much needed to help me rally back. At the same time, there was exactly zero risk. I was already at the bottom and there was nowhere but up, so what the hell? What risk? To hell with it! Let's go for it! I had already lost everything, so what else could they take? I no longer had to worry about the downside. I was there. I bundled it all together, the self-believing, the believing of others in me, the small victories, the baby steps, one more day, turning setbacks into opportunities—and it all came together.

My four decades of entrepreneurialism was now ready to start a new chapter. I was on the road back and the past was long gone. I was moving forward and it was all becoming a reality. I was still broke but my spirit was not. I was broke, but I was never broken. I no longer saw the downside. All I saw was the upside. It was time to make dreams come true. I made it clear to all: *"Don't judge me by my past. I don't live there anymore."* I had the ingredients necessary to rebuild the winner that had almost given up. *Yes! I was broke, but I was not broken. I believed again. I believed in me.*

Chapter 15

Anatomy of a Comeback

The mark of a great player is in his ability to come back.
The great champions have all come back from defeat.

—Sam Snead

As I continued to write the Daily's, I was gaining strength. I soon found out that there were important players who believed in me and our young company. Jon Moffitt from Bank of America, a friend of twelve years, put together support for our self-storage company. He helped us identify the lenders necessary to acquire assets and brought in strategic investment partners. With the B of A banner and Jon's support, we were finding a pulse. We worked on simple success models. I put on my armor, and the whole team went to work.

176

Speaking of *armor*, which is the term I refer to as my suit and tie, I wear a suit and tie every day and I never underdress for any meeting, even meetings at home. I strongly believe that by dressing your best, you will give your best, and it has time and time again provided me with a distinct advantage in business and in life. Dale Carnegie was never wiser than when he said, "Dress for success." *I would rather be criticized for overdressing than underdressing.* It is a clear sign of respect when you attend a meeting dressed well. It shows respect for the attendees, but it also demonstrates respect in yourself. It felt good to be in the working world again and, more importantly, to be wearing a suit and tie. I was proud again of whom I was and who I could be. I arose every morning with a hop in my step. I looked to the skies as I put on my tie and into the world I did go. I had confidence, confidence leads to momentum, and momentum leads to success. The biggest single piece of advice I may ever give is *"Never ever show up to a business meeting underdressed unless it is your goal to lose in that meeting."* The purpose of meetings is to advance yourself, not reduce yourself. Every meeting has a purpose; it is that simple. If you are going to a meeting, you have a plan, and you should always dress up as opposed to down.

Some folks argue that you should dress like the others in a meeting so you are on their level. BS! Do you really go through life thinking you are on everyone's level? *Nope!* You want to believe you are at least a teensy-weensy little bit above. People who dress down to match others are just making up excuses for their lack of effort. Give your best always. There is not a justification in the world to not give your best. *Ever!*

Dressing well is exactly like a judge's bench. The reason the judge sits up high and the rest of the folks in the court sit low is so the judge can have a position of respect, a clear advantage of elevation or superiority and/or authority, add to this that the judge wears an impressive black robe, further supporting his position of importance. The judge gets most of his respect from the robe he wears, and the seat he sits in, and that seat is always higher in the air than yours. This same advantage can be and is delivered by dressing well. I wear my armor with dignity, respect, and pride for myself and for others.

Thanks to my armor, my power of belief, belief in me, my formula for success and the confidence that comes with it was returning. Jon was opening doors, the team was making the extra effort, and the armor was working.

As the momentum was building, a fella by the name of Joe Bardin decided to write an article about me that he published in *Phoenix* magazine. The story was their feature and entitled "Anatomy of a Comeback." The story was about my collapse and rebound, or in the process of rebounding as it were. Like this book, it was very direct and very gritty. It was a fairly accurate picture of my life focusing on the collapse and the fight on spirit. It hit the presses, and the phone lines lit up. My friends and family were calling. They loved it! I chose not to read it, and in fact, to this very day I still have not read the article. I don't read my press clippings. My good friend Reggie Fowler advised me I should never read articles about myself, and I heeded his advice. Reggie received a lot of negative press when he was buying the Minnesota Vikings and it was very unfair to him. He refused to read the reviews as he stated his family and his business success spoke for himself and he needed not to sell himself beyond that. Reggie is a very smart man.

In spite of the fact that all reviews have been very positive, I, for some reason that I myself am not even sure of, still have not read it. The rave reviews my friends and family were giving me were enough for me.

I believe sometimes we read about ourselves to satisfy our egos. While it may appear I have an ego, I really do not. There are two rules you should follow if you want to succeed in business. Rule 1: Do not have an ego; it will work against you. And Rule 2: Do not become emotionally attached to a deal. These are killers. Make the deal about the deal; never make it about your love for the deal. I get emotional after we own the deal and not a moment before that. An ego will cloud your judgment. People can like me or not, but I like me, and how you feel about you is the most important decision you can ever make.

As "Anatomy of a Comeback" hit the stands and my friends were proud to finally be my friends, I felt good about life. I knew I had made a difference and that I would continue to be the good guy that was fighting for his family and friends, but most importantly, fighting for himself. The article provided one very unusual benefit that I never saw coming. I made four new friends. There were four folks who read the article and called to thank me for helping them to believe in themselves again. They were all at the door of uncertainty, and the article allowed them the understanding they could win and that they should never give up. All four wanted me to know how important it was to them. One fella's wife read the article in a doctor's office and brought it home for her husband to read. That fella is Perry Best and his wife, Cheryl. Perry and Cheryl have since become two of my best friends in the world. They introduced me to a few of their friends, including Dr. Rose Richards, who is also a very dear friend. I could not believe these folks would call me just to tell me thank you! They were all great people, the best of the best. And "Anatomy of a Comeback" gave them just the hope they were looking for. Then there was more. There was James.

"Anatomy of a Comeback," our team, Jon Moffitt, and most importantly my belief in me helped me make a difference and allowed me the privilege of rebounding and rebuilding. The ladder was before me, and I had climbed a few more rungs. I remained fixated on my goal of making a difference in at least one person every day. I was on target, but when I received James's letter, I felt like I had went into hyperspace. I never expected what I read. I soon made a new friend to which James and I remain very close today. James is, without doubt, a warrior who needed a little help in a dark moment. Having been in a dark moment, I knew the exact help he needed.

James's Story in the Daily

Actual Daily

Good Morning,

I know that we all go through life and we hit certain turns that are not always the best. We want to sometimes give up and we even think that maybe this world would be better without us. THIS IS THE BIGGEST MISTAKE YOU WILL EVER MAKE IN YOUR LIFE. Today there are no clever quotes! Today there is no did you know? In fact there is not even a name for you guys, my heroes. Today I simply want you to read and think about the e-mail I received last night from someone I have never met. It is his words and not mine. Here you go.

Dear Mr. Roberts:

Without going into much detail, I have been out of work for almost 2 months. It is depressing to say the least. I am a great guy, absolutely NOWHERE in your league as far as higher education and accomplishments are concerned, but nonetheless the best customer service professional ever. I have always been the guy who sees the glass half full. I am the guy friends come to when they are troubled, I always look at the bright side, yet this time, I am fighting for my sanity and in some aspects have been fighting for my life.

Yesterday was a low point for me. I was just so down in the muck, I couldn't leave my house or answer my friend's calls. I just sat in the dark. I picked up the new Phoenix magazine from my coffee table and flipped thru and found your story. I read it once, then later took it outside and read it again, and later when I went to bed read it one more time.

For someone who's had so much success in his life, for someone who has had everything and lost it. For you to share the fact that you were vulnerable to thoughts of suicide, for you to share in detail that moment that brought you so close to ending your journey here on earth was profound, humble, scary, inspiring. You did not go thru with it and I am thankful. For your children, your friends and for you.

Last month I researched methods of suicide online. I found a medical university where I could will my body to, so my friends wouldn't be saddled with my funeral expenses. I picked out the photos I wanted shown at my memorial. I started preparations. I had it all planned. The only thing I feared was survival. What if I were to survive a suicide attempt, what if I failed at this and lived the rest of my days on life support, or forced into the care of people I know who would give up their own lives to see me live.

I am not done with this life. Your story reinforced this for me. I live simply, I don't have much, so if you can come back full force, so can I and I can come back even stronger. All day long today, I thought of you and I feel I have rediscovered my ambition.

So, thank you. Thank you for sharing. Thank you for being honest, thank you for telling that brutal personal story. I will start over again tomorrow with my job hunt. Everything is temporary, right?

God Bless.
James Hanson

Whenever you think that the chips are down, they are not. Life will always be different, but if you are not here, you will never know. I will call James today while I am on my way to Las Vegas. I will try to explain that this is the greatest world and that his friends and family need him. I will also explain that life is God's greatest gift and that it should be cherished and worshiped, not taken. Folks, you and I made a difference.

James's story moved the readers as they read it. With respect to a typical Daily, I usually receive five to ten responses. But after this Daily, I received thirty-eight, the highest one-day response total ever.

I connected with James as he had connected with me. I knew that no matter what level you are fighting, that is your level and you must fight on. You cannot give up. James was as helpful for me as I was for him.

No matter how well you are doing, you never forget the down moments you lived through to get to here. Those great moments of despair can be very harsh. Use those moments to make sure you stay positive, build away from those moments, and by all means, when it comes to the negative moments, do not build on them.

James helped me reflect on the value of fighting, never giving up. I knew I couldn't give up, but reading James's letter pushed me even harder. I was in the fight of my life. *I knew the steps to take, but the key is taking the steps and never giving up.* I was so beat up that quitting seemed a lot better than moving on and starting over. *"Retreat? HELL NO!"*

There are things in this life that people believe in so that they feel better about themselves. There are things that people believe in that make them fight their battles and rise above their weakest moments. James was ready to cash in, and for some reason, he was slow on the trigger. He decided in his mind that there had to be a reason to not give up, and then James read "Anatomy of a Comeback," and it pushed him to the next level. It pushed him to read it three times and say, "If this guy can come back, I know I can." He believed in himself again. I knew this feeling because it was my own self-belief that saved me from the bowels of purgatory. Thanks to James, the mission was bigger than ever. I knew I had to give my best because people like James needed me to win. I gave them something and someone to believe in. My own children and my mother were very important to me as an inspiration to win and to fight on, but I also knew there were others. Lots of others! I guess quitting for me would be easy and giving up was something that I considered, but when it came to the others who needed me to do my best, well, I just could not quit on them.

It may be easy to quit when no one needs you, but the more people need you to do well, the more you have to. I needed my mother to see me win; it was what gave her the strength she needed to look up to the stars. As for my newfound friend James, I owed it to him to do my best and to let him see me win, for it is one way he wins. This is for James; it says the system works and Mike Roberts is a winner, and since Mike Roberts is a winner, then James Hansen is a winner. He fights incredible odds but he fights them, and he wins. If he can do it, then I can too.

When I read James's letter, I did not think I saved his life. Most readers did, and James said I made the difference, but it was James who made the difference. One friend said it was proof I was sent here to do God's work. I just never saw it that way. In fact, if anything, I believe God sent James to me, that God needed me to keep after it and not give up. I thought very simply that James saw me as a reason he could do it, and at the same time, I saw it as James needed help; therefore, I had to stay the course so James could stay the course. He saw me as a reason to fight the battle and fight to win. I really, deep down, immediately thought, *"Mike, you have to continue the fight and win because there is another person who believes in you and who needs you to win so they can win!"* It was that simple. I knew my responsibility and my work was a little bit bigger and was very important not only to me but to others. It is this need to help others that drives me to always do my best without exception.

The Momentum Continues

I wake up in the morning and upon my wall are several Post-its that have the names of the people who need me to do my best. I read their names every day and I tell myself, *If I get weak, think of these names and find the strength to give that extra step.*

I kept reminding myself of all the reasons I needed to do my best and the reasons I needed to come back and win again. It was for me, it was for others, failure was not an option. It was less than twelve months prior that I was sitting there with a gun in my mouth. I often wonder what would have happened had I took the coward's way out. I know that my family would have been destroyed, and my children would be scarred for life.

My favorite movie for many, many years has been *It's a Wonderful Life*, and at this moment in time, I felt like George Bailey. I was on the bridge ready to jump in, and at the last minute, I was saved. It was not an angel named Clarence; it was me. I did not return home to find my wife and children surrounded by all my friends and a Christmas tree, or a friend named Sam Wainwright who wired me $25,000. No! I got up off the cold damp floor, I put the gun down, and I looked in the mirror. I sat there and thanked God for showing me a firsthand look at death and giving me the strength to pick up the pieces and fight again. It does not work in real life like it did for George Bailey, especially when you hit the point I hit. It is a Mike Roberts recovery and not a George Bailey Hollywood movie. There is no one with a fistful of cash, and you don't come home to a house full of loved ones and friends. You are usually alone, and the happy faces are the ones you dream about. Believe me, this makes the fight harder, but you can beat it, It is up to you to beat it. You must refuse to give up and surrender. Life is not Hollywood. Life is life. Life is your own reality show, and you are the star, the only star with a contract.

The good news was plenty and the fact that I was still in the game was awesome, but the reality that the game was getting better was spectacular. I was well-known for being a persuader, and I became known as the Marshmallow Bulldozer because I was not pushy but I never gave up. I stayed with it and *no* meant *yes* no matter how long it took me to get the *yes*. I am known for being persistent and folks hung in there with me because they saw I was not going to give up. I was not going to hurt anybody, and I was not going to give up. When I financed the big home in Scottsdale, I was turned down thirteen times before I finally got a yes. I never quit, and I made it happen. Then a year later, B of A bought the paper from the original lender and became my new lenders. A $3 million loan, thank you very much.

I found with every new day there was another reason to go on and every little battle was a round of championship golf. My values changed. The things that were so important to me, mostly material, were not anymore. I had lived all the dreams and had all the toys. The goal was to win again, to rebuild the champion within. The meltdown brought me to the brink of hell, but the rebuild brought me to realize what the real values are; it is no longer the biggest house and the most exotic car.

As I raged on, it was the warrior unleashed returning to the field of victory. I was a warrior on the battlefield who was fighting not for the spoils of war but for the thrill of conquering. A true warrior is a great warrior because he wins on the field of battle and relishes the fight, not the treasures they get from the fight. It no longer was important to win so I could drive the nicest car. Winning on the battlefield and the way by which I fought was how I was to be measured. Now that was the real glory.

My motivation shifted from being a man of wealth to being a man of value. It was now the dream to win and to win for those who needed me to win that mattered. My family and friends became more important, and in reality, it was through them that I measured my true riches. I became the wealthiest man on the planet. I had the best of children, the best of mothers, my family and friends were all behind me, and the time with them became extra special. The meltdown had become a blessing in disguise. I soon realized that the key to my life was understanding all the misfortunes, and the most important part of my rebuilding was to realize I would never be the person I am today without the collapse. Those experiences were critical to me being the best I can be. I would not be the person I am today without having gone through the financial Armageddon; that turned out to be my biggest growth component.

My whole attitude shifted. I had spent so long crying, "Why me?" and feeling self-pity that I could not find the man inside me. I had decided instead of saying, "Why me?" I started saying, "Why not me!" This helped me with my victory process and my rebuilding process. I now believed, and I started living the "Why not me?" life. I had always known I could do anything in the world, but after the beating I took, the odds seemed against me. Every day I continued telling myself, "Why not me!" and it worked. You bet your ass "Why not me!" The power was back: "I can do it and it needs to be me."

We were working hard, and we were doing all the right things. I was now in the world that said, "Why not me!" and "I can do it." It was this world that changed everything. Instead of doubting I could do a deal, I went into every deal knowing I could do it.

I was back full steam ahead, and the path to victory was clear. The path was all about believing. It was turning the negatives into positives. It was doing the right thing and never giving up. It was about doing it for those who believed in me. It was about never quitting even if I wanted to quit because the ones who believed in me needed me to march forward and they needed me to win. The ones who needed me became that invisible hand that pushed me to take an extra step even when I had nothing left with which to take the step. I kept in my arsenal a little bucket of blood and guts, and when I knew I was fresh out of strength, well, I would reach down into the bucket and find just a little something extra that allowed me to push on. I still did not know my future or where my next dollar was going to come from, but I knew I would not be defeated, that I would believe and I would take the extra steps until I find the mountaintop. I knew, more than ever, that I was a warrior, and that I was again on the battlefield. It felt good. I was now fighting for the smell of the napalm in the morning and not for the riches. I had focus. The thrill of the fight and the thrill of knowing I could win was the biggest victory of all. I knew that I had my armor and that I could win the war. I took the mighty sword and I thrust it as hard as I could and I came to respect the warrior in me and the glory of the battle. I was winning. I had been broke, and I was still broke, but I was not broken.

Chapter 16

The Warriors Dance

If you can accept losing, you can't win.

—Vince Lombardi

It was exactly one year to the day after I filed bankruptcy that we caught our first big break. We were in the process of acquiring fifteen stores in Cincinnati and we needed funding. Jon Moffitt and Bank of America delivered a terms sheet for $32 million. I could not believe it; it was exactly one year to the day after my BK and here on my desk sat a terms sheet for $32 million. We had hurdles to jump through but we could do it. The realization of thinking big had paid off. The Bank of America terms sheet was the power of believing and not the power of luck or anything else. It was purely belief— believing it could be done and then going and doing it.

I yelled score one for the good guys. To all those people who told me it would never happen and that I must give up, I wanted to say, here it sits on my desk, and it is in living color. I looked over and over at that beautiful Bank of America red, white, and blue logo. A year earlier, I was ready to sell out, but then I crawled off that floor and decided I was ready to buy in. Instead of "Why me?" I was living and breathing "Why not me!" Now B of A was ready to buy in. Just the fact that we were able to get the bank to look at the assets and consider doing a deal with us and then put it in writing was a huge milestone. It was a terms sheet filled with many conditions and many outs for B of A, but they took us seriously enough to go to terms. We were now beyond a pulse; we had a strong heartbeat. We were no longer lying on the gurney with an IV shoved into our arm. We were taken up to the boardroom, and we were forty stories in the air.

The power of knowing we could do it was the most important part of the process. If you believe you can do it and act as if you are going to do it, then the simple reality is you will. Once again, Henry Ford's words echoed like a saber in the night. *"Either you can or you can't, and whatever you pick, you are right!"* I had always approached everything in life as it can be done, and it is that attitude that has served me very well. Abraham Lincoln said, *"If you feel you can't do something, then you have already lost."* I never felt it could not be done, and now here it was—a terms sheet from B of A. Even if we did not move forward with it, at least we had a huge weapon in our arsenal. If Jon believed, then we knew others would follow. It is exactly as had been put into the master recovery plan. I knew I needed to believe in myself, but I would need others to believe and here it was. *Shazaam!* Others were starting to believe.

Momentum was growing and it was all positive. I could no longer let the setbacks outweigh the momentum of success. Setbacks are always going to be there, and if you let them take charge, you will never grow. I had to put them in perspective. I had decided anything short of death would not stop me, and we tore into it with a

189

vengeance. My appetite for success was hungry as hell, and it needed to be fed. It needed to eat now, not tomorrow, but now. My thirst and my hunger were growing with every victory. The warrior within knew his purpose and would not yield.

As I stated earlier, my values had changed, and with these, my resolve strengthened. I became relentless, and it was not for the prize but for the fight, the fight to be a champion. I felt like the caped crusader fighting for truth and justice and the American dream. My compromises were fewer, and every opportunity had my full attention. I started to live by my theme *"Don't do tomorrow what can be done today."* I littered my desk with Post-it notes, all written to inspire me in life and in business. I would ask myself at the end of the day, "Have I done everything this day that I could?" and if I answered no, I would get up and go hit it again until I could say yes.

My sleep became less than four hours a day, never longer than two hours at a stretch. I have always required very little sleep. I thought about counting sheep and then I reasoned, hell, the sheep should count me. I pushed and took every extra step I could. I learned to work smart and not work hard. I would ask myself, "Is what I am about to do a good use of my time?" If I answered no, then I moved on. I challenged myself to business meetings. "Is that meeting a good use of my time?" If I answered no, I would not accept the meeting. I was brutally honest with the person, too. I explained that the meeting was not a productive meeting and to pass on it. Everything I did needed to have value and add to the growth of the company and the growth of my family, as well as myself. I needed to be productive. I also needed to accept that Rome wasn't built in a day but that through hard work and persistence I could accomplish my task. Vince Lombardi said he never lost a game, he just ran out of time. I too believed I could not lose and that I had all the time in the world. I used time to work for me instead of against me.

Even though I was building my strength from momentum and success, I always used my difficulties to guide me. I used adversity to feed my passion and to make me greater. I would say as quickly as I hit a speed bump, "It is only a test," or, "It will make me stronger." I welcomed adversity with open arms.

It is surmounting difficulties that make heroes.

—Louis Pasteur

My focus would only allow me to use my adversities as building blocks. Pretty soon I was saying, "That's it! Is that all you got? Shit, that ain't nothing." I am here all week. I was determined and I would not lose. All you have to do, folks, is believe in yourself and you will win. If you are in control of your mind, then you are in control of everything. You will win, and you will become the person you want to become.

I looked back at my previous successes and used those experiences to my advantage, but I looked even harder at my failures and made sure to grow from those with even greater conviction. I looked back at my values in the past and realized again they served me differently than the warrior I was today. A clear example of my values changing was the importance I placed on relationships in the past that were phony, whereas today, my relationships were very real and they were critical.

There are two simple rules for success. As easy as this sounds, it is in fact that easy. The first is passion. If you do not have passion for what you are doing, then don't bother. Second, your values must be in order. Your cause must be just. Both of these ideas reflect on you as a person. Passion comes from within, as do values. You can thrive off of other's values and passions, but it is your own internal drive with these two factors that will make you the king or queen of your world. To appreciate my values being in order, I have to share with you my time as a member of the very elite, of a very special group, which I call the phony rich.

191

The Phony Rich

I was a big member of the phony rich. Hell, I was their chief. I nearly ran for the top slot in the corporation. I was so phony I cannot believe that I was even that person. You know the type—nice to your face, talk about you behind your back, pretend they are the nicest people in the world, and then they serve the soup to the homeless on Sundays. Of course you will never be invited to their house for crumpets and tea on Sunday.

I attended many charities, and before I knew it, I owned three custom-made tuxedos just for the phony-rich charities I was attending and contributing to. The charities were and are great; it was the phony rich who attended these events that brings me to this writing—all these rich folks throwing their money around just so they can be seen as the aristocrats, the rich, and the wealthy, and as I call them, the phony rich, giving to charities so they will be seen as good guys and gals. Most of them give to charities and are not even sure what charities they are giving to. I know I never did. I should probably not expose them as they were once my friends, but then again, when I took my bow from grace and fall from glory, they ran the other way and acted as if I had leprosy. In addition, on my next go-around, I won't be signing on for the phony rich.

I can remember going to charities and writing checks for ten grand and not even knowing what the name of the charity was, let alone the cause. We were going to two and three charities a month, and there I was in my custom Armani tuxedo with my trophy wife meeting the other phony rich and writing checks for ten grand just to be in the club. I was trying to be something I was not. I was trying to buy my way in, and as long as the check cleared, I was in.

My values have changed. Every dollar I donate today, I know exactly where it goes, and I carefully pick my charity. It almost always involves children or students. It is not as much as it used to be, but it is from the heart, and I am not keeping up with anyone else. I am not putting on the custom-made Armani tuxedo either as I am writing the check.

The closer you were to the charity, the bigger you were in the phony-rich club. You gave because it made you feel like you were doing well. I can remember going to the events and spending time with the rich guys at the wine bar while we watched our wives work the crowd. The poor schmucks, myself included, were there against our own free will. About Monday, we would get a reminder that we had a charity Thursday or Friday. Yes, dear! Pretty soon, I was making friends with the other fellas who were giving their money to the charities that they thought they might know. They did not even feel the check, and they were just going about their lives doing the things that their brides signed them up for.

I love the charities in all reality because they usually benefit those who need the help, and what a better way to get the phony rich to pony up, or in this case, *phony* up. There were a lot of good people at these charities, so it would be unfair of me to categorize all of them as the phony rich, so let's leave it at most of them.

My favorite charity event was Fight Night. Oh man, did the celebrities come out! Fight Night is a very worthwhile cause, I think, and its face is Muhammad Ali. It deals with Parkinson's disease. This is the priciest of charities I have ever attended. We had a table of ten and my good friend paid $250,000 for the table and the extra goodies (this is what he told me he paid and I never questioned it), to which he gave my bride and me a seat to the show. We, of course, made a sizable donation to the event. Our table was right up front next to the celebrities' table. Included was our VIP room greeting. We arrived two hours early for the VIP welcome. I will confess here and now, that was one of the greatest events I have ever attended in my entire life. On that night, I was proud to be there among my peers.

Upon arriving to the JW Marriott Resort and Spa, Phoenix, via private limo, we were whisked in, compliments of a red carpet entrance. We were escorted to the VIP room and sailed through security to safety. Once in the room, we were treated like royalty. Everything over the top and no cash allowed. Premiums liquors and hors d'oeuvres that you see on the food channel and in fancy magazines. Then the stars started to show up. The VIP list of guests was small but, without doubt, the best part of the evening. It was the first time where I think I have been anywhere where there were more celebrities than guests.

It was the celebrity list that was way over the top. The celebrities filled the room and you went and spoke with them at will. I don't believe that anyone asked for autographs as that is kind of classless, even for the phony rich, so I did not ask, but looking back, maybe I should have. In came Kareem Abdul Jabbar. Man, that dude is tall. And then Michael Irvin, Jim Kelly, Emmitt Smith, Tony Hawk, and by far my favorite, Shawn White (the redheaded ski board gold medal champ). I spoke with Shawn for thirty minutes and that dude is for real. He is the nicest guy, and he could not have been more polite, so well-spoken and full of life.

Michael Irvin, since the cocaine days, had found God and he was very pleasant. Larry Fitzgerald was, without a doubt, one of the classiest guys I have ever met. Tony Hawk has a good thing going on. In came the Champ and that was very brief. He was really suffering hard from the disease. This to me was a heartbreaker, a pure tearjerker. Then Diana Ross, I could just marry that girl. Wow, is she special! Michael Bublé, Josh Groban, John Elway, Reba, Sharon Stone, Billy Crystal, Donald Trump. Speaking of Donald, he was auctioned off for an evening with Donald. Scott Coles, who I mentioned earlier in this book, the guy who took his own life, had on this Fight Night paid, at auction, in cash, $250,000 to have dinner with Donald Trump in Manhattan. Trump delivered; Scott and his bride had dinner with Donald. Just imagine paying $250,000 to have dinner with Donald Trump? Scott told me it was the best money he ever spent. Scott said that Donald was very gracious, and in fact, the dinner turned into a very long evening. He loved Donald after that meeting, even more than before the meeting. Scott was the ultimate marketer. He sponsored portions of almost every major charity in town. *This was where he found investors to fund his company that eventually crashed. It was a very target rich environment for Scott and he knew how to work 'em, and work them hard he did. When Scott's company collapsed, he had almost 1 billion dollars of private money placed, and the bulk of it raised through the charities. He was everywhere and he was doing a lot better than the charities* themselves.

The list also included Steve Nash, Alice Cooper, Whitney Houston, and on and on. It was, without doubt, one of the most beautiful events ever and I found it to be the one charity dinner I would never miss. The support its founder Jimmy Walker had garnered for the battle his best friend Muhammad Ali was fighting was amazing, and Jimmy himself was a tremendous person.

As the event unfolded, we were swept to our table that was front and center. Our seats were better than Jim Kelly's, John Elway's, Michael Irvin's, and Steve Nash's. These guys are all heroes and well above my place in life, but that was okay—this will be our little secret. My seat was elbow to elbow with Emmitt Smith and less than five feet from Michael Bublé and Josh Groban. The event was truly amazing, and being a member of the phony rich paid heavy dividends that night.

The Aliens Returned Me Home

Earth to Mike! Earth to Mike! This was not how I was raised, and it was time to realign my values. Find the values that connected my passions and put me back on the right road. I was carried away with the fame and the glory of being in the same room with the super celebrities. All I did was build a bunch of houses and make a bunch of money. I think maybe you can see how it makes sense after being seated among folks like Diana Ross, Billy Crystal, Michael Bublé,

Josh Groban, Shawn White, Sharon Stone, and Reba McEntire that I could easily be lost in the moment. This is something I discovered to be the biggest challenge. As you rub elbows with these folks, you actually forget from where it is you came. I was this guy from Flint, and all of a sudden, I was among the elite royalty of this country's socialite. I was a victim more than a success.

I knew my grandfather would not be proud of who and what I had become. He lived a simple life, and it was much better than this. I had been a member of the phony rich too long, and it was time for me to return back to reality—to find the hero that had slipped into obscurity. I had to find me. I turned in my badge, got my two hundred, and back I went.

After being among this group of people, I am sure you can feel why when I hit rock bottom and I was alone in my bedroom with a divorce and bankruptcy filed, I was ready to check out. My strength was weak. This part of my life was not real and I abused the power. However, I needed to understand this as it helped me to be the strong, focused person I am today. I know my values and I know my passion, and they are not being a member of the phony rich. I am a member of the real rich and I owe it all to understanding that with my family and friends, I am the richest man on the planet. Back then, the money was nice, but it has a different place today. I am not alone. I believe that this meltdown of the world has made everyone realign their priorities.

The bankruptcy, without a doubt, was the best thing that ever happened to Walt Disney, and it was the best thing that ever happened to me. It gave me an inner strength I never knew I possessed. I knew I was strong, but I never realized I was that strong. I was a hero, and I was now fighting for all the right reasons. In short, I needed to depart the phony rich and come back to who I really was and who I really am today.

I will also share with you that when you hobnob with the royalty of the Fight Night folks, you feel like you are one of them. You feel like you belong and you are on top of the world. This euphoria is embellished by the underlings who worship the phony rich. These people are the masses who put you on this pedestal, and they do it as a way to live out their own fantasies. Everyone wants the American dream. I felt like I was on top of the world, but it soon turned, and I felt like the world was on top of me.

Unfortunately, the downside is that the underlings can turn on you every bit as quickly as they place you on the pedestal, in fact even quicker. When I filed for BK, I was about to see the other side, the side where the underlings put you down and treat you like trash. Unfortunately for them, I grew up in Flint and started out as white trash, so I knew how to handle these folks. I grew up in the 313 like Kid Rock and Eminem. I knew how it felt to be treated like shit by the underlings.

The reality is that when you are on top, they treat you well because they're hopeful something is in it for them. It is like touching a great baseball player thinking this somehow will make you a great baseball player. It doesn't work that way. Then as you crash, you are like a disease and even the underlings avoid you. They look down on you. You will get the true feeling of "What have you done for me lately?" Or, "You have no value! See ya!" It is like you are now the third-string quarterback and you serve them no purpose. Be ready for the ride down, folks, it is a tough one. It is difficult to go from god status to a mere peasant with no visible value.

Grandpa Van had a few simple rules for me when I was growing up. He always advised to treat everyone very well and hear them out no matter their lot in life. Everyone has something to say, and the chance to be heard should always be given. He further argued that I should be especially nice to everyone on my way up because I would see them again on my way down. I was very fortunate I heeded his advice. Grandpa Van proved himself to be right, as I saw both parts of the journey. Up and down! I also saw the same people as I headed both directions.

People look at you differently on both paths, up and down. As quickly as they treat you like royalty on your way up, they are even quicker to treat you like trash on your way down, and it is money that guides the whole process. The amount you do not have or the amount they think you do have will be their guiding light. This is the difference between a dog and a man. Feed a dog and he will never bite you, but good luck with man.

The fear of failure was worse than the failure itself.

I was back on the right path, and my trip to stardom only helped me realize my true self. I was fighting again, and I was in control of my life. I was following all my steps and I was back on the winning trail. I believed I could win, and I was thinking big. I was convinced that I could do anything, and even if I could not, I must try. You must always fight for what you think is right and you must believe you can do it. And I believed more than ever. The signs were clear. Doing well was my plan, and I was succeeding at it.

I used all of my resources to find myself again and return to the winners' circle. I followed my plan, and I stuck to it. If for even a single second I started to deviate from the plan, I would immediately correct myself. I would read my wall of fame and the many quotes I had collected. It would take me as many as fifteen to twenty minutes to go through the ritual, but the ritual paid off. I would push myself to go the extra step, and I would reason I needed to because everyone who believed in me, including myself, needed me to give my best. If for a minute I would feel defeated or weak, I would stop and thank the Lord for the gift of life and for my beautiful family and friends. I would say things to myself and still do. "Strength and Honor," "Stick to the plan," "I need to go forward!" "You can quit tomorrow," "Hannah and David *need* you too," "Give your best," "Now, not later," "You can do it," "Now is not the time to stop!"

Winning and success was now a habit, and it was paying off. I had every reason to win, and the reasons to lose were long gone. I had changed my whole attitude, and I had returned to the basics and they were paying off. I was now looking in the mirror and was seeing the winner I wanted to see. I had reasoned with myself and was a true believer in myself again. I was seeing the change I wanted to see and was becoming the person I wanted to become. I was thinking BIG and was not thinking small anymore. I was coming into the opportunity and saying, "I can do it," instead of "Maybe," or, "I don't know," or, "I can't." I screamed, "I can!"—and can I did.

I was near the worst brink of defeat I could have ever imagined. I made a choice, and that choice was to fight and to win. I needed to fight, I needed to believe, and I was doing it. I was broke, but I was never broken. I realized that I could become the person I wanted to become, and if I failed, it was simply because I did not try. Failing was not an option, and not even trying was absolutely unacceptable. The warrior's formula was complete, and the results were coming in by the bucketful. The little victories were adding up, and the big victories were all coming our way. Life was good, and I knew I could do it. There was only one person in the world that could save me, and that person was me. I had jumped into the water to save me and was on my way back to shore.

CHAPTER 17
THE BATTLE WAS WON

Remembering you are going to die is the best way I know to avoid
the trap of thinking you have something to lose. You are already naked.
There is no reason not to follow your heart.

—Steve Jobs

It was hard to believe that as I was changing seats on the *Titanic*,
not many months ago. I wanted an out; I went looking for the OFF
switch, but I never was able to find an out. There was no escape
hatch, but what I found was me. I found that the answer was not an
out but a through, going right through the mess. I was going through
pure hell and I wanted to quit—quitting seemed easy. I understand
what Winston Churchill meant when he said, "If you are going
through hell, then just keep going." I had clearly gone through hell,

and without a doubt, I needed to keep right on going. I was beat so hard that I could not even get up off the floor. I looked to the ground and said, "Why bother?" I had filed the bankruptcy of a lifetime. My wife was gone and the divorce was brutal on both of us. I had been through several audits and investigations by just about every agency. I was going from one deposition to the next. The world needed a bad guy, and I was it. I was featured in the newspaper on several occasions, again as the bad guy. I was front-page news. I went from one 2004 exam to the next 341 review and then over to another hearing. I had to produce piles of documents. I was accused of everything there was. The investors formed lynch mobs and I was at the bottom of the world. I was evaluated from every corner there was. The economy had collapsed, and it was hard for people to ante up and admit they were a victim of the failed economy. It was too hard to admit a loss, so they wanted to blame it on me. Guess what, I was down $131 million. The examinations continued. These exams made my visits to the proctologist seem like a vacation.

When the dust settled, they could not find the stuff they were looking for. I had no hidden cash, no offshore accounts, no money stuffed in the mattress. I never once used investor money to pay other investors. The Ponzi scheme accusations were soon proven false. The facts showed all the investor dollars went into the real estate that crumbled and was later taken back by the banks. The empire was gone, and I lay on my floor broke and wiped out with no glimmer of hope. More than willing to give up and quit, I somehow found the hope and strength to go on. Maybe it was not strength, but more of survival. I believe in each of us there is a natural survival instinct, and that was what was taking me to the next step. I was on autopilot survival mode. I was numb to the world, and I was looking for anything that made me think I was alive. I was so badly beaten that I was not recognizable. I had been so verbally abused and attacked that even I began to wonder about myself. Through it all, I knew I was a good guy, and I would ride again. I had to. I could not quit; it was not in me. I had surrendered to everyone and everything but I could not surrender to the final defeat. It felt as if I was Jason from the horror movie *Friday the 13th*, and even though it looked like I had been killed, I kept coming back to life. When they looked out the window for my dead body on the ground, it was gone. It was truly a mystery at this point.

After tearing my world apart and finding out that I was as much a victim as the rest of the investors and that there were no scandals as they had hoped for, not one person came back and said, "We are sorry! Our mistake!" No! They just moved on to the next guy and left me to rot in my own hell. They almost pulled it off. If it were not for the faces of my children, I may have given in. In the end, I was the biggest loser, far bigger than any of the people who lost their investments. They lost an investment; I nearly lost my life. They got to write off their losses and go back to their lives. I spent the next three years being mutilated in every sense of the word. When it came time to give up and quit, I found the strength to go one more step. That one extra step saved my life, and now I am back. I am alive, and I am a winner. I will not give in, and I will not give up.

I think often of the man who almost gave up, the man today who now loves life, and prays for a chance to help any way he can. A man who knows his values and who chases his passions. A man who experienced one of the greatest meltdowns ever and rallied to learn and improve from the worst of the worst so that he can deliver the best of the best. So now let's share the ride one last time before we end this book.

In the movie *8 Mile*, Eminem was coming down to the championship round and he was heavily outmatched. Eminem knew he was going to lose if his trailer-trash background was exposed. He could not deal with the personal attacks. He was most vulnerable about his personal life. So in the movie, he does the smartest thing in the world. He goes out, and in his performance, he acknowledges he is trash but he is a fighter. He took away any ammunition that his opponent had against him. He was brilliant. When his opponent came out, he had nowhere to go because there was nothing left to expose. Eminem won and was the champ. *In our case, this is very valuable because it has to be your number one strategy—to always be honest.* Tell them everything about you that may be a deal killer. Flush it out now. Be brutally honest; in fact, be over honest. In my case, I do not go into a meeting unless everyone in the meeting already knows I have filed bankruptcy. To this book, the same is true. This book allows me to be Eminem and tell the world everything there is to know. Now I go into the championship round of my life, and I build the life of a winner. Now everyone who does business with me knows everything there is to know, but they get a bonus—they now get to win with a winner. I am a champion and needed to experience the worst pain imaginable to become the winner I am today. I am clear on my values and clear on my goals. I know what it takes, and I am willing to step up and make it happen.

I make all my weaknesses crystal clear and known right up front. In fact, I turn these weaknesses into positives. For instance, allow me to share with you why banks like that someone has filed bankruptcy. That's right. They actually like it. The idea is that you have already filed so you cannot file again, and if you have filed, you have made all your debts go away, so there are no hidden debts that can affect the success of loans you might take with the bank. They actually like it. It is about finding the positives, but more importantly, it is about being honest right up front. I tell everybody I know I filed for BK. Why not? I did. All they have to do is Google me and I am the number one person that comes up on Google. I am not ashamed or embarrassed. It happened, the economy collapsed, and I went with it.

In the spirit of Eminem, I am totally upfront and totally honest. This is the right thing to do. Keeping secrets allows people to know that is the type of person you are, and besides, if you keep secrets or conceal the truth, do you really want to have people find out on their own? Bad plan!

I had found my dreams and my warrior spirit. I had found the person I knew I could become, and it was time to unleash the beast. It was time to move forward. I had everything in order, and the opportunities and the victories were piling up.

I believed in myself, others believed in me, and I was taking every step to victory. I was not going to give up nor was I going to give in.

The number one reason I wrote this book was because I had to. I had to let someone know, anyone I could, and even if it's just one person that I let know, they would know they can win. And no matter how bad it gets, there is always a way to make it better. If you believe in yourself and if you can get others to follow you, then you will win. Do your best and give your best, but most importantly, be your own judge. If you want it bad enough, you can achieve it, and with every single victory in life comes success. Do not leave anything to chance and do not count on luck. I strongly disagree with Donald Trump. Luck has nothing to do with it. Donald credits luck with his success and often writes that it is all a matter of luck. BS! Donald, you are full of shit. I, however, do agree with Donald on another more important matter—*Think big!*

My whole life I had known what was required to be a winner, and I had always performed as such. For the first time in my life, I was faced with failure, and to make matters worse, I was under constant attack. Every single time I would try to rebuild, three more shingles were ripped off my roof. Fortune knocks but once, but misfortune has much more patience; my patience was to be stronger. I finally said I can't give up, and no matter what it takes, I must fight on. Once I made the fight the mission, I knew I would not be beat, and I knew I would not lose. I was so ready to give up but I could not. I think to myself what a travesty it would have been if I did give up. I am a warrior, and I am meant to fight. What if Walt Disney would have given up? After seven bankruptcies, he finally found his dreams. He fought with a passion and never surrendered. You know there were plenty who doubted Walt Disney and he had to spend many hours questioning himself. Today Disney is a $38-billion-a-year corporation and the hearts and minds of tens of millions of children are forever in the debt of Walt and his dreams, for Walt and his passion and for Walt and his never quitting.

Any winner will tell you exactly as I have, and as guys like Walt Disney and Henry Ford lived their lives, we had passion, a burning passion, and a fire so strong that it would burn you just at the mere mention of it. They had to give their best all the time, not just some of the time; they never missed, and they never quit. They used their failures to build from and not to surrender to. Their failures were speed bumps that they raced over. Number one above all else: *They never ever doubted themselves and they believed it could be done.* They also knew it took time and they would stay the course no matter how long it took. As Vince Lombardi would say, he never ever lost a game, he just ran out of time. He firmly believed, given enough time, he would win every game. He was right. Henry Ford, Walt Disney, and Mike Roberts all have one thing in common—they know it takes time and they will not and they never have surrendered.

Success requires many ingredients; hard work is number one, you need passion, you need this to win, and you have to believe in yourself and what it is you are doing. You need others to believe in you. You have to wake up and say, "Why not me!" instead of "Why me?" Winning does not happen; it is up to you to make it happen. You have the power right inside of you. You can do it, and you can do anything you set your mind to. You need to do it today, not tomorrow, and you need to do it with the grace of a champion. You must take every step, no matter how small or how big, in the right direction and you will find your dreams. You will achieve, and you will be victorious.

Never give up, and never give in. Give your best and know that your hard work will take you to the Promised Land. Don't rely on luck, and do not rely on others to do for you what you must do for yourself. It is all up to you, and the decision to be a champion is yours and yours alone.

You will always find a way to win. Had I given up, I would have never ever been the winner that I know I am today. I fight with a vengeance, and I fight with a passion. I will not lose because I cannot accept loss. You should win every single time you suit up, and for a minute, if you give up and if you say it is okay to lose, then you will not win. You must win and you must defeat failure. You make winning a habit and you win at everything you do.

I am living proof that you can do it and that it can be done. Winners win and quitters quit. It is that simple. Winners start where quitters stop. We are all people with the same gifts; we get dressed the same way. We all have the same talents, and the second you realize how powerful you are is the same exact second you become the person you want to become, the person you know you can become.

I had two choices: live or die. Dying is easy; it is living that takes the work. I choose to work, and I choose to live. This is without doubt my greatest triumph. Your life is your greatest triumph, and you have a gift that is to be used.

Do not ever let anyone tell you that you cannot do something, especially if that person is you. You must always believe that you can do it no matter what anyone says or thinks. I know you can, and if I can do it, then you can for sure.

Tony Robbins once said there are two things that motivate people to make dramatic changes in their lives: *inspiration and desperation.* As crazy as it might sound, there is actually tremendous power in hitting rock bottom or a low point in your life. It is through this desperation that I found inspiration. Tony is one of the greatest motivators on the planet, and he is amazingly right—my greatest inspiration ever came from hitting rock bottom. Thank you, Tony, for all the lives you have saved. Hitting rock bottom gave me both inspiration and desperation.

It's only after we've lost everything that we're free to do anything. I came to this realization, and the simple truth is that no matter what I had gone through and the beatings I had taken, I was still alive and I still had me, and now I was free to do anything.

I wrote two sets of power systems for myself and I hope that they help you. I call them "I believe" and "I can."

I Believe

I believe...that if I get knocked down 9 times, I will get up a 10th time.

I believe...that if I hear *no*, they are simply saying they don't *know* and that they need more information to say yes.

I believe...that you can win the baseball game in any of the 9 innings as long as you do not give up.

I believe...that if 100 people tell me I can't do something, I can still do it as long as I am not one of those 100.

I believe...that I would rather have a long kiss than a short good-bye.

I believe...that this world is pretty darn good and I would not trade it for any other.

I believe...that if everyone threw all their problems in a pile, I would run and ask for mine back.

I believe...that there are a lot more good people in the world than bad and that the good will always win.

I believe...that if I give my best, I will never hang my head in shame.

I believe...that if I try and lose, I am far better ahead than to have not tried at all.

I believe...that no matter how bad it gets, it will always get better.

I believe…that no matter how good it is, it can always get better.

I believe…that a friend who is there in bad times deserves to be there in good times.

I believe…that every time I fall down, when I get up, I am stronger than the time before.

I believe…that my successes come from my adversities.

I believe…that when someone tells me I can't do something, it is because they are afraid I will.

I believe…that when someone says it can't be done, they are already defeated.

I believe…that we can do anything we put our mind to.

I believe…that the microwave, cell phones, computers, cars, and airplanes were all deemed impossible and only fools believed. Thanks to the fools, we have all these things.

I believe…that technology will exceed the capacity of the human brain but it will never dream like the brain.

I believe…that when it rains, it is a good time to dream.

I believe…that no matter how hot it gets in Arizona, I will not melt.

I believe…that I have the ability to be the very best person I can be.

I believe…that I can do it.

I believe…that you can do it.

I believe…that the best part of the race is being in it.

I believe…that we can all find happiness if we are willing to look inside ourselves and discover it.

I believe…that this life without family and friends would be no life at all.

I believe…that the good we do today will bring more good tomorrow.

I believe…that we are all equal, and we wake up with the same ability to *make it a great day.*

I believe…that either you can or you can't, and whatever you choose, you are right.

I believe…that the sun will always come out.

I believe…that I always have a chance as long as I believe.

I believe…that the moment I stop believing is the moment I have lost.

I believe…that my attitude is mine to create and develop and that I should count on my own input for my attitude and not the external sources.

I believe…that I am what I eat.

I believe…that my favorite part of the day is the whole day.

I believe…that taking one extra step is often the margin between failure and success.

I believe…that I will never give up.

I believe…that 100 nos always lead to 1 yes.

I believe…that if I give it everything I got, then I will know the meaning of belief.

I believe…that I can't stop after I cross the finish line as this is the point when I must start.

I believe…that winners start where quitters stop.

I believe…that I can never ever give up.

I believe…that no matter how many years it takes, you still have time to do it.

I believe…that the best part of the dream is your vision.

I believe…in visions and outcomes, not goals.

I believe…that everyone of us has the same chance and that we can all do it.

I believe…that an education is important, and no matter what happens in life, you will always have your education.

I believe…that there is a reason for everything and my reason to write is so I can make a difference.

I believe…that if I show up believing I can do it, then I will do it.

I believe in you and I believe in me, and no matter what they do, they will never take that from me.

209

I Can

My last paycheck was twenty-seven years ago. That is right! Twenty-seven years ago, I went to work as an entrepreneur. I would say I have been on commission for the last twenty-seven years. I loved the steady paychecks from Mt. Bell and Bell Atlantic, and the ones from Chevrolet were especially nice, but the glory of working with my dreams, well, that paycheck is unmatched. The good days outweigh the bad, and every time I want a raise, I simply work harder. Here is the secret: you have to be prepared to take the bad with the good. You have to realize that on some days you eat Spam or you don't eat, but on other days, you eat filet mignon. As for me, I would not have it any other way. I love this great big old world, and even with its bad knocks, there are still many more good knocks. I wrote about believing; now I think it is time I write about the power of "I can." So in my words, I know "I can do" this.

I can...get up whenever I have been knocked down.

I can...keep going when the world tells me to stop.

I can...do anything I put my mind into.

I can...become the person I want to become.

I can...no matter how old I get, still reach my visions and realize my outcomes.

I can...do things that other say can't be done.

I can...choose to see the cup half full with room to add to it.

I can...dream a little dream.

I can...turn my dreams into reality.

I can...finish the job and take the extra step.

I can...be kind to someone even when I do not like them.

I can...forgive but not forget.

I can...be there to dance in the storms instead of waiting them out.

I can...go to a sporting event almost every single day of my life.

I can…call my mother at any moment to tell her thank you and that I love her.

I can…call my children and tell them I am proud of them and that I love them.

I can…thank the Almighty for taking my dad so that I was able to become the man I am today.

I can…know the difference between trying and not trying.

I can…call any one of my friends and say hello, just to say hello.

I can…smell the roses and feel the sun on my face.

I can…hug a stranger.

I can…start where others stop.

I can…know the value of a friend over the value of a dollar.

I can…offer a helping hand even if my own hand is broken.

I can…listen even when I think the person speaking is 100% wrong.

I can…fly a kite and write a poem.

I can…offer a smile and share a laugh.

I can…give more than I know I had.

I can…learn far easier that I can teach.

I can…be thankful for what I have as opposed to being sad for what I do not have.

I can…walk on beaches and sing with birds.

I can…lift someone up even if I am unable to lift myself up.

I can…give my best even when I am unsure my best is good enough.

I can…put the needs of others ahead of the needs of myself.

I can…take the extra step.

I can…always find an answer.

I can…do everything that they said I could not do.

I can…take the blame a whole to easier than I can take the credit.

I can…give every single thing I have and still find a little extra.

I can…always find a solution, there is always a way to get it done.

I can't…there is no such term, and to me, it is the true dirty four-letter word.

We all have the power, and in each of our minds, we hold the key. You must always believe in yourself and your abilities. No matter how tough it gets, you have the ability to change it. It may take years, it may take days, but no matter what it is, it is all up to you. You can never give up and you can never stop believing, because the minute you stop believing is the very minute you have lost. We are all winners, and each day we are given the privilege to work our magic. We are warriors, and we are champions. We fight to win, and we fight hard. We never give in, and we never give up. We are warriors. We are champion warriors and our resolve is unmatched. We are clearly "I can" people.

Thank you for reading this book. It meant everything to me to write it. It was an honor to have you read it. I know that dreams do come true. All you have to do is pursue them.

Falling down is how we grow. Staying down is how we die.

THE DAILY'S

Daily 1: Chris Sabin

Good Morning Surprise Winners,

Nearly 18 years ago, I buried one of my very best friends. Bill Sabin died of an inoperable brain tumor. 2 days before Bill slipped into a coma that would lead to his death 7 days later and while we were alone, he asked me a very important favor. Bill asked me to make sure his 2 children, Angie, a recent high school graduate, and his son, Chris, a high school student about to graduate, were looked after. I am not sure what "looked after" meant—but then again he never needed to ask. Chris and Angie worked in our video stores for quite some time after Bill passed. Chris worked all the way through his four years of college and graduation from NAU.

What I never realized at the time was that his son, Chris, would become my best friend in life. To this day, Chris and I speak several times a week. We have not missed since Bill left us. I now hold Chris true and dear to my heart. Chris is every bit a winner as is his sister, Angie. I would say that in my life I spend more time with Chris than anyone. I promised his dad that I would take him to his first girly joint. I never kept that promise, but I have always been there for Chris as he has for me.

I will tell you the one thing I remember the most about Chris. After Ann and I divorced, I faced that first Christmas alone. For anyone who has divorced, there is nothing sadder than the first Christmas without your family. It is absolutely terrible. On this first Christmas alone, I received three gifts. One from Hannah (a handcrafted ceramic coffee cup that I still drink from three to four times a week), one gift from David (a handcrafted ceramic football which I keep my shirt stays in this very day). Thank you, Ann, for seeing to those gifts, and the third and the final gift a Jersey from Chris (which of course I still wear). Gifts don't really matter but the thought does. Chris pulled me out of a pretty big lull that Christmas, for which I will never forget.

Chris, like his father, is and always will be one of my best friends. Chris, like his father and I, have never had a bad word or a bad thought about the other. Chris wanted to do something that was very important to him. He wanted to write the Daily. He has a story he wants to share with you, so today's Daily comes to you from Chris Sabin, one of my best friends in this whole wide world. Chris, thank you!

From Chris:

First and foremost, I would like to thank Mike for allowing me the opportunity to write to his audience. Mike was one of my father's best friends prior to his passing, and is now one of mine. Back in March of this year, Mike incorporated my family into one of his Daily's. It was truly special and it meant a great deal to me.

My profession background is not conventional, as I am a probation officer for high-risk sex offenders in Northern Arizona. I have been working with this specific criminal population for seven years now. The driving force behind this madness is that in 10 years I will be able to retire, and hopefully have my brain erased from all of the incidents and accounts I have experienced over the years! When my career first started, I was a standard probation officer to a variety of criminals, and my region was Camp Verde, Arizona. I was fresh out of college and excited for my career to start. Most people envision Camp Verde as the "pit stop" from Phoenix to Flagstaff or Sedona. When I was assigned this region, I thought to myself, "How much more can there be to Camp Verde, than a couple of gas stations and fast-food establishments off of I-17?" Boy, could I have not been any more mistaken.

Deep in this region was a defendant I was assigned, and his name was Rick. Rick was sentenced to probation right around the same time I started in my department. By conventional standards, he should have never been given the opportunity to prove himself with such a sentence. See, Rick was originally a gang member from Los Angeles, and his prior criminal record was one of the worst the sentencing judge had ever seen. Starting as a juvenile, until his early 40s, he had been incarcerated for most of his life. When Rick was not in jail, he was abusing illegal drugs and committing new and illicit crimes. Prior to sentencing, he was facing 18 new felony charges. I was not present for sentencing, but Rick talked the judge into giving him one more chance on probation. Hardly any of his charges were thrown out, so if Rick did violate, he would more than likely serve the rest of his life in prison. The judge verbally made this known to him while on the bench. It was a risky game to play, because his plea called for 8 years in prison.

When Rick came in for his first office visit, my supervisor handed me his file and told me, "I don't know how or why this guy got probation, but he lives in Camp Verde, so he is yours." After reviewing the file, I was intimidated before even meeting him. This was a criminal you read about, and I had one on my plate fresh out of college. When I got the call that he was in the lobby, I swallowed deeply and brought him into my office. The first words out of his mouth were, "Look at you . . . I am old enough to be your father." I then started to give him a pre–thought-out speech. He then interrupted and said, "You don't need to worry about me," and smiled. Feeling very uncomfortable, I had him sign his initial papers and got him out of my office. Weeks and months went by without a hiccup from Rick. On paper, he should have been the defendant I worried about the most, but after a year of progress and full compliance, he was my finest client.

About a year and two months after I was hired and Rick was sentenced, I started to teach an orientation class for incoming probationers as to the ins and outs of being on community supervision. When the program started up, all new incoming probationers had to attend the class once, and sadly had to sit through me lecturing for two hours. Rick sat in on one of the classes, and told me it was awful, boring, and it made him want to go out and commit a new crime. While joking, this was important to me, because I wanted these incoming defendants to get something out of this mandatory class. I asked Rick what could/would make it better or even bearable. He said, "Chris, I have done just about everything, let me teach/lecture the class." I quickly staffed this suggestion with my supervisor, and the idea went forward with caution.

Being green and new to the Criminal Justice System, I was very anxious to see this play out. Rick was such a success; he basically ran the class for a year and a half. His message was simple, "If I can do this, anyone can do it." I heard his story time and time again. Most importantly, he provided incoming probationers with personal tools as to how not to make that next mistake. After each and every class, we talked afterwards about everything except why and how our lives came together.

Eventually, the time came when I was transferred to another office. I had to move from Sedona to Prescott. The program and format was given to another officer as a result. Before moving on to my next assignment, I spoke with my chief and asked her if I could present Rick with a plaque of appreciation. She liked the idea, and I had one made for his honor. After our last class together, I presented him with the plaque that my chief signed. Rick broke down in front of the class, and said it was one of the greatest gifts he had ever received.

After moving to Prescott, I tracked Rick's case. He was granted an early term off of probation in 2006, as he was let off two years early. Earlier this year, I wanted to reconnect with Rick. I placed a call to my mentor where I started out, and inquired about him. It was at this time that I found out that he passed away from cancer earlier this year. I was able to obtain his obituary. The write-up was consoling and it put a smile on my face, as it revealed his 10 years sobriety, his strong family values and how he contributed to society over the last 10 years. Nothing was hidden, just like the story I had heard on so many occasions.

The one thing I love about these Daily's is that plaques are given out routinely. Mike individualizes and personalizes his relationships with any and all who are worth the effort, and he takes the time to write about the good in his family and friends on this forum. Thank you, my great friend.

Thank you, Chris and Angie, for making your father proud every day of your lives.

The key is to keep company only with people who uplift you,
whose presence calls forth your best.

—Epictetus

Daily 2

July 30, 2011! (For me, this is the one I go back to time and time again!)

Everyone and their brother is telling me to settle . . . to take the first thing that comes my way . . . I'm being stupid and hardheaded they say. For me, their words are foreign, I can't come to terms with what it seems everyone around me wants me to do . . . "give up."

I just can't do it! I know my ship is coming and if I give up, and "settle," it is going to sail right past me. I love the 7/30/11 Daily and it keeps me focused. And for all those nonbelievers out there, I am getting by . . . I choose not to just "get by" and that is why I search for my ship every day. It will come, and when it does, I will not only continue to get by but soar with the eagles.

Here is one of my favorite quotes:

"Excellence is the result of caring more than others think is wise; risking more than others think is safe, Dreaming more than others think is practical and expecting more than others think is possible."

Cheers and always,

Cheri' Valentino

Daily: July 30, 2011

Good Morning, Conquering Heroes,

This is a daily you want to make sure you read. Don't glance, read it. Read it if you ever needed a reason to believe. A reason to believe that from bad comes good. From adversity comes victory. From failure comes success. If you are good without it, then go to the quotes. Everyone needs a reason to believe. Today I am so inspired that I got out of bed and jumped up. I did not drag, limp, crawl. I literately jumped and I yelled: "Lord, let me at 'em." This is going to be another great day! Yay! Feels good. I raced to this computer and I hit the keys and the following will be truly inspirational. I know, I thought out in advance of what I am going to write.

From failure comes victory! I have often written about Walt Disney. Walt literately filed BK 7 times and he also had several small business successes. Walt had many battles but he never lost focus. He always chased his dreams and he used every set back as a step forward. This pattern is common amongst the giants. Abraham Lincoln, Thomas Jefferson, Hershey, Ford, Goodyear, Ulysses S. Grant, Mark Twain, Heinz, Donald Trump . . . all filed bankruptcy. They all faced many adversities and yet they are the most revered men in US history. Men of great honor.

Henry Ford went out and convinced investors to invest with him. He found them and then away he went. Unfortunately, the lead investor, William Murphy, brought in Henry Leland to babysit Ford. Ford finally found the right group of investors and his safety net, so it seemed. Unfortunately, or fortunately, Henry Ford would not be the second Henry on the team, and upon Henry Leland's arrival, Henry Ford left. Ford left and created the monster we know today as Ford Motor Company.

Ray Kroc, a high school dropout, who took over the small-scale McDonald's Corporation franchise in 1954 and built it into the most successful fast-food operation in the world started penniless. He convinced the MacDonald brothers to sell him their hamburger shop and after hundreds of nos they finally said yes. Ray never gave up. Ray had several jobs, all failing him. Ray was the salesman for Hamilton Beach Multi Mixers. Ray was convinced that the multi mixer should be in every restaurant. He soon realized he should own the restaurants himself. Ray was frustrated with the brothers' slow growth and he wanted to sell more mixers. Ray envisioned millions of hamburgers being sold daily with malts compliments of his mixers. Ray faced tremendous adversities before he created the biggest chain in the world. His many failures led to his biggest success.

The point is that these heroes had to take chances and they had to endure many adversities to find their successes. We all have to and it is a matter of doing it. A matter of believing and never giving up. Walt Disney filed bankruptcy 7 times and yet today the Disney is valued at 600 billion dollars. Hmm? 600 billion. Wow! Hershey, Heinz, Goodyear. McDonald's, Ford, are you seeing a pattern here? All men with a dream and determination. A willingness to start where there was no place to start. All men who picked themselves up and hit it again. From adversity came greatness.

Now I am going to tell you about me because you know me. Because you believe and because you must believe. You all know that over three years ago I filed bankruptcy for $131 million. $131 million. Wow. That was July 15, 2008. On June 19, 1995, Ann and I sold our video stores for $9.8 million dollars and a check was presented to us on that day with our names on it. A check handwritten by Dan Potter and cashed by Ann and me. It was an amazing day. I have been at both spectrums and I have fought hard. I have never given up win, lose, or draw. My last adversity has given me the greatest strength I have ever known. I am strong! I am a beast and I will not lose! You would be wise to bet on me every time.

I truly practice what I preach. I have said it is better to go for it and chase your dreams than it is easy to take the easy road. Here is my proof. Two years ago when I started our company I was offered a job that guaranteed me $10 thousand a month. A good job! I was broke and I could not even find 10 cents for a cup of coffee. It was so incredibly tempting but I knew if I took it that would be where I would stay. Stuck in a job with no life. To add to it, the offer came at an extremely challenging moment in my life. The day I was offered the job I was taking Hannah and David up north, in the car, with their friends, for a mini vacation. We were all loaded in the car, on

221

our way I stopped by the bank to cash a check that I had. The check was for $500 and it represented everything I had. The bank needed to hold the check for 24 hours and would not cash it. I had to go to the car and tell Hannah and David trip cancelled, no money. I did not lie to them and we went home. It was one of the worst moments in my life. That night I said maybe I should take the job but I KNEW DEEP DOWN IT WAS A MISTAKE. I knew I had a dream and it would come true. I knew I could never give my passion to the job like I could my dream. I wanted to cry, but I turned my self-pity to strength. I knelt at my bed and I said a prayer, I then said I am going to do this thing and I will not quit. I have never looked back. Not once! Every day I am one step closer to my dream.

Two days ago we closed our first two stores. One in northern California and the other in Phoenix. We have close to another $800 million's worth of opportunities in our arsenal. We will close a number of these stores. Today! We have 8 million dollars' worth of assets on our books. Wednesday we had 0. One year from now the number will be $200 million. Why? Because I believe and because I have used all my adversities to find my victories. Because I never gave up and because I never took the ten-thousand-dollar-a-month job. Also because I have been in business for myself for 27 years and I know what it takes. I know exactly what Ford, Heinz, Hershey, Goodyear, Disney, Kroc and Jefferson knew. It took believing in your dreams. It took never giving up! It took starting where others stop. It took defeat to understand victory. It took despair to understand glory, but more than anything in the world it took themselves.

A fella the other day said to me: "Mike, I understand where you are coming from and you want to get back to where you were." Firstly, he did not even remotely understand where I came from, and until you have been where I have been you never will. I came from private jets and estates to one dollar in my pocket. More than the loss of power or the flight of a private jet is the place your mind and your heart go during these times. It is understanding the harsh and grim reality of not being able to take a simple mini vacation to the north with your children. It is knowing that as bad as it gets you may be the only person in the whole world who knows you can do it.

Being alone with your thoughts in your weak moments will either make you a winner and stronger or a quitter and loser. I cannot and will not quit. No! I am afraid he did not know where I came from, and secondly he has no idea where I am going. I am not trying to get back to where I was before. I have every intention of going well beyond those prior successes. They were nothing as compared to what I will accomplish. I am not trying to get back at all where I was before, I have no interest. I have every intention of being bigger. Not for the money! Not for the glory! But for me and for you and for my family. You need to believe and you can believe in yourselves through me.

Every time we see a success we become a success. Walt Disney is to be my greatest success and I use his success every single day to drive me. I want to drive just one of you. I WANT TO MAKE A DIFFERENCE IN JUST ONE OF YOU. I WANT JUST ONE OF YOU TO BELIEVE AND TO GO ONE MORE STEP IN YOUR LIFE TO BE THE HERO THAT YOU ARE. I want you to win because every time one of you win, I win. Every time one of you wins, we all win. With each victory, we become champions. We become conquering Champions.

Did You Know?

Facts about millionaires:

- Only 3 percent of them inherited wealth. Over half of them got that way by starting their own business while a third had a professional practice (doctor, lawyer) or worked in the corporate world.

- They rent stuff. More than 50 percent of millionaires say they plan to rent luxury goods within the next twelve months, according to a survey by Prince and Associates. Handbags topped the list, followed by cars, jewelry, watches and art.

- They weren't good students; the median college GPA of millionaires is 2.9, and the average SAT score is 1190. 59 percent of millionaires attended a state college or university

* * *

Today's Funny: How can you get four suits for a dollar? Buy a deck of cards.

* * *

All your dreams can come true if you have the courage to pursue them.

—Walt Disney

If you work just for money, you'll never make it, but if you love what you're doing and you always put the customer first, success will be yours.

—Ray Kroc

If you're not a risk taker, you should get the hell out of business.

—Ray Kroc

I am looking for a lot of men who have an infinite capacity to not know what can't be done.

—Henry Ford

224

There is no man living that cannot do more than he thinks he can.

—Henry Ford

The best thing about the future is that it comes one day at a time.

—Abraham Lincoln

The power of you is amazing.

—Mike

In war there is no substitute for victory.

—Douglas MacArthur

Michael Roberts

CEO / Chairman

Sure Storage USA

DAILY 3

Good Morning Heroes of Virtue,

It was July 1st, 1965. A Happy little family from the Midwest was preparing for the holiday weekend. They were heading up north to Houghton Lake, Michigan. The Mom was readying the bags and the four little children for the big weekend. The Dad was getting the car washed and gassed up for the big trip. The Dad, a very proud man, was excited to take his wife and children for a well-earned vacation. July 2nd arrived without a hitch, at first. After work the happy family would head north where they would meet more family and friends for the famed Fourth of July weekend in Northern Michigan. Next to Christmas there is not a more important holiday in northern Michigan, the lakes are full, the hot dogs are sold in bulk and the beer goes by the galloon. Actually, in Michigan Deer Hunting holiday may be more important. Michigan is the Midwest. It is where some of the finest people in this country are from. A Midwestern is easy to spot; they usually carry jumper cables in case you need a jump and they are quick to offer coffee and a smile.

The proud dad, a good man, a man of faith went off to work this day, as he had every day. It was July 2nd, 1965; he was hard at work in Plant 2A at Chevrolet Manufacturing in Flint, Michigan. As he worked on the machines and kept the production lines running, he drifted back to the thoughts of the fabulous weekend ahead with his family. As the day progressed his excitement built and the day was to be his. Suddenly, he fell to the ground. His heart had attacked him. At the age of 28, he was rushed to the hospital.

The phone rang and the young mother of four answered it. It was a call she wished would have never came. It was McLaren Hospital, her husband was there. She rushed to his side. He was dying. The young bride held her husband's hand and tried not to cry. The nurses pulled the curtain and they came in and out. They told her that Dr.

Gorne was on his way. The nurses knew they could not do anything for this young man. The Mom sat there waiting for Dr. Gorne, holding the hand of her dying husband. They spoke, but those words have never been shared with anyone. They were their final words together. As she held his hand, he closed his eyes for the last time. Dr. Gorne arrived after the young man passed, but he could not have done anything anyway. The bride cried and the family began to pour in to assist her. Four little children sat at home not knowing that their father had just died. It would be quite some time before they would know. This was nearly 46 years ago and my Mother has never been to a hospital since. She does not have what it takes to enter one. Also in those that 46 years Mom has never been to a doctor, nor will she go. She has never taken any medicine. Mom will take her final breath at home if she has her way, and she most likely will. Mom never remarried and she never seriously dated. On this day a hero died and another was born, in fact, two heroes were born—Mom and Grandpa Van.

Mom never looked back. Mom knew that we had to survive. *The fight was before us, not behind us.* With Mom we looked only in front of us. In this almost 46 years Mom and I have never spoke of Dad. We never really had to. We both knew she loved him and he was a good man. I guess for me that was everything I needed and for her it was the way it worked best. At 6 I became a dad, as put into play by Grandpa Van. I did not understand until later what it all meant, but I do today that is for sure.

Mom never yelled at me, she never hit me, she never put me in time out. Mom only told me that I could do it. If I fell she did the smart thing, she did not pick me up, she let me get up on my own. When I got up, and I did every time, she said I knew you would. Mom never said you can't do it, she always said you can. I stunned Mom when, at the age of 8, I calculated what we were charged for some slop at a McDonald's and discovered we were over charged. I marched in there demanded a refund and got it. That day she said I needed to be an Attorney, a career I considered right through college. I even took the LSAT. I will probably go get my Law Degree when I retire, if I retire. Mom has never in my 51 years criticized me for anything. I guess she always figured I was a smart kid and I would figure it out. My hero she is and always will be. I guess Mom's most famous words are these: "You can never go back!"

I grew up in a home where there was no criticism, there was no fighting, the 5 of us pulled together as we were fighting for survival, together, as a team. I remember one of the most important things Mom ever said to me. Mom said: "Mike! We are not trying to keep up with the Joneses, we are just trying to keep up!" I will never forget it. The best thing that happened to me was that I became a man with the loss of my father, and I was raised by Grandpa Van and Mom— my two greatest heroes.

It was a famous fight and to this day Mom and my sisters are still in it. We never fight against each other but always with each other. My sisters may snap at one another but they still know they are in it together. Here is a story that will help to shed light on moving forward and being a team. When we were all growing up, I mean the 5 of us, as mom was growing up too, back in flint there was one particular moment when I knew we were working forward. In the winters it gets cold back in the Midwest. I can remember as a young man of about 12 that I would wake up and I would be freezing. I mean it would be so cold that I was awaken out of a sound sleep. I soon realized that the heat was not on. I usually was the first to figure it out. The heat was not on because we did not have the money to pay for the fuel oil to keep the furnace going. I would go into the kitchen and I would open the stove door and gather the chairs around. I would turn the oven on broil so it would get hot immediately. I would then get my sisters and mom up and we would all sit around the stove in the kitchen to stay warm, until we could run off to school. Mom was simply too proud to beg and borrow so we would have to wait until her check came in, and then order oil. By the way, this is where I first learned about COD, as that was how the heating oil arrived. We would sit there and shiver, but we would laugh and I would tell jokes to pass the time. It was the best of times. We were a family of 5, and we were fighting to not keep up with the Joneses, but just to keep up. I would never trade those moments for anything in the world. Mom never claimed one day of welfare in her life, nor have I. We knew we would always figure it out. Mom never gave up and she never looked back. She never said, "If only your father were here it would be better." Not Mom! Mom knew we could not go back, so let's move forward and make this work.

I have had the best life imaginable and every minute of it is a gift. My Mom is my best friend and I got to learn from Grandpa Van. I love my sisters, as they love me. We all talk all the time. We all remember sitting by the stove, as a family, fighting together for a better tomorrow and ignoring the past. The past was gone but the future was on its way.

This picture was of our family and it was taken less than a month before Dad died. Look at that big smile on Janet and I. Little did we know our family was about to change, forever. Mom's face is so serious I wonder if she knew something we did not?

Ladies, be honest, Dad was a handsome man!

I look not to the loss of Dad but to the growth of our family. As he looks down on us I am sure he is proud, I know that I am!

Mom, thank you for always being there for us. I tried to be the best son I could be and a dad at the same time. We all learned from you, the very best. Thank you for making sure we looked to the future.

Now you can see, why like Phyllis and Rose, Mom is my hero. These three heroes were heroes because they had to be. They found courage when that was all there was.

Here is a picture of the 5 of us. I was a senior working at Chevrolet. I worked in Plant 2A, the very plant where my father worked up until the day he died. Five great smiles. Dad, we love you.

First Communion at St. Pius X, age 8. My junior year at Michigan State, age 21. Notice my car. I am prepared for the abuse I will get for that car. Hit me with it.

Did You Know?

Charlie Chaplin once won third prize in a Charlie Chaplin look-alike contest.

At the time of the U.S. Revolutionary War, Philadelphia was the second largest English-speaking city in the world, surpassed only by London.

Although the Pony Express was one of the most famous chapters in U.S. history, it only lasted one year, from 1860 to '61.

* * *

Today's Funny: Frank Layden, Utah Jazz president, on a former player: "I told him, 'Son, what is it with you. Is it ignorance or apathy?' He said, 'Coach, I don't know and I don't care.' " (1991)

* * *

The harder you work, the harder it is to surrender.
—Vince Lombardi

Adversity causes some men to break, and others to break records.
—Source Unknown

Face your deficiencies and acknowledge them. But do not let them master you.
—Helen Keller

Courage is the discovery that you may not win, and trying when you know you can lose.
—Tom Krause

God places the heaviest burden on those who can carry its weight.
—Reggie White

If my mind can conceive it, and my heart can believe it, I know I can achieve it.

Promise me you'll always remember: You're braver than you believe, and stronger than you seem, and smarter than you think.
—Christopher Robin to Pooh

The need to go forward will always exceed the need to stop or look back.
—Mike

DAILY 4

Good Morning Miracle Workers,

We all need a miracle so how about I give you a few today or at least reminds us of a few. I don't know what was bigger the US beating the Russians in the '80 Olympics or the Arizona Cardinals making it to the Super Bowl a few years ago. Of course both were highly unlikely. The odds were so low that the Vegas odds makers did not even post them. I am sure they did but they had to be 1,000 to 1 at best. True miracles can happen. We believe in the impossible, that is exactly why we all love underdogs. That is why I rooted for the Diamondbacks baseball team this year. Not because I am from Arizona, beside we all know I am a Detroit Tiger fan, no I rooted for the D'Backs because it was a team filled with young guys who made no money and played with all their hearts. Three of the players who started all the playoff games were in the minors 60–90 days prior. We all love an underdog. We all love the impossible to become possible. Believing in the impossible is what sets us apart.

Ever notice that there are those who believe anything is possible and there are those who believe nothing is possible? It is all in our attitude and our mind set. I was in Michigan recently while there I was speaking with a friend of my moms. I was enjoying the beauty of the fall leaves and their colors changing. It was so nice and pretty. I commented on how much I enjoyed the colors of the leaves. She quickly said: "That's because you do not have to be here to rake them up." I saw the beauty of the leaves and she saw all the work. It was raining and I told her how much I loved the rain. "I could sing and dance in it all night long. We don't get rain in Arizona so to see it here today is a beauty that mere words cannot describe." She said: "You have to be kidding me! The rain! It just makes the roads and my car dirty. We get too much of it." At that point I decided to enjoy all of life's miracles by myself.

It truly is why we love miracles, because they are the things that dreams are made of.

I read a quote the other day that I thought was so perfect. It went like this: "Why does no one ever root for Goliath?" I thought it is not that I don't want to root for Goliath, I choose to root for David. David was fighting impossible odds and won. It is like the 300 Spartans who fought 800,000 Persians. They fought with their hearts and they fought a situation they could not win; problem for the Persians is the Spartans did not think that they could lose. Heroes who never thought they could lose, although everyone else thought they could not win. Rudy for Notre Dame. He never gave up believing in himself. He had no business on the team yet he was. Or Vince Papali, from the Eagles, a walk-on who played, against impossible odds.

We all need to believe in miracles, it is our heartbeat, but no matter if it is a miracle or just everyday life, we need to believe. It is in our attitudes and it is in our hearts. If you choose to see the beauty of the leaves or the work from their falling, it's a choice we all make, every day, in everything we do. If you love the crispness of the rain or you hate that your car gets dirty again comes from you and nowhere else. The more you see your car dirty and the less you see the rain, the harder it is to bring a miracle to your heart. I guess for me I get up every day and I start out with a miracle. I get to write to you, the readers, of the joys of life. How awesome is that?! I know that every day I arise I can be part of a miracle, I can make a difference and I can and I will believe. I know that I can see the beauty of the fall leaves and not worry about the rake work that will have to come. The price of raking a few leaves does not compare to the days and hours that we get to enjoy them changing colors. Their splendor and their beauty will always outweigh the little bit of work, besides good things require work and it is often that work that makes them special. We earn the privileges of life through hard work and to me that is the best reward there is.

It is between our ears that all the beauty of the world can be discovered and it is between our ears where miracles happen. For this reason we arise every day and every day we look for miracles and on some days we realize that we are the miracle and that the miracle is from us to us. I believe in miracles and I am not alone.

Did You Know?

USA

Languages: English 82.1%, Spanish 10.7%, other Indo-European 3.8%, Asian and Pacific Island 2.7%, other 0.7% (2000 census)

Population: 301,734,134

Religions: Protestant 52%, Roman Catholic 24%, Mormon 2%, Jewish 1%, Muslim 1%, other 10%, none 10% (2002 est.)

* * *

Today's Funny: How do you tell when you run out of invisible ink?

* * *

A grandchild is a miracle, but a renewed relationship
with your own children is even a greater one.
—T. Berry Brazelton

Before I do a play I say that I hope it's going to be for as short
a time as possible but, once you do it, it is a paradoxical pleasure.
One evening out of two there are five minutes of a miracle and for those five
minutes you want to do it again and again. It's like a drug.

—Isabelle Huppert

Birth is the sudden opening of a window, through which you look out
upon a stupendous prospect. For what has happened? A miracle.
You have exchanged nothing for the possibility of everything.
—Willie Dixon

Could a greater miracle take place than for us to look
through each other's eyes for an instant?
—Henry David Thoreau

It is a miracle that curiosity survives formal education.
—Albert Einstein

It is a true miracle when a man finally sees himself as his only opposition.
—Vernon Howard

A miracle happens every day and it comes from us to us.
—Mike

During my 18 years I came to bat almost 10,000 times.
I struck out about 1,700 times and walked maybe 1,800 times.
You figure a ballplayer will average about 500 at bats a season.
That means I played seven years without ever hitting the ball.
—Mickey Mantle

DAILY 5

Good Morning Motivated Maniacs,

Yippee! Let's get this train rolling.

TODAY WE WILL TAKE THE READERS' OATH. IT IS OUR CREED!

I will win because I believe.

I will succeed because I will try.

I will find the strength to take the extra step because it is that one extra step that so often makes the difference.

I will begin where others stop.

I will work harder when I reach the top, not just to get there.

I will know that Visions may take YEARS BUT THAT THEY WILL ALWAYS COME TRUE IF I STAY THE COURSE.

I WILL KNOW THAT THE Champions are the ones who give their best and never stop giving.

I will know that to try to do something and fail is infinitely better than those who try to do nothing and succeed.

I will always know that the value of family and friends is more important than any deal.

I will know that when I die I can look back in honor for being the father and son that I was and am.

I will not live by regrets but successes.

I will not seek do-overs but do-agains.

I will know that as long as there is a will there is a way.

I will take the time offer a thank you and leave the frowns to the clowns.

I will not complain but praise.

I will catch someone doing something right as opposed to catching them doing something wrong.

I will spend the evening with a friend as opposed to watching *Dancing with the Idols*.

I will find reasons "Why I can" as opposed to reasons "Why I can't."

I will spend more time connecting and less time correcting.

I will walk on the beach instead of talking about it.

I will care to know more.

I will learn and listen.

I will stay the course even when others don't believe in me.

I will not be afraid to try.

I will help with my hands and my heart and not just my wallet.

I will remember that I have a very special life and that it is gift to be cherished and protected.

I will not put off until tomorrow what I can do today.

I will count the number of moments that take my breath away and not the number of moments I breathe.

I will realize that life is a Journey not a destination.

I will always remember I may be one person in this world but to one person I may be the world.

I will know that I can always do better but that I have given my best and that is a mighty fine place to start.

I will never ever apologize for doing my best.

I will not lie to those whom I love because they care and I will not lie to those I don't know because they don't care.

I will be patient.

I will smell the roses instead of complaining about the weeds.

I will become the person I know I can become.

I will have visions and outcomes and I will reach them.

I will know that no matter how bad it gets it will always get better.

I will always find time to fly in the back Country with Crazy Dan.

I will dance in the rain and not wait out the storm.

I will always find one more I Love you.

I will be thankful for what I do have instead of unhappy for what I do not have.

I will offer a smile as I can always afford one of those.

I will be positive as I know it is contagious.

I will always find the time to find the time.

This is our creed. A Winner's creed. I am going to ask that you write me with more items to put on our creed. Please!

Did You Know?

Of the total 80 German Nobel Prize winners to date, 68 won the prize for services to the natural sciences or medicine.

The first Wimbledon took place in 1877 solely as an amateur competition. Men's singles was the only event that took place.

Today, only the Great Pyramid of Giza survives as one of the original great wonders.

* * *

Today's Funny: After you've dated someone, it should be legal to stamp them with what's wrong with them so the next person doesn't have to start from scratch (Rita Rudner).

* * *

I'll put you through hell, but at the end of it all we'll be champions.
—Bear Bryant

The integral part of being a star is having the will to win.
All the champions have it.
—Betty Cuthbert

The mark of a great player is in his ability to come back.
The great champions have all come back from defeat.
—Sam Snead

True champions aren't always the ones that win, but those with the most guts.
—Mia Hamm

Don't say Aretha is making a comeback, because I've never been away!
—Aretha Franklin

Anyone can give up, it's the easiest thing in the world to do. But to hold it together when everyone else would understand if you fell apart, that's true strength.

We are the Champions of the World.

—Freddy Mercury

To succeed…you need to find something to hold on to, something to motivate you, something to inspire you.

DAILY 6

Good Morning Super, Super Heroes,

To all of the many, many readers. I would like to thank you for all of your support. I know that many of you have been with me for over two years and some just got into the groove in the last 30, 60, 90, 120 days. Over the course of these Daily's I have often referenced my greatest hero, Grandpa Van. I have used many of his quotes and shared with you many of his beliefs. I shared his wit and his respect for his fellow man. I spoke of his kind heart and his love of life. I have written of his wife, my Granny Van, his partner of 55 years. I have spoken of his honor and of his commitment to his family. Today I will provide yet another glimpse into the man I call hero.

First, I must share one very important lesson that I received from Grandpa Van. Grandpa Van always made it a priority that you love all family members equally. I have one sister, and 10 cousins who read the Daily's. They all know of Grandpa Van and they know what a hero he was, as was Granny Van. They also know that my relationship with him was not different from theirs. Grandpa Van always loved everyone equally. He had many different special relationships but he cherished all of his grandchildren. There were really two of us who got just little more of his time, but not love. My cousin Susan was very close as well. Sue earned her teaching degree and she student taught one semester up north. During this time she lived with Grandpa and Granny. This made Grandpa Van so happy. They greatly enjoyed her company. Grandpa Van always found time for all of us and he loved each and every one of us. Although he never said it, he did not have to. You see, back in the Midwest growing up, hugging, kissing and I love yous were only accepted with thy neighbor's wife. Ha! Love was always understood and displays of affection were fairly uncommon. They were not needed

I salute Grandpa Van, because of the loss of my father he jumped in to help me. My Uncle Leonard, my Uncle Bob, and my Uncle John, all three great, great men took care of their families, but Milton, my Dad, was gone. My Mom was also the baby. I realized a lot about my Grandpa Van that never made much sense until later in life. Regrettably, a lot of what sunk in was after he had passed. I was 28 and he was 83 at the time of his death, almost 23 years ago. I always saw him as my mentor, as my father and my grandfather. I never thought to think how he saw me. I was too busy thinking about me. What I figured out as I got older was that Grandpa Van saw me as all of these things, but he also saw me as his friend.

My first real important memory with Grandpa Van was when I was 6 and he took me out to the garage on Court Street, he had me sit down with him. He flipped over the milk crate and there I was. Grandpa Van said: "Mike, your Dad is gone and you have to be the man of the family. Now! You have to take care of your mother and your sisters!" It was a remarkable thing he said, and I bet every bit as hard for him as for me. How do you tell a 6-year-old his Dad is dead and he won't be coming back . . . ever?

The good news is that it was all downhill from there. Grandpa liked my father a great deal and he too was grieving my Dad's death. He decided he had to help me, and for whatever reason, and there were many, he did. How he helped me was he became my hero. He took the time with me that a father would give a son. He watched out for me. Grandpa Van was a man of much substance. He did not take to the drink or womanizing. I saw him of drink once, at his 50th wedding Anniversary. Grandpa Van always had a joke, and never for a second did he find the difficulty of the day. He always found the brightness of his life, his good life. He stood behind family. Right or wrong. I only saw him mad once, and he was not even mad, he was disappointed. He rattled his wife now and again, just to keep her on her toes, but he loved her and he protected her.

I learned another important lesson from him. He would never cuss in the presence of a lady. NEVER. He always felt that when a fella cussed it was because he was not smart enough to find a good word to use. He would do it around me, more to get a rise out of me than anything else. I still remember the first time he dropped an f-bomber around me. I was speechless. He later apologized. He never yelled at me nor told me I could not do something. He always gave little life lessons. He always kept his tongue and his anger in check. He did so by both patience and humor. He would tell me it is always easier to tell a joke than it was to run off and get angry. It took less work and the less work he did the better. This of course was not the exact truth because he always worked so hard. He never would sit the ax down if there was wood to cut. He also taught me the value of a hard day's work. So many days we would work all day long knocking off only to watch his beloved Detroit Tigers. Now you know why I love the Tigers so much. Grandpa Van and I watched some 300 to 400 hundred games together on his TV. He loved those Tigers.

Grandpa Van always believed that there was good in everybody. He would say, "Sometimes you may have to look a little harder in others to find it but it is there." My biggest Grandpa Van lesson was and is my all-time favorite. "Mike! Always remember you can never feel inferior to anyone unless you give them your permission." "Worry about who you are and not what people think you are." He liked me because I worked extremely hard for him, and with him. My reward was not money, as I was never paid nor would I have taken a cent. My reward was I got to be a big buddy and hang out with my hero. He treated me like a young man instead of a kid. He liked my company and I loved his. Grandpa Van saw me as an investment. He knew that I was like this sponge and anything he would say to me would be absorbed. He knew that as they day came to a close I would say, "What else can we do, Grandpa Van? What else needs working on?" I never looked for the out but I was all about the in. Because,

Grandpa Van was my hero, my best friend. When Ann and I got married, in June 1988, I asked him to be my best man. He was aged and getting ill. He died later that December. The trip to Pennsylvania would have been too much. He said, "You do not want me as your best man 'cus when you are not looking I will run off with your bride."

I can never remember Grandpa Van saying a bad thing about a person. He always figured everyone was doing the best they can and it wasn't his place to judge 'em. Grandpa Van had tons of friends, he knew everybody and everybody liked him. However, he held his family closest and he was very careful to be too good of friends to too many folks. He was always the first with a smile and a joke but he protected his family. When folks saw Van coming, they waved and said hello.

I have so many favorite Grandpa Van stories. Wow! One time Granny, Grandpa and I were playing B-rummy and it was late at night. We were up in Gladwin and Grandpa was losing at the game. He could not stand losing. Oh boy! Did not matter who it was either. As we sat there a spider descended down from the ceiling above us on its web. It landed on Granny Van. No one saw it at first, and then Granny saw it and she jumped sky high and was flicking all over her body to get the darn thing off of her. Grandpa looked at her like, "Woman, what in the heck are you doing?" Granny is yelling: "Van, didn't you see that spider on me."

Grandpa Van never missed a beat, looked right at her, and said: "I don't know what you were worried about by the time that spider crawled all the way around you it would have died of exhaustion anyway." I laughed for hours. Poor Granny could not help but laugh and she never dropped one of her playing cards through the whole ruckus. He loved her.

At the end of the dirt road where the pavement started on old 18 was a Sinclair station. Grandpa would always get gas there. The owner who was also the pumper guy was blind. This was absolutely true. Grandpa Van would fill up and talk to this old guy while he pumped the gas, he then would get back in the Chevy pickup and say we need to hurry. "I just gave him a dollar bill and I told him it was 20." He did it every time and he would laugh. Finally, one day he told me that he always gave him the right amount, but one day he would slip a one just for fun.

My favorite time was rat/bear night at the dump. We would go to the dump off of 18 and watch for bears and rats. We would watch the rats run through the trash and out would come the 22. Bang! Another rat bites the dust. Grandpa Van never missed. Sometimes on the way home from the dump we would go by the cemetery and Grandpa would point out his school hood friends, who were now there. It would be somber but it gave him some serenity.

I use to be the first one in his Chevy pickup. Man I could not wait to go for a ride with Grandpa Van. Did not matter where. You had to be a little careful in the Chevy as that is where he kept his spit can. He would put a Maxwell house coffee can between us and use it for his chew spit. Man, I looked in that can a couple of times and each time I was ready to toss cookies. Man was that Gross. He would say: "Mike, can you grab my spit can out of the truck." Oh man! For real? Ouch! I would go get 'er with my eyes closed the whole way back.

I remember the hardest thing for Grandpa to do was listen to others be picked on. He never had much call for that. He pretty much worried about his family and never really offered a bad word about anyone. If folks got to gossiping he would either change the subject, get quiet or move on. It was always pretty simple for him. He always had a joke to tell and it was hard to tell your jokes if you are picking on people.

I will tell you one final thing about my hero. When I was 19 and working for Chevrolet I lost my driver's license due to too many points. Speeding! I continued to drive anyway and I got caught. I was sentenced to a weekend in jail for driving on a suspended license. I paid a friend of mine, Rick Chamberlain to go sit in jail for me while I worked. He agreed and I paid him the agreed upon $75.00. Upon his release they needed a fine paid, his brother Randy came down to pay the fine and get him released. Randy then told the coppers they had the wrong guy. The ruse was up and we were on the front page. I went to the judge immediately and he threw the book at me. He gave me 30 days. I sat in the holding tank to begin my 30 days and cried. I was in there doing 30 days when on the 10th day they came and got me, and then released me. I thought they had made a mistake but I elected not to point it out and depart. I never understood until several years later when Granny Van told me why I had been released early. You see, Grandpa Van drove into town in his Chevy pickup and he went and saw that old judge. He told the judge: "You do not know my grandson the way I do. He is a good boy and he works hard. He does not deserve to be in your jail another minute longer and I want you to let him go now. I will vouch for his character and I will see that you do not see him again." The Judge immediately released me. Grandpa Van never said a word and he made Granny Van keep it to herself. After he died she then told me. I could never properly thank him, not that he ever really much cared about being thanked. This was the kind of man he was. He always protected family and right was right. He did not want me in that jail because he knew I was a good person, nor did he want any credit for setting me free. He asked me to quit driving and do good by it all. I did quit driving and I spent the next year on a bicycle and bumming rides.

Grandpa Van always would say, "If you have given your best, Mike, then you are almost there." There are so many wonderful Grandpa Van stories and my cousins and sisters could tell just as many. We all enjoyed a very special relationship with Grandpa Van. He and Granny lived for their family and to them there really was not much more to it.

One last thought. Granny Van never missed a day of church. Never! Grandpa Van felt that by here going the family was taken care of so he would sit home. I asked him one time why he never went? He said: "Granny takes care of that but besides I need to be home on Sundays!" "You see, Mike, I go out on the front walk and I throw all the money in my pockets up in the air and what God keeps he can have what falls to the ground I put back in pocket until next Sunday." He always laughed when he would tell me this.

My father, my grandfather, my hero, my best friend, Grandpa Van.

My junior year at State. Grandpa Van and me in front of Granny's Cadillac. No arms around each other; that is just how it was then.

Did You Know?

That the real Rudy from the movie *Rudy* had a cameo role in the movie. He stood in the stands with Rudy's brother and father.

Rhythms is the longest English word without the normal vowels, *a*, *e*, *i*, *o*, or *u*.

Second string, meaning "replacement or backup," comes from the middle ages. An archer always carried a second string in case the one on his bow broke.

Speak of the Devil is short for "Speak of the Devil and he shall come." It was believed that if you spoke about the Devil it would attract his attention. That's why when you're talking about someone and they show up people say, "Speak of the Devil."

* * *

Today's Funny: Eagles may soar, but weasels don't get sucked into jet engines.

* * *

If a child is to keep alive his inborn sense of wonder, he needs the companionship of at least one adult who can share it, rediscovering with him the joy, excitement and mystery of the world we live in.
—Rachel Carson

It is not a lack of love, but a lack of friendship that makes unhappy marriages.
—Friedrich Nietzsche

Good friends, good books and a sleepy conscience: this is the ideal life.
—Mark Twain

I always felt that the great high privilege, relief and comfort of friendship was that one had to explain nothing.
—Katherine Mansfield

Our heroes lead us to being a better person.
—Mike

DAILY 7

Is there a God?

Hmmmm? Don't judge me for who I use to be I don't live in that neighborhood anymore....

Today is going to be a very gripping story of truth and understanding. It will by no means be your normal Daily. I have decided that there are forces at work beyond me and I must share those with you here today. I was told yesterday that my being alive is a miracle which medicine cannot explain. It seems I too cannot explain it. Today I am going to try. I think I have been very gritty and I have been very direct but today I am going to go beyond that.

Is there a God? I believe there is and I believe it every day. There are many times in my life, because I could never see or touch God I believed he was created by people. I have many times argued that he was created as a way to serve the weak and as a vehicle to give power to the tyrants of the world. Cynical I know but I gave it merit. I also subscribed to the simple logic that we are star dust. I believed that our creation was a simple process as a result of the Big Bang, and that the conditions prevailed just right, and as a result of star dust, and due to reasons that astronomers accept as a fact, we were thus created.

Well what happens if there is a heaven and I die and then I go there and I say oops: "Well I would have believed in you if knew there was really a heaven?" Voltaire when asked to renounce Satan on his death bed simply replied with his last words: "Now is not the time to make enemies!"

As a child I could not believe that if there was a God he could take my dad away? I went to catholic school as a child and as they pushed that shit down my throat about the Lord and all that I never quit asking "Why did God take my Dad?" I did not like God as a child and refused to accept him. As I got older I just simply let God go about his business and I went about mine. I Figured you do your thing and I will do mine. Grandpa Van and my mother were my two biggest influences and their commitment to religion was more for appearances than commitment. I am not sure Grandpa Van every really truly believed that there was a God I think maybe he feared the alternative. He was a good man by nature and he gave his best every day and to this he was my God. Mom followed his trail almost to the tee.

As I got older in the public school system I got heavily involved in drugs and trouble. All petty stuff but, nonetheless, in trouble. I was the kid parents would not let their children hang around. I always had a good heart but I was always cutting edge if not on the cutting edge. I had grit, true grit.

Is there a God? I went to college and I kept going on in life. My heart was filled with dreams and hopes. I found an opportunity at every turn but still I neither credited God nor blamed him. Am I here today going to give you my big speech about my becoming a born again Christian? NO! Because I am not nor will I ever be. I will never be a Bible thumper but today I will ask you to examine a few facts and just maybe you will draw the same conclusions I have drawn.

Yesterday I had a heart procedure in the hospital. It did not go well. We had hoped to inflate a few balloons and send me home. Unfortunately, I have four blocked arteries and they require a lot of work. Three of the arteries are over 80% blocked one being 99%. The cardiologists stopped the procedure and sent me into recovery. He came and spoke with me and said he is not sure how I was still in the game? I go back tomorrow to have four stents put in my heart arteries. I will be there and it will go fine. Tomorrow I will have a very good strong heart and the chance to live another 40 years. A chance that was about to go away. I was told yesterday that it was a miracle that I am still here. The cardiologist assured me I would not have seen my next birthday. I had no clue. I felt no pain, no warnings. Hell! I weigh 178 pounds I am 5'11" and I feel like a million bucks. I can't wait to get up and hit the day. I had no chest pains. No shortness of breath. No groggles or goggles. I mean I really felt great yet I was walking around waiting to die and I had no clue. So I ask you, is there God?

It all started with a broken foot or did it? So let me understand this a little bit more so keep on reading and maybe, just maybe, you will see something that I am seeing today. First and foremost I am alive....

I had not had health insurance for the last four years. I was broke and with the BK how could one afford it? I had it for Hannah and David but not for me. Hannah and David's health care was paid every month before I paid my power bill. As for me I am in good health I thought. I will be ok I reasoned not realizing each day I was dying. As the company finally got health insurance and for the first time in four years I was covered. It seemed no big deal. Then two weeks after we were insured my foot broke. I do not know how it broke? It swelled up and I went to the doctor, we tried some infection treatments that did not work. Finally after a month I went to a Podiatrist on my own. Or maybe with the help of God. My doctor was sure it was an infection, so without telling him I went and saw a podiatrist; in 5 minutes the podiatrist said, It is broken and you will need surgery. Surgery was a terrible decision but I did not know that at the time. I was sent to a foot surgeon. This woman should not be allowed to practice medicine. She is the worst person every allowed into medicine. As it turns out after checking up on her, her license is under review on two separate investigations and she is going through hearings as we speak. Why her? Why was I sent to her? God sent me to her. Well a normal foot surgeon would have never recommended surgery and without her I would have never known what was going on with me. You see she took me into surgery and while I went under anesthesia my blood pressure went down so low they were unable to get it back up and they stopped the surgery. It was touch and go and they almost lost me on the table. They almost lost me to a surgery that should have never happened. It led to the problem being my heart. It forced me to stay in the hospital two days and do heart tests. The cardiologists did not pick up anything that concerned him and authorized me to go back into surgery. I said NO! I knew something was not right. I went home and I immediately went to another foot surgeon. The new doctor I now use has fixed the foot without surgery and could not believe surgery was even a consideration. The foot was not strong enough for a surgery. He could not figure out why a surgery had even been considered. Is there a God? I have had 7 surgeries and never once a problem. Why this time did I have a problem? Was God in that room with me that day? I think so! The surgery was stopped not for the foot but for my life. Truly a miracle!

Thanks to the botched surgery and a terrible medical decision I have my life back. The real culprit which was waiting to take me away has been defeated. This is all pretty simple or is it? I need to go further. Why did God take my dad from me? I think maybe he did not I think he gave me to you. I think he needed my mother to be strong and I think he needed my Grandpa Van to be the good man that he was. I think it was a plan. I also had to learn I was here to serve others and not serve myself. So why I am alive? I was told I should not be and that it is a miracle I am.

You see folks this is what concerns me even more. These Daily's? I keep writing them and I never stop. I am like a machine—a machine that has to reach out to each of you. I am a tool.

Here is the inner most thought. When I filed BKI prayed to God to take my life. I wanted to die. I put a 9mm in my mouth and said "Fuck this world." As I was about to pull the trigger I saw Hannah and David's face in my head and I pulled the gun out of my mouth and I cried. Here is the worst part I was so high on Cocaine and wallowing in self-pity I lied by my bed naked and I hated everything in this world and most of all I hated God. My soon-to-be ex-wife

Colleen tormented me so bad that I had accepted I was a failure. She verbally abused me so harshly that I began to believe her and I began to believe her words. I was so blitzed on the coke and filled with hate for Colleen that pulling the trigger seemed so easy. I had been a success my whole life and for the first time I hit rock bottom. I had filed BK, I was going through a bitter divorce and my life had become meaningless. Dying was easy; it was living that was hard.

I had never hated before in my whole life. Even in my weakest moments of being mad at God for taking my father I never hated, but Colleen taught me to hate. I thought it was the devil who brought Colleen to me but I was wrong it was God. God needed me to hate so that I could fight to live again. I could not kill myself that night but I wanted to .to. I could not do it for three reasons, Hannah, David and my mother. I was prepared to die and I had accepted in my heart it was time. The drugs took away reason and hate justified action. Since I could not do that to my mother and my children, I then prayed that God take my life, kill me with cancer or something but he refused. I wanted to die of the cancer so I could go out and people would pity me, I would be gone and it would not be at my own hand. I did not want to go on in the harsh cruel world anymore. I was so absorbed on self-pity I no longer knew who I was. I welcomed death and raised my hands out to it.

I put the 9mm down and I cried. I got off the coke and I refused all contact with Colleen. Each day I became stronger. Each day I told myself I have to fight. I began everyday telling myself I have to be strong because my children and my mother need me to be strong. I soon realized the reason God took my dad was to make me strong. To make me a better person and to help as many people as I could. So is there a God?

My whole mind changed I no longer wanted to die. I prayed every day to the Lord and I would never accept one single reason to not give my best. The reason God took my father was so I would know what it was like to lose a father and so that in my weakest moments, with a gun in my mouth, I would know that feeling and not put my Hannah and David through it. To this day this is exactly the reason. I could not end it all because I knew the feeling and I could not do that to Hannah and David. I also watched my mother fight her whole life and never give up or give in. She always faced the challenge as much as she did not like it she faced it so I too knew I must face it for her.

The Daily's evolved and I have never been clear until this day. It is my job to help whomever I can whenever I can. I am no longer in this world for me but for all of those I touch. I want to live more than any other time in my life. Today the fight for life is stronger than it has ever been. I truly care about living and I love everything this world has to offer so I make the choice to live and I make the choice to love this world. I make the choice to write to you every day.

So I ask you, is there a God? It all adds up for me. God stopped a surgery that would have been a disaster; he kept me alive and got me in front of the right people. He pulled that gun out of my mouth. He taught me to hate so that I could love. He taught me to fight and to write. I am alive and that is exactly how I intend to stay. I want to live more than anything in this world. I want to give my best. I know that when I wanted to die I was sent down that road but by a miracle he kept me alive so that I can be what I must become and what I will become.

Even more to the point, was I was invited to a dinner a few years back and at the dinner I met Dr. Rose Richards. Rose is clearly an angel. Rose is now my PCP and she watches me like a hawk. She is not about to let me die. Last Friday my insurance company refused to pay for the procedure yesterday; and requested additional authorization steps. This would have caused at least a 2-wk delay in scheduling of the procedure. Without my procedure yesterday we would have never known how close I am to death and without it I would surely soon be leaving. My cardiologists called the insurance carrier and they pushed him back, he accepted it and said we would schedule this later. Dr. Richards would not accept it. She got on the phone and relentlessly pleaded my case. Once they understood the gravity of my situation they threatened that should anything happen to me she would make it very well known their failure to cover me. They quickly approved the procedure and yesterday I was given my life back. Is it a miracle? It is truly so. Here is the best part of all of this. I know Dr. Richards through the Daily's. She has read every day for the last two years and written in on many Sundays. If it were not for the Daily's I would have never maintained a friendship with Dr. Rose Richards and I would surely be days, if not minutes from my death. My choice to live is the most important choice I have ever made. I will do everything in my power to be alive, to be there for my mom, for Hannah and David and for all of you. Is there a God? You better believe it! I am alive and I intend to stay that way. It is through a collection of miracles and to these Daily's that I am alive. Do I believe in Miracles, it would appear I am one....

"There is no force more Powerful Than the Will to Live."

Made in the USA
Charleston, SC
17 November 2012